CONSPIRACY THEORIES

THE FACTS AND THE EVIDENCE BEHIND
THE WORLD'S GREATEST COVER-UPS

THIS IS A SEVENOAKS BOOK

This edition published in 2018 by SevenOaks
First published in 2004 by Carlton Books Limited as *Conspiracy Files*
20 Mortimer Street
London W1T 3JW

10 9 8 7 6 5 4 3 2

Design © Carlton Books Limited 2018
Text © David Southwell 2004, 2018

A CIP catalogue record for this book is available from the British Library.

ISBN: 978-1-78177-859-3

Printed in Dubai

CONSPIRACY THEORIES

THE FACTS AND THE EVIDENCE BEHIND THE WORLD'S GREATEST COVER-UPS

DAVID SOUTHWELL
+
GRAEME DONALD

SEVENOAKS

CONTENTS

INTRODUCTION 6–7

CHAPTER 1:
POLITICS
8–33

CHAPTER 2:
ORGANIZATIONS
34–53

CHAPTER 3:
SECRET SOCIETIES
54–71

CHAPTER 4:
HISTORICAL
72–87

CHAPTER 5:
TRAGEDIES
88–109

CHAPTER 6:
TECHNOLOGY
110–123

CHAPTER 7:
PLACES
124–149

CHAPTER 8:
CELEBRITIES
150–169

CHAPTER 9:
EXTRA-TERRESTRIALS
170–185

CHAPTER 10:
MURDERED OR MISSING
186–205

INDEX
206–207

CREDITS
208

INTRODUCTION

Conspiracy theories range from the mundane and unbelievable to the jawdropping and terrifyingly true.

Some conspiracy theories are born of a departed celebrity's fans' unwillingness to accept their idol's fate – mainly because extraordinary people have never been allowed to enjoy an ordinary death. The theory that purports "Elvis lives!" was perhaps best summed up by the American medic who, having performed the autopsy on the star's body, wryly opined: "If he is then he's walking around without his heart, liver and brain 'cos I took them out." However, such conspiracy theories are nothing new: 15th-century France was buzzing with tales of the so-called Joan of Arc, who, having eluded her "Rouen-ation" (she was burnt at the stake in Rouen) slipped away to a life of married bliss in Metz after finding some willing doppelgänger to burn in her stead …

Was Princess Diana murdered? Probably not. This is not because this writer does not firmly believe that every administration keeps kennelled dark-ops characters ever willing to undertake the unthinkable – but there was no real need for anyone to take such drastic measures. Besides, no serious assassin attempts to engineer a car-crash – too many random variables and too unpredictable an outcome – as demonstrated by the bodyguard surviving the incident, thanks to his safety belt, as would have Diana had she been wearing hers in the rear. Although it is beyond doubt that the limo carrying Diana clipped or was clipped by a white Fiat Uno shortly before the crash, it was an accident, pure and simple. Let's face it, should anyone wish – for whatever reason – to ram a heavy limo at speed and kill the occupants, a Fiat Uno would not be the first vehicle to spring to mind; a Hummer, maybe – but not a Fiat Uno.

Moving on to theories addressing frightening realities, sometimes these concern plans or actions conceived or carried out by those at the very top of the greasy pole of politics and sometimes by elements within an administration determined to shield the eyes of their Chief Executive from the details of their machinations. Take, for example, War Plan Red – of which US President Franklin D. Roosevelt was unaware, as it was never presented for Presidential or Congressional approval. This was clandestinely hatched by his own Military Chiefs in 1947 after the United States and Great Britain had fallen out at the Geneva Naval Conference; the US delegation wished to impose restrictions on Britain's

increasing naval power – something that the British delegation refused to even consider. A blueprint for an all-out and pre-emptive strike against the United Kingdom and her dominions, Plan Red's first move – Operation Crimson – provided for a massive ground-and-air thrust across the Canadian border. Much later on, it was very much a case of red faces all round when this audacious plan was de-classified in 1974.

Was US President John F. Kennedy assassinated in Dallas by covert operatives? Very likely. Was "9/11" inflicted by shadowy elements within the American administration? Possibly. However, before any reader is tempted to dismiss theories in this category as nothing more than eye-rolling bunkum, they would do well to ponder the sanity of Operation Northwoods. This military venture was proposed by the American Joint Chiefs of Staff in 1962, when they were anxious to mount what they euphemistically termed a false-flag operation.

Signed by all the Joint Chiefs of Staff – including the chairman, Four-Star General Lyman Lemnitzer – Operation Northwoods proposed the unleashing of black-ops squads who, dressed up as Cuban activists, were to hijack several domestic flights, shoot up several schools and colleges and bomb some shopping malls, prior to the release of false intelligence that implicated Cuban leader Fidel Castro as the puppet-master. This operation, the Joint Chiefs proposed, would give President Kennedy ("JFK") the excuse he needed to launch an all-out and overt attack on Cuba. Considered by Kennedy and his inner circle, the plan was mercifully rejected – not because it was mad, bad and dangerous to know, but because there were too many open variables in its conception, bringing with them the very real possibility of the true orchestrators being revealed. No one thought to temper the Joint Chiefs' extreme ideas and no one proposed quietly retiring them all. So, we can only conclude that there really are highly placed, state-serving psychopaths out there who are willing to put in danger those they are appointed to protect – and for no other reason than self-serving political expediency. To paraphrase the second-century AD Roman poet Juvenal: "Who will protect us from our guardians?" We would all do well to keep that maxim in mind.

Strange elements in NASA's moon photos have caused many to believe the lunar landings were faked.

CHAPTER 1:

<u>POLITICS</u>

THE TRILATERAL COMMISSION

Formed in 1973 by private citizens from North America, Europe and Japan, the Trilateral Commission was born to create closer ties between the three geographical areas and to share leadership responsibilities on a more global basis. One of the principal founders of this was David Rockefeller, the wealthy American banker. Apparently inspired by Prof. Zbigniew Brzezinski's book _Between Two Ages_, in which Brzezinski proposes an alliance between North America, Western Europe and Japan, Rockefeller went about trying to establish such an organization In reality.

With a membership supposedly gleaned from the elite echelons of society, the Trilateral Commission is said to be composed of some 335 prominent figures in the media, politics, academia and business. Its membership is supposed to include such dignitaries as Paul Volcker, erstwhile head of the Federal Reserve System; Akio Morita, chief executive officer of Sony; Count Otto Lambsdorff, leader of Germany's Free Democratic Party; Henry Kissinger, and Bill Clinton. Top executives of such companies as AT&T, Pepsico and the Chase Manhattan Bank, among many others, are also members.

The Trilateral Commission meets once a year, in spring, to discuss world problems and hopefully to come up with solutions. The Commission is nothing more than the political power behind the formation of the New World Order (NWO), according to conspiracy theorists who believe that the Commission has one aim: to wipe out all political sovereignty on Earth and place its people under the rule of one government and one bank. Others see the Trilateral Commission as a group that is merely trying to ensure that global financial interests (such as those of AT&T and the Rockefellers) are protected. While hiding behind a mask of benign kindness, the Trilateral Commission's real aim is not to protect the interests of the lower classes but to convince people, subtly, that they must bow to the needs of the banks and corporations ...

THE STRANGE PART

Given that the Trilateral Commission's membership includes some of the most important and powerful names in the worlds of politics, business and the media, many conspiracy theorists find it hard to believe that their role is purely consultative. The theorists feel that US presidents, world leaders and other members of the globe's power elite would not find time in their schedules to attend something that only serves as a talking shop – especially when the mysterious lack of media attention on the Commission means that they do not even get the chance for a photo opportunity.

USUAL SUSPECTS
The Freemasons

Theories abound that the Freemasons control the agenda of the Trilateral Commission, shaping its decisions and influences on global policy to ensure total Freemason domination of the Earth. By slowly moving the world into the straitjacket of the New World Order, the Freemasons could, by crushing all dissent under the tight rules and brutality of the NWO, finally achieve their ultimate goal.

The Illuminati

Another mysterious, shadowy group that is feared to be behind the scenes in all governments, the Illuminati is another candidate for running the Trilateral Commission. Like the Freemasons, the Illuminati's goal is total global domination.

Also suspected: the Bilderberg Group, another alleged "discussion group" based in Geneva, Switzerland, and apparently partly financed by the Rockefellers.

UNUSUAL SUSPECTS
Aliens

According to this view, an unnamed alien power is trying to take over the planet. It is working in conjunction with the Trilateral Commission, the Bilderberg Group, and the Council of Foreign Relations. Clearly, conquest will be much simpler for the aliens once all governments, and all armies, have first been absorbed into the single New World Order. Those who work with the aliens will be spared the horrors that are due to befall the rest of us.

Knights Templar

The high number of bankers and financiers involved in the Trilateral Commission have convinced some that the group was put together at the behest of the Knights Templar, the world's first truly international bankers, who still secretly organize all the secret muscle in the world of global business. The Commission serves to help the Templars keep the world's political climate at the right level for their control to remain solid with profits booming.

MOST CONVINCING EVIDENCE

There is a curious lack of media attention surrounding meetings of the Trilateral Commission, which seems extremely odd considering the profiles of many attendees. In a world where the President of the United States is bombarded with flashbulbs and microphones when he does something as innocent as walking his dog, it's interesting to note that when he attends a meeting of the Trilateral Commission, it barely merits a mention on the evening news. Despite the Commission's insistence that it is merely a "discussion group" and that all of its discussion papers are available to the public, this shadow over its activities is disquieting. Considering how President Clinton could not control the media circus over the Lewinsky affair, where does the Trilateral Commission get its power to muzzle the media when it sees fit?

MOST MYSTERIOUS FACT

Without explanation, the Commission's 2003 conference in Seoul marked a sudden departure from its 30-year-old focus on the interdependence of nations to a more global perspective – conference titles included, for example, Current Global Trade and Global Aspect of New Terrorism. The fact that many members and associates – such as Shirley Temple (d. 1992) and Barbara Walters – broke links with the Commission without public explanation fanned the flames of debate about the true objective of the organization.

SCEPTICALLY SPEAKING

If there were going to be a New World Order, would the Trilateral Commission even have to exist as a public entity? While it can be argued that the best place to hide is in broad daylight, which could be the Commission's credo, why create such an organization that would inevitably lead to suspicion and fears of conspiracy? In an age of encrypted communications and underground government bunkers, there is no need for the power brokers of the world to meet in full view of a suspicious public to discuss their future enslavement. There is every evidence to suggest that the Trilateral Commission is nothing more than an excuse for rich people to get together, swap stories, drink expensive wine, and maybe sneak in a few rounds of golf. Perhaps world domination isn't their goal: maybe just getting away from the office is.

The Trilateral Commission claims to be "A non-governmental, policy-orientated forum" dedicated to "world improvement".

MALCOLM X

If you were a controversial political figure in America during the Sixties, it was highly probable that your life would end in a hail of bullets. Malcolm X, the fiery leader of the Organization of Afro-American Unity, who outraged white America with his pronouncements on racial matters, was yet another man cut down in his prime because of the dangerous power of his beliefs.

The Audubon Ballroom was deserted after the shooting. Today it is a business centre.

Malcolm X was born Malcolm Little in 1925. His father, a Baptist minister, was murdered by white racists six years later and the family was broken up and put into care. Although he was a bright student, Little's dreams of becoming a lawyer were crushed when a teacher explained to him that he was only a "nigger", and should consider becoming a carpenter instead. Disillusioned with education, he drifted into a life of petty crime. While serving time for burglary, Little began to read about the Nation of Islam. The NOI's beliefs of black self-reliance and the need for racial separation intrigued Little, and when he was released, in 1952, he joined the Nation of Islam, dropping his surname because it was a vestige of slave ownership, and replacing it with a simple "X".

Malcolm X rose quickly through the ranks of the Nation, becoming the organization's chief spokesperson. But after his inflammatory comments about the Kennedy assassination, its leader, Elijah Muhammed, suspended him from the NOI.

Malcolm X took this opportunity to create his Organization of Afro-American Unity (OAAU), and did not return to the Nation when his suspension was over.

Where Martin Luther King believed in non-violence and the integration of the black man into white America, Malcolm X angered white society by stating that blacks were superior to whites in all ways. He travelled the world, speaking in the Middle East, and generating support for a United Nations resolution condemning both South Africa and the United States for human-rights violations in their treatment of blacks. Such views, as well as animosity from the Nation of Islam, made Malcolm X a man who was widely hated. This hatred came to a head on 21 February 1965, at the Audubon Theatre and Ballroom in New York.

At the beginning of the meeting, a fight broke out in front of the stage where Malcolm X was speaking. As he tried to calm things down, a group of five assassins stood in the audience and shot him. Malcolm X died shortly afterwards, another figure cut down in America's cull of leaders who threatened the Establishment in the not-so-groovy sixties.

THE STRANGE PART
Even though there was a hospital across the street from the Audubon Ballroom, it still took close to half an hour for an emergency crew to arrive, following X's shooting.

THE USUAL SUSPECTS
The FBI
J. Edgar Hoover, the cross-dressing head of the FBI, distrusted Malcolm X; indeed, he distrusted all other Black Power movements, which had no place in his somewhat blinkered perception of the American political landscape. Perhaps "Mary" – as Hoover liked to be known at the transvestite parties he attended, held at the New York Plaza Hotel by liquor-baron Lewis Rosentiel – had good cause. In the week before Malcolm X's assassination, an undercover NYPD officer named Raymond A. Wood, who had infiltrated the Black Liberation Movement, was instrumental in foiling a plot to blow up the Statue of Liberty, the Liberty Bell and other national monuments with dynamite that Wood himself had helped smuggle in from Canada. One of the leading lights of this terror-cell was Walter Bowe, who also served as Chair for the Cultural Committee of Malcolm X's OAAU – and Malcolm X was known to have been nothing if not militant. Perhaps Hoover decided, on that basis alone, that X was no longer required on the political landscape.

The prime assassin arrested at the scene, Thomas Hagan – a prominent NOI activist and a man who never denied his part in the killing of Malcolm X – consistently denied that the other two men who were later arrested, Thomas Johnson and Norman Butler, had anything to do with it. Right up until his release in 2010, Hagan always insisted that the plot had been hatched with two other men. He refused to name them, other than stating that neither were members of NOI nor Muslims. However, when undercover officers are added to the mix to act as provocateurs, nobody can ever be quite sure who they are dealing with. Therefore, it is odd that witnesses to Hagan's arrest at the scene also spoke of another man – Ray Woods – being bundled away from the Audubon Ballroom by the police, yet there is no record of any such arrest. Also, Gene Roberts, the man who was photographed apparently trying to resuscitate Malcom X after the shooting, was also later revealed to have been an undercover NYPD/FBI operative. Of course, he could just as easily have been getting close to Malcolm X to ensure that he died, as opposed to have been rendering assistance.

The US Government
The prospect of a UN resolution condemning the US along with South Africa for human-rights violations seemed a clear possibility. This would have been seriously embarrassing for the US. By taking out the chief proponent for this resolution, Malcolm X, the States could then spin-doctor the whole messy business away.

THE UNUSUAL SUSPECTS
The Mob
In an effort to clean up black neighbourhoods and institute a lifestyle of clean living, Malcolm X verbally attacked the drug trade. This threat to the profits that could be made from the despair of the ghetto may have sealed X's fate.

The Nation Of Islam
The schisms between the Nation of Islam and Malcolm X's own group ran deep, with some people feeling that X was unfairly criticizing Elijah Muhammed and other Nation leaders, such as Louis Farrakhan, if not outrightly blaspheming. This could have resulted in a murder that had both political and religious overtones to its motive as some in the Nation of Islam openly fanned this hatred of X.

MOST CONVINCING EVIDENCE
Leon Ameer, a leading light of the OAAU, a fitness-freak and a martial-arts instructor, announced on 10 March 1965 that he was in possession of documents and audio tapes that conclusively identified X's killers. Ameer stated: "[They] aren't from Chicago (the HQ of NOI); they're from Washington." Having sent his wife and child away to a safe house, Ameer approached the FBI with his evidence – and was then found dead in his apartment on 13 March. At first it was declared that he died of an epileptic seizure, but when his doctor came forward to state he was not an epileptic, the official explanation for his death became an overdose of sleeping pills. When this theory was also ruled out, Ameer's death was recorded as being due to "natural causes", which of course seems highly unlikely.

MOST MYSTERIOUS FACT
To this day, the NYPD and FBI both refuse to release any of the files detailing the actions of agents Raymond Wood and Gene Roberts. This is despite more than 50 years having elapsed since their involvement in the death of Malcolm X. Additionally, the fact that both men are dead makes the professed rationale for the authorities' refusal to release details – the protection of the agents and their families – seem very weak indeed.

SCEPTICALLY SPEAKING
In the US, if you're black and speak out about human rights, you're a radical asking to be shot. If you're white, you're a humanitarian and get asked to Rotary dinners. No conspiracy is needed to explain this awful truth.

NIXON, WATERGATE AND E. HOWARD HUNT

Watergate is the most famous political conspiracy of the modern age. The exposure of attempts to cover up a failed conspiracy led to Richard Milhous Nixon becoming the first US President to resign from office. It gave new meaning to the term "Deep Throat" – now an anonymous source of classified information as well as a sexual act – and no current political scandal is complete unless it is given the "-gate" tag.

In 1995, when renowned conspiriologist and filmmaker Oliver Stone produced *Nixon* – starring Anthony Hopkins as the unfortunate President – he was not the first theorist to speculate that Watergate was only the visible surface of a much larger and more sinister plot. Like Stone's other conspiracy-fuelled opus, *JFK*, the film was condemned by those it portrayed and by the establishment – a sign taken by Stone's fellow conspiriologists to suggest that it may have contained a great deal of truth.

The facts regarding the outer layer of Watergate are well established and form the basis of the official version of the scandal that is even taught in schools – one of the few conspiracies that the education system acknowledges. In the early hours of 17 June 1972, James McCord – a man with links to the CIA – led a group of four anti-Castro Cuban exiles in an attempt to burgle the Democratic National Committee (DNC) headquarters. The burglars were discovered and arrested as they attempted to tap the telephone system in the Watergate office and hotel complex in Washington, DC.

Charges were also eventually laid against two more people: G. Gordon Liddy, finance counsel to the President and the power behind Nixon's Committee to Re-elect the President (CREEP); and E. Howard Hunt, a former White House aide and ex-CIA operative. Over the next few months, what initially appeared to be a third-rate burglary quickly escalated into a full-blown political scandal. Nixon's involvement in the conspiracy to cover up a conspiracy led to America's gravest constitutional crisis and climaxed with his resignation as President on 9 August 1974.

However, in the national aftermath of distrust following Watergate, conspiracy theorists began to examine the details of the case. They discovered an assortment of facts that suggested the real reason behind the downfall of Nixon was a conspiracy to hide the truth about the assassination of President John F. Kennedy.

THE STRANGE PART

On the Watergate tapes that provided the damning evidence of his involvement in the cover-up of the original burglary, President Nixon says: "Look, the problem is that this [Watergate] will open up the whole Bay of Pigs thing again." John Ehrlichman, Assistant to the President for Domestic Affairs, who served 18 months in prison for his part in the conspiracy, has admitted that "Bay of Pigs" was Nixon's code phrase for the John F. Kennedy assassination.

Dorothy Hunt, the wife of one of the key players in Watergate, E. Howard Hunt, may have been blackmailing the White House and have demanded more than a million dollars to keep silent about information that would "blow the White House out of the water". Many conspiriologists believe that there is photographic evidence to suggest that Hunt, a long-time CIA agent, was one of the famous "Three Tramps" photographed on the grassy knoll immediately after the shooting of JFK.

THE USUAL SUSPECTS
James Jesus Angleton

Director of CIA counter-intelligence from 1954 to 1974, James Jesus Angleton is suspected by many of being the mastermind behind JFK's assassination. His uncharacteristic refusal to help Nixon cover up the White House involvement in the burglary definitely helped seal Nixon's fate. Was Angleton willing to sacrifice a president to hide his involvement in the "whole Bay of Pigs thing"?

The Mafia

It is well established that the Mafia and their Cuban allies had strong links to the CIA and probably played a part in the death of John F. Kennedy, so it is probably more than coincidence that four anti-Castro Cuban exiles were among the Watergate burglars. If the role of high-placed mobsters in the JFK conspiracy were in danger of being exposed by

Watergate, they would have a solid motive for wanting Nixon to take all of the blame.

THE UNUSUAL SUSPECTS
Federal Reserve Bank
Lee Harvey Oswald's widow has pointed the finger at the US Federal Reserve Bank's mysterious role in the JFK affair. A private corporation that controls the creation of all American money, the Federal Reserve Bank (FRB) is owned in part by the Rockefellers. Given that the hugely influential Trilateral Commission was set up by David Rockefeller in 1973, some have conjectured that the FRB had the financial and political muscle to stage Watergate to depose Nixon – a possible obstacle in its plans for world domination.

Howard Hughes
In 1972, eccentric millionaire Howard Hughes asked the White House to send the team that eventually bungled the Watergate burglary to break into the office of a Las Vegas newspaper editor, Hank Greenspun. Their task would have been to steal certain papers that formed allegedly devastating blackmail material. Given that some have linked Hughes and his fellow oil barons with Nixon and a plot to kill JFK, his role in Watergate is suspicious to say the least.

MOST CONVINCING EVIDENCE
On 8 December 1972, Dorothy Hunt – aka "The Watergate Paymistress" – met with Michelle Clarke, the lead CBS journalist on the Watergate investigation. The pair were joined by George Collins, a Congressman from Chicago, and the three then boarded United Airlines flight 553 from Washington to Chicago. Also on board were ten other people who were in some way linked to the Watergate scandal. For reasons that are not clear, Hunt was carrying over $2m in cashier's cheques and money orders; understandably reluctant to commit the case containing the money to the untender mercies of the baggage handlers, she purchased an extra seat to keep her booty next to her. The plane then crashed and burst into flames on its approach to Chicago's Midway International Airport, killing 43 people on the plane and two on the ground.

No prizes for guessing who was first on the scene: the FBI. Before any of the emergency services could get to the site of the crash – and they were in rapid-response mode – 150 FBI agents had secured the area to keep all rescue services at bay while they rummaged through the wreckage. Dorothy Hunt was proclaimed to have been carrying $10,000, yet none of the traceable cheques were in evidence. The suspicious mind might be tempted to consider the possibility that the FBI knew where and when the plane was going to crash and were ghoulishly waiting for it. Cyanide levels found in the bodies of the flight-crew were five times higher than what is considered "normal" in such incidents (the inhalation of fumes from burning plastics and so forth can increase them) and although Dorothy Hunt's death certificate was dated 8 December 1972, the coroner's signature is dated 4 November 1973. All very odd and largely inexplicable.

MOST MYSTERIOUS FACT
A mysterious letter written by Lee Harvey Oswald on 10 November 1963, has been the source of much heated debate. In this note, Oswald asks a "Mr Hunt" for a job within his organization. More than one researcher has come to the conclusion that the letter supplies additional evidence for Hunt's role in the JFK affair.

SCEPTICALLY SPEAKING
Watergate traumatized the American psyche and its scars run deep. The events, which started with that "third-rate burglary", have been described as the root cause in America of the current distrust of government as well as the tendency to believe in conspiracies. Hardly surprising, then, that Watergate set off further speculation into the JFK assassination.

"You won't have Nixon to kick around anymore!" Nixon shouted at his farewell press conference.

PEARL HARBOR

There are crossroads in time – nexus points – when the actions that take place have the potential to shape the course of history on a grand scale. The events that took place at Pearl Harbor before dawn on Sunday, 7 December 1941 form such a nexus point. They influenced not only the course of World War II, but also the way world history unfolded.

The US lost 19 ships, 188 planes and 2,335 men. Japan lost 29 planes and 64 men.

The infamous "sneak attack" by Japanese forces on Hawaii resulted in 2,403 American deaths and 1,178 wounded servicemen; 18 ships, including three battleships, were sunk and 188 aeroplanes were destroyed with a further 162 suffering severe damage. By contrast, the Japanese lost only 29 planes, five midget submarines and 64 men. The direct result of this allegedly surprise attack was a US declaration of war on Japan, which immediately led to Adolf Hitler supporting his Asian allies – an act that finally brought America into the war against the Nazis.

However, some of America's most respected historians have joined forces with the conspiriologists to suggest that the real reason why Pearl Harbor should be remembered is because it was the tragic outcome of a massive conspiracy to ensure that the US joined Britain as a full combatant in World War II.

By 1941, the US President, Franklin D. Roosevelt, was faced with a massive and seemingly insurmountable political problem. He wanted America to become involved in the war with Germany but US public opinion was unsympathetic – Americans felt it was a European affair, and that Britain, Russia and Germany should be left alone to sort it out without any American lives being put at risk. Conspiracy theorists, and some historians, feel that Roosevelt knew Pearl Harbor was going to be attacked, but allowed it to happen as it would give him the perfect excuse for declaring war on Japan – an action that his intelligence services had told him would provoke an identical response from Germany on the US.

THE STRANGE PART

In 1941, Roosevelt had been warned by his admirals that cutting off the supply of petrol to Japan was likely to involve the US in a Pacific war. In July, Roosevelt cut off those petroleum supplies and began to withhold intelligence information about Japanese activities from Army and Navy officials based in Hawaii. The governments of Britain, Holland, Australia, Peru, Korea and the Soviet Union all warned the US that a surprise attack on Pearl Harbor was coming, so it is even more odd that this information was not passed on to the military in Pearl Harbor.

THE USUAL SUSPECTS
Franklin D. Roosevelt

The most obvious suspect in the conspiracy is the President himself. It is no secret that he wanted to bring America into the war with Europe, but was being held back by domestic political concerns. His position meant that he had the power to manoeuvre events in such a way that the US would not have to fire the first shot and be seen as the aggressor.

Anglo-American Cabal

There is a widespread belief, at least in certain sections of the conspiracy field, that there is a powerful Anglo-American cabal in operation determined to keep the "Special Relationship" in existence. Believed to involve members of the American and British intelligence services, as well as major figures from business and finance and top politicians, the cabal may also have counted Roosevelt as a member. He could have been instructed to cover up the impending attack on Pearl Harbor so that the US could be brought into the war to defend Britain.

THE UNUSUAL SUSPECTS
The American Banking Community

At the time of Pearl Harbor, Britain was in debt to America under the terms of the lend-lease agreement. If Britain were defeated by Germany there would be no chance of her ever repaying the vast loans she had taken out. Therefore, members of the American banking community had a vested interest in British victory and may have pulled strings behind the scenes to ensure America lent more than financial support to their client.

International League of Communists

American conspiracy theorists with a very heavy right-wing bias have believed for some while that Roosevelt was secretly a communist. Their conjecture also makes him a vital member of an alleged International League of Communists, which conspired to take the US into a war with Germany.

America's entry to the war would not be to save democracy in Britain and Europe, but to ensure that the world's first communist state, the Soviet Union, was not crushed by the might of the Nazi war machine.

MOST CONVINCING EVIDENCE

In 1932, a joint US Army-Navy exercise saw Pearl Harbor being successfully "attacked" by 152 planes half an hour before dawn on a Sunday – catching the defenders completely by surprise. This was duplicated in 1938, so there can be no doubt that the military knew the potential risk to Pearl Harbor. Furthermore, the US had cracked the top Japanese Naval and diplomatic codes – a fact not lost on a top-secret Army Board. In 1944, the Board reported: "Numerous pieces of information came to our State, War and Navy Departments in all of their top ranks indicating precisely the intentions of the Japanese including the probable exact hour and date of the attack."

MOST MYSTERIOUS FACT

On the day in question, the Opana Radar Observation Station up on Kauku Point, above Pearl Harbor, was being manned by radar-rookies Privates Joe Lockard and George Elliot. This was because the regular operators – Privates Lawrence and Hodges – had been surprised to be given 24-hour passes that they had not requested. At 7:02a.m., Pvt Elliot spotted an enormous "blip" on the radar screen, moving steadily in his direction. He phoned the Tactical Office but, strangely, got no answer. With the in-bound blip by now almost filling the screen and Elliot in a state of panic, he phoned the Admin Office and spoke to Private Joseph McDonald, who informed him that both the Tactical Office and the Information Office were deserted.

Unnerved by Elliot's obvious panic, McDonald collared the Duty Officer, Lt Kermit Tyler. He showed a strange reluctance to phone Pvt Elliott, but eventually did so to dismiss Elliott's reaction as being down to his lack of training in "reading" a radar screen and to further suggest that what he had seen was probably a flight of geese. Elliot told Tyler that if it was a flight of geese it was the biggest and fastest in the world, as it was approaching Pearl Harbor at a steady 180mph. To Elliot's amazement, Tyler told him in a flat and monotone voice to shut the facility down – "Don't worry about it; go and get some breakfast." Then everybody's breakfast was rudely interrupted at 7:48a.m. by those in-coming "geese" ...

SCEPTICALLY SPEAKING

It is hard to be sceptical over many aspects of the Pearl Harbor conspiracy, but it is also hazardous ever to underestimate the levels of incompetence that can be achieved by the US military and its commander-in-chief – the President.

RUDOLF HESS

Having arranged for his Messerschmitt Bf-110 to be fitted with long-range fuel tanks, German Deputy Führer Rudolf Hess took off from Augsburg-Haunstetten airfield in Bavaria at 5:45p.m. on 10 May 1941, setting course for Scotland. In doing so, he set in train one of the most bizarre and convoluted tales of World War II.

Hess's destination was Dungavel House in southern Lanarkshire, home of the Duke of Hamilton – but he ran out of fuel and had to bail out over Eaglesham, a mere 12 miles short of target. Awoken by the crash at about 11:10p.m., farmer David McLean wandered out into the night and, finding Hess sitting in his field, took him home and phoned the Home Guard. Naturally, all were well and truly amazed when Hess identified himself to the Home Guard, telling them he had come with an important message for the Duke of Hamilton.

Hess had been led to believe – wrongly, as it transpired – that Hamilton was a pivotal member of a group of British elite keen to arrive at some kind of peace deal with Germany. The conventional version of events has Hess suffering from some sort of breakdown and undertaking his mission entirely of his own volition, with Hitler going berserk when told of his departure. However, Hess's Adjutant, Karlheinz Pintsch, tells a different story. According to Pintsch, not only was Berlin in secret and protracted talks with London on the very same subject, but when he handed Hitler his boss's "By the time you are reading this I shall be in England" letter, Hitler simply nodded quietly and dismissed him. But had Hess simply been sucker-punched by British Intelligence?

Hess was allowed to meet Hamilton the next day, only to be told by the duke that he had been misinformed and that Hamilton was not in favour of any appeasement or any deal with Berlin. At this juncture, Hess does appear to have become slightly unhinged – as might be expected, as he thought he was flying to a pre-arranged and sympathetic meeting. Now realizing that he looked for all the world like a deluded lunatic on a fantasy mission, Hess was transferred to a series of prisons, including the Tower of London.

While he was being held in the Tower, Hess expressed a desire to meet Winston Churchill. The history books tell us that Churchill refused this request out of hand, but can this really be true? Could Churchill have resisted the chance to interrogate his enemy's second-in-command? Hess was next detained in Camp Z at Mytchett Place in Surrey, where he became increasingly depressed – even attempting suicide. Soon it was his turn to stand in the dock at Nuremberg, after

which Hess was despatched to Berlin's Spandau Prison, where he spent the rest of his life under the watchful eyes of Allied and Soviet jailers working in rotation.

By 1966, Hess – if indeed it was him – was the sole prisoner of the massive complex at Spandau, mainly due to the Soviets' steadfast refusal to sanction his release. Finally, on 17 August 1987, at the age of 93, Hess allegedly took the flex from a table lamp in the summerhouse of one of the prison gardens and hanged himself from a window catch. Or did he? Not everyone accepts that the man in Spandau was actually Hess and, whoever he was, few accept that he committed suicide.

THE STRANGE PART

A concern that Spandau Prisoner Number 7 was not in fact Rudolf Hess was first raised by Doctor W. Hugh Thomas, appointed Consultant General to the British Military Hospitals in Berlin in 1972, and not a man given to flights of fancy. The first thing to strike Dr Thomas about the man believed to be Hess was the fact that he bore no upper-body scars from his well-documented World War I wound. When Dr Thomas first examined Hess, he commented on his war wounds having healed remarkably well, whereupon the patient quickly replaced his shirt before beating a hasty retreat from the examination room.

Keeping his suspicions to himself, Dr Thomas travelled to Bavaria in the autumn of 1978 to meet Frau Ilse Hess at the family home, where, professing to be on a routine visit to get a rounded picture of his patient's general health, he casually asked if his old war wounds bothered him. Frau Hess said that, in the early days, having been shot through the lung sometimes affected his love of hillwalking but that, in the main, the only reminders were the unsightly scars on the front and back of his torso. Dr Thomas also discovered that at Nuremberg, Hess had failed to recognize either of the two secretaries who had worked closely with him on a daily basis until his flight. Additionally, on one occasion when an Allied officer had gone to his cell to interrogate Hess, he simply started to laugh, saying, "Sir, there is no such person as Hess here!"

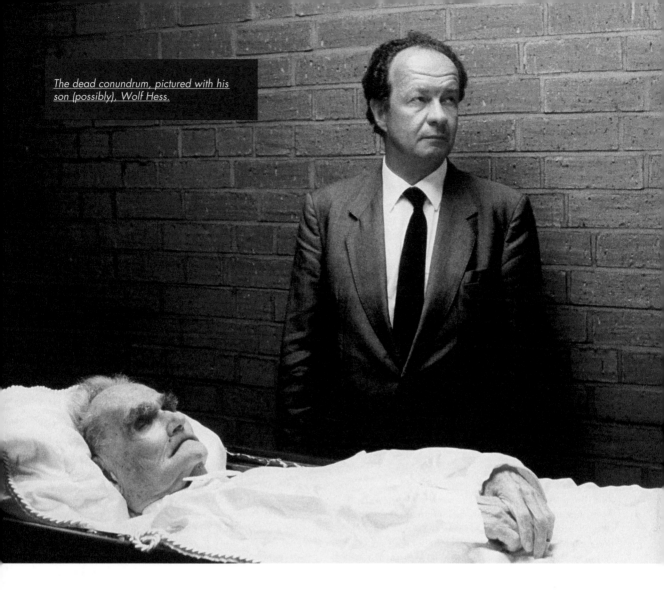

The dead conundrum, pictured with his son (possibly), Wolf Hess.

THE USUAL SUSPECTS
British Intelligence

In 2004, declassified MI5 files revealed that in early September 1940, Hess had tried to open up a clandestine dialogue with the Duke of Hamilton by getting his close friend and advisor, Albrecht Haushofer, to write to the duke. The files revealed that Hess proposed a meeting in neutral Lisbon to discuss a peace agreement between London and Berlin. However, British Intelligence intercepted the letter. They waited and considered a "sting" operation by making the reply themselves and luring Hess into a trap. The idea was abandoned, they say, but not according to the diary of the wife of Frank Foley, the pre-war Head of MI6 Berlin and, during the war, the agency's leading expert on Germany in general. On 17 January 1941, Kay Foley records her husband and his aide suddenly, and without a word of warning to her, flying out of Whitchurch Aerodrome near Bristol on a

clandestine flight to Lisbon, where he spent two weeks under wraps, not returning until 1 February. The suspicions of Kay Foley – and quite a few others – are that Frank Foley met Haushofer in Lisbon to send word back down the line that all was set for the Duke of Hamilton to welcome Hess with open arms and a deal already on the table.

The House of Windsor

The British elite and even the Royal Family were riddled with avid supporters of Hitler, desperate to forge some sort of accommodation or even an alliance with Berlin. The links between Hitler and the abdicated Edward VIII and Wallis Simpson are as well-known as they are documented – but less so those of Prince George, Duke of Kent and the king's brother, and those of his mother, Queen Mary.

The Duke of Kent was a voracious bisexual who was addicted to cocaine. His lovers included Anthony Blunt and the singer/actress Jessie Matthews. British Intelligence also listed him as a Person of Special Interest. On 25 August 1942, the Duke took off in a Sunderland flying-boat from Invergordon in Scotland, ostensibly bound for Iceland on a "Special Mission – Non-Operational". Not long into the flight but far off the correct route for Iceland, the plane crashed in flames on Eagles Rock above the small Caithness village of Berriedale. The dead duke was found handcuffed to a case stuffed with 100 Swedish Krona notes, which would suggest the actual destination for his flight was neutral Sweden, for a meeting with representatives from Berlin.

By some miracle, the tail-gunner on the duke's flight – one Flight Sergeant Andrew Jack – survived the accident. The tail section of the Sunderland snapped off on impact and Jack escaped the explosion. To his dying day, he insisted that there were 16 passengers on board and not the 15 listed on the flight manifest. Jack's testimony fuelled suspicions that the additional passenger was Hess, who was brought along to lend gravitas to the meeting. If a Hess look-alike was shoe-horned into the equation, then this would have been the time to make the switch. Interestingly enough, in the closing days of World War II in Europe, a young British Intelligence officer flew into Germany to retrieve letters of "a sensitive nature" that had been sent by members of the Royal Family to high-ranking Nazis. That officer was Anthony Blunt, who later achieved great infamy in his own right.

THE UNUSUAL SUSPECTS
Vril Society
This theory states that Rudolf Hess was kept imprisoned by the Germans because he held vital information about secret Nazi Antarctic bases operated by the occult Vril Society, which included many top Nazis among its members. Although this sounds bizarre, it should be remembered that James Bond creator and member of MI6 Ian Fleming recommended that master occultist Aleister Crowley should lead the interrogation of Hess.

MOST CONVINCING EVIDENCE
Britain always made a show of supporting moves for the release of Hess, safe in the knowledge that the Soviets would always oppose them. However, their bluff was called in the late 1980s, when Soviet Premier Mikhail Gorbachev, announcing his programme of glasnost and perestroika, proclaimed that the lifting of any Russian objection to the release of Hess "would be accepted worldwide as a gesture of humanity". Whichever secrets Prisoner Number 7 held were about to come out so, from a British perspective at the very least, Hess – or his double – suddenly became a political liability.

As previously stated, on 17 August 1987, the 93-year-old Hess had supposedly hanged himself with an electrical flex in a small building in one of the prison gardens. However, his Tunisian medical orderly, Abdallah Melaouhi, stated that

the flex to the only lamp in the so-called summerhouse was still plugged into the wall when he arrived, to be confronted by two taciturn men in American army uniforms.

According to Melaouhi, what little those men did say was wholly lacking any trace of an American accent. Hess's attending doctor also expressed surprise that his patient could have tied the flex about his own neck, as the arthritis in his hands was by then so severe that Hess could not tie his own shoelaces or dress himself.

Most damning of all was the conclusion of the independent autopsy, conducted by Dr Wolfgang Spann, who stated that Hess had died of strangulation, not by hanging from an electrical flex. Dr Spann further stated that, no matter his findings, it could not be proved that any other party was involved in the death. However, self-strangulation is notoriously difficult to achieve – especially with arthritic hands locked in gnarled fists – because the party involved tends to pass out before they actually expire.

MOST MYSTERIOUS FACT
With regard to the "suicide note" that was presented to the public as if it had been found beside Hess in the summerhouse, the orchestrators of Prisoner 7's death really shot themselves in the foot.

Doubtless overjoyed at reading the first line, the investigators of the death failed to spot the glaring and damaging anachronism that was embedded in lines below the heading of "Written a few minutes before my death". This was as follows: "Tell Freiburg I am extremely sorry that since the Nuremberg trial I had to act as though I didn't know her. I had no choice, because otherwise all attempts to gain freedom would have been in vain. I did get the pictures of her, as of you all."

Apart from the fact that in 1987 Hess's arthritis was so severe that it precluded him writing anything at all, that note had in fact been written nearly twenty years before his actual death. This was at a time when Hess, at death's door with a perforated duodenal ulcer, was about to be taken off for surgery that nobody thought he would survive. The pictures of Freiburg – one of the two secretaries he apparently failed to recognize at his trial – and members of his family had been sent to him for the Christmas of 1969! While Hess was in surgery his cell was "sweep-searched", as was normal, and the note was taken into custody. As Hess did in fact survive his surgery, the note was not forwarded to the family but kept in a drawer for a rainy day.

SCEPTICALLY SPEAKING
There is not much to be said here. Presumably, in order to prevent forensic examination of the death/crime scene, the summerhouse in which Hess died exploded in a ball of fire shortly after the discovery of the body. This fact definitely hands an advantage to the conspiracy theorists …

SADDAM HUSSEIN

On the face of it, the first Gulf War in 1991 was a straightforward conflict. Traditional analysis stems from the view that Saddam Hussein was a classic megalomaniac dictator, who tested the will of the world to halt his expansionist policies by invading Kuwait in August 1990.

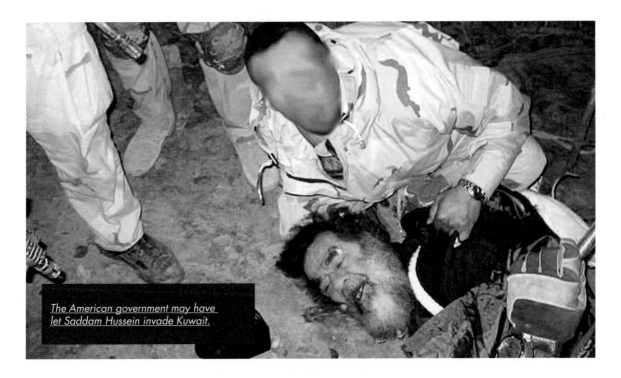

The American government may have let Saddam Hussein invade Kuwait.

In response, a global coalition, led by the US and UK, united against him. George Bush Snr referred to this coalition as a "New World Order". During the Gulf War, the US organized enough military and political power to successfully defeat Saddam and free Kuwait. Yet all is not what it seems when the conspiracy researchers turn their questioning gaze to the Gulf War, which up until the second Gulf War in 2003, was the largest military campaign undertaken since World War II. A number of significant puzzles develop when certain questions are asked. For instance, why did Allied forces stop when they could have easily driven into Baghdad? If Saddam was another Hitler, why wait over a decade to bring about the "regime change" that Bush, Jr was determined to bring about? Accusations and rumours that began when the conspiracy world started to question the established view have now been brought out into the open as accepted, mainstream facts. Even before the tanks hit the

Baghdad highway for a second time, in 2003, more than one revisionist heavyweight commentator on international politics had begun to wonder if the first Gulf War was set up and carried out for objectives other than freeing Kuwait.

THE STRANGE PART

Saddam believed that the US State Department had given him a "green light" to invade Kuwait. This happened when an Iraqi Ambassador raised the subject of how the US would react to a potential Iraqi invasion with American Ambassador April Glaspie, in August 1990, just before Iraqi tanks rolled across the sand.

While debate rages as to the exact details of what occurred at that meeting, whether by intent or accident, it seems certain that Saddam thought that the US would not object if he went ahead with his invasion plans. Given that a number of US Senators had recently visited Baghdad and declared support for Saddam – including at least one staunch Jewish liberal and champion of Israel – it is a conclusion he could be forgiven for making.

THE USUAL SUSPECTS
New World Order
The "New World Order" was an expression first used in the Twenties by Colonel Edward House, who believed in world government. President George H. W. Bush brought the phrase into the public spotlight when he described the coalition gathered against Saddam as a sign of an emerging New World Order. Most conspiriologists view the NWO as a form of One World government that secret forces are working to introduce. For a New World Order to hold power over nation states, it would need to be able to justify its existence. The type of international operation of joint political and military force seen in the Gulf may be the first example designed to convince the population of the globe that the NWO is an idea whose time has come.

Military–Industrial Complex
With the fragmentation of the Soviet Union, in 1989, and the spectre of a communist menace a thing of the past, people were beginning to question whether the US and its Western allies actually needed to keep spending billions on defence. Conspiracy theorists believe that the invasion by Saddam Hussein, in 1990, is just too much of a coincidence. They believe that he was put up to the attack on Kuwait by the military–industrial complex, so that he could be presented as the new enemy that needed opposing – hence justifying continued massive spending on armaments.

THE UNUSUAL SUSPECTS
KGB
It is well known that the Soviets and the KGB had developed a very close relationship with Saddam over the years. Some conspiracy theorists believe that the demise of the Soviet Union is merely a diversionary tactic to allow the KGB to develop plans for communist world domination – it was the KGB that arranged the Gulf War. By setting up Saddam as the main bogeyman, the KGB's strategists ensured that American attention would be focused on Iraq, leaving them free to pursue their machinations unmolested by the US.

Oil Companies
If nothing else, the first Gulf War managed to push the price of crude oil up to the type of figure that the oil companies had not enjoyed since the days of the 1973 oil crisis.

George Bush, Sr made his fortune as an oil baron and, with petrochemical industry–intelligence community connections, some have speculated that financial gain may have been the true motive behind the staging of the first Gulf War. With "Boy George" following in his father's shoes and

with his own oil-based fortune, it is not surprising that this is still a popular theory to explain the second Gulf War, too.

Most Convincing Evidence
On the CIA payroll since 1959, Saddam Hussein had most certainly been in Washington's pocket from the very beginning. The CIA bankrolled his Ba'ath Party coup of 1963 and gave him the "green light" to attack Iran in 1980. They even supported him in his gas bombing of the Kurds, with the prevailing attitude in Washington best summed up by the old adage, "He may be a son-of-a-bitch, but he's our son-of-a-bitch."

In the weeks leading up to the Iraqi invasion of Kuwait on 2 August 1990, both Saddam Hussein and his deputy, Tariq Aziz, had several meetings with April Glaspie, US Ambassador to Iraq since 1988. During their meeting of 25 July 1990, Glaspie told Saddam, face-to-face, "We have no opinion on your Arab–Arab conflicts, such as your dispute with Kuwait. Secretary Baker has directed me to emphasize the instruction, first given to Iraq in the 1960s, that the Kuwait issue is not associated with America." With the Americans knowing full well that Iraqi troops were already massed on the Kuwait border and both Saddam and Aziz knowing that they knew, Glaspie might just as well have stood on the Kuwaiti border herself, waving a green flag to signal the start of the invasion.

Given that Mussolini was on the MI5 payroll as early as 1917, to the tune of £100 a week – or £8,000 at today's values – perhaps Mary Shelley's *Frankenstein* ought to be obligatory reading for all intelligence chiefs. This might remind them that while they can build any monster they like, they should always bear in mind that one day, sooner or later, their creation will turn on them.

MOST MYSTERIOUS FACT
In the aftermath of the Gulf War, an intriguing book entitled *American Hero* by Larry Beinhart was published by Ballantine Books. Purporting to be fiction, it details how the war was the idea of a Republican dirty-tricks expert designed to boost the popularity of President Bush. For a novel, its unearthed facts and extensive footnotes provide a damning level of evidence for the conspiracy view of the Gulf War. One question it raises is why did the American, British and Soviet ambassadors all leave Kuwait two days before the invasion?

SCEPTICALLY SPEAKING
As the second Gulf War showed, America has never shown much inclination to come up with good excuses not to throw its weight around, so allowing the invasion of Kuwait seems a little unnecessary. Maybe the reason why Saddam was left in power at the end of the first Gulf War was because George Bush, Sr wanted to leave his son something to get his teeth into when he became president?

HILLARY CLINTON

That there is a broad-fronted and multi-faceted conspiracy hounding the Clintons in general – and Hillary (HRC) in particular – is beyond doubt, but which way are we peering through the telescope? Are we looking at a conspiracy justifiably founded on their political machinations and wrong-doings or, as claimed by Hillary herself, a cynically constructed conspiracy of lies aimed at them/her by elements determined to bring them/her down?

Since her husband elected to slowly fade from the political limelight so as not to overshadow his wife's public ambitions, Hillary per se has become the focus of some rather dark and largely unfounded attacks on every front – including her sexuality. She is strident, firm and unflinching in her opinions and likes to wear trouser suits so she must be lesbian – well, they do say that the top three things that men hate is a smart woman.

In fact, HRC herself first went public in 1998 with the notion that she and Bill were the focus of "a vast right-wing conspiracy" and subsequently used that expression so many times that its origination is attributed to her whereas she "stole" it from Chris Lehane, one of her husband's then consultants. But she did invite some justly-levelled ridicule for ushering under that umbrella the Monica Lewinsky scandal, as if Bill was somehow a passive victim in it all. As things turned out, with Lewinsky being canny enough to keep certain forensic

Where will Hillary Clinton's political ambitions take her next?

samples in her freezer for a rainy day, she was propelled into the celebrity status she still enjoys; as Shakespeare opined through the mouth of Malvolio in *Twelfth Night*, some are born great whilst others have it thrust upon them!

But there is a much darker element of the conspiratorial ball-and-chain that HRC is condemned to drag though the public arena – the attempt of stunted imagination to brand her and Bill serial killers, albeit by proxy. Just Net-search "Clinton Body Count" and you will get something approaching 2 million results! But how did this conspiracy-based libel/slander get started? It first reared its head in 1994 when the right-wing – and slightly delusional – American politician William Dannemeyer of the House of Representatives sent a list of 24 names to Congress with the demand that their deaths be investigated in an attempt to implicate the Clintons. He in turn had received the list from its compiler, the even more delusional Linda Thompson, a conspiracy-buff who, like Dannemeyer, believed the world to be under threat from a Zionist-backed New World Order. Her life dogged by depression and suicide-attempts, she once made a film featuring what she claimed to be a concentration camp built by the Federal Emergency Management Agency (FEMA) to contain citizens unwilling to bow to the New World Order, but the featured compound turned out to be the rolling-stock repair yards of Amtrak. Oops!

Congress ignored Dannemeyer but the list has since grown as others have added names willy-nilly – even Hillary Clinton's mother's hairdresser – who allegedly died "mysteriously" in her late 80s – was included as was Dr Stanley Heard, a chiropractor who once treated Bill's mother and step-father, he dying years later in a plane crash.

THE STRANGE PART

… is that nobody bothered to check the names or the details of their deaths as the list, like Topsy, just grew and grew, to include, for example, James McDougal, who was arrested for financial malfeasance in the real-estate fraud known as the Whitewater Scandal. Although investors in the same, the Clintons were cleared of any wrong-doing. In fact, McDougal had serious cardiac problems and died of a heart attack in the Medical Centre of the Fort Worth Federal Penitentiary. How spooky is that? Also on the list is Gandy Baugh, one of the lawyers who defended restauranteur/ entrepreneur Dan Lasater, who, a significant contributor to the 1980s Clinton political bandwagon, ended up doing time for cocaine distribution. Years later, in 1994, Baugh killed himself – as did his law partner a month later, which would suggest they were up to no good and considered suicide a preferable alternative to that which might come their way.

Also included are four FDA agents who died in the shoot-out at the Branch Davidian compound in Waco because all four had, at various times, been attached to the White house bodyguard detail. Then there are the six sailors who met Bill Clinton on his three-hour visit to the USS *Theodore Roosevelt* in 1993; all from the same ship's unit, they later died together in a helicopter crash. The famous meet so many that, statistically, some of those are going to die, get murdered or commit suicide. You could draw up a similar list for the Pope – indeed, someone probably has!

THE USUAL SUSPECTS
The Fourth International
Because some other conspiracy theories maintain HRC has historic links to radical groups such as the Black Panthers, she is, by extension, thought to be linked to the Fourth International, a one-time hard-line communist cabal imagined to be determined to put a fellow traveller into the White House. But, existing only in the minds of some conspiratists, the Fourth International effectively died in the 1960s – there is even a small UK group called the Workers International to Rebuild the Fourth International! As for HRC having supported in any way the Black Panthers, those who voice this should be aware that she tends to reach for a lawyer when such is suggested. At the time of the 1970 conspiracy trial of a group of Panthers, known as the Chicago Eight, Hillary Clinton was still Hillary Rodham and, not yet a lawyer, she was one of a small group of law students sent to monitor the trial as an exercise to watch for civil-rights infringements, such as one defendant, Bobby Seale, having to sit bound and gagged on the orders of the judge. At no time did she support, represent or act in any way to facilitate their acquittal.

THE UNUSUAL SUSPECTS
Feminist Lobby
The most disturbing things about the conspiracy to bring down HRC – and there most certainly is one – is the twisted imagination of those driving such a juggernaut. From the moment she had the temerity to step out from 'Teflon' Bill's shadow and stand in her own right – in a trouser-suit, the hussy! – she attracted such a tirade of frothy-mouthed flack as to defy description. With her marriage branded a sham – which by now is more than possible – and her daughter Chelsea believed by some loonies to be an actor hired in for the role, there are those who claim she is spear-heading a "petti-coterie" of matriarchal activists determined to take over the world. Even if true, would that be such a bad thing? Let's face it, the men have been making a Horlicks of it for millennia.

MOST CONVINCING EVIDENCE
That the Kill Bill 'n Hill lobby is determined to twist any event in order to lay it at their door was perhaps best illustrated by the sad death of one-time White House intern Mary Caitrin Mahoney, who was one of three staff gunned down in a Washington branch of Starbucks during a robbery-gone-wrong in the July of 1997. Brandishing two handguns, the soon-arrested Carl Cooper burst in at the end of their nightshift but Mary tackled him, resulting in her being shot several times; having done that in front of the other two, Cooper dispatched them also.

This shooting came in the run-up to the breaking of the Monica Lewinsky scandal when Mike Isikoff of *Newsweek* kept putting it out there that "a former White House staffer, with the initial 'M'" would soon be going public on her dalliance with the president. Everyone ran away with the idea that Mahoney had been the target of a Secret Service "hit" to shut her up, resulting in her name gracing the Body List, as indeed it still does. But the anti-Clinton lobby really missed a trick here: what they did not know at the time was that Mahoney was a lesbian activist so they would have been better off trying to conjure up some imagined link between her and Hillary, not Bill. But before anyone tries, the two women never even met.

MOST MYSTERIOUS FACT
Why does no one ever ask the obvious question: why are those who have done the Clinton's most harm still walking about voicing their accusations and imputations, why are they not riding high on the Clinton Body Count? The following – and indeed many others still alive – could have been bumped off before they said a word: Monica Lewinsky, Paula Jones and Gennifer Flowers, just three of Bill's indiscretions; Kathleen Willey, who claimed sexual assault, and Juanita Broaddrick, who went the whole nine yards with allegations of rape; and then there was Linda Tripp, the "friend" of Lewinsky, who secretly taped her reminiscences of White House manoeuvres in the dark, and gave them to Kenneth Starr, the solicitor general who brought about the impeachment of Bill Clinton.

SCEPTICALLY SPEAKING
Whilst the Clintons might not reach out to swat those who displease them, just to be on the safe side, many associated with this book have changed their identities and "gone dark" after becoming aware that Griswold Zachariah Finderflop of Moosejaw, Alabama, died "mysteriously in his bed" exactly three years to the day after the Clintons overflew his town in a commercial airliner bound for Washington. Flinderflop was only 96!

GEORGE BUSH, SR

Anyone elected to the office of President of the United States of America becomes the centre of attention for an army of conspiriologists. George Bush, Sr was something of an exception – even before he was elected as Ronald Reagan's Vice-President, in 1980, he was already at the heart of several major conspiracy theories, including Watergate, the Bay of Pigs and the assassination of JFK.

Before becoming President of the USA, George Bush had already served as the Director of the CIA.

Officially, George Bush only worked for the Central Intelligence Agency from 1976–77, when he was its Director. However, there is a large body of evidence to suggest that George Bush was working for the CIA as early as 1961. He was a member of the bizarre Skull and Bones Society at college – a known recruiting ground for senior CIA agents. Running his oil company meant visiting rigs across the world – perfect cover for an agent. His company was named Zapata, which was also the codename for the CIA's Bay of Pigs operation; the two Navy ships re-painted as civilian ships for the aborted invasion attempt were renamed *Barbara* and *Houston* – the names of Bush's wife and of the town in Texas where his company was based.

When the US government released nearly one hundred thousand pages of documents on the Kennedy assassination, in 1978, conspiracy researchers found a memo among them from the State Department to "George Bush of the Central Intelligence Agency". This memo warned of the possibility that anti-Castro groups in Miami might stage another invasion of Cuba in the aftermath of the JFK murder. President Bush has denied that he was the man in the memo and that it was intended for another "George Bush" who also had a similar address to him. Conspiracy buffs believe that the memo was sent to the CIA because of the previous invasion attempt and to George Bush because he was involved in the planning of other invasions, including the Bay of Pigs.

Another significant Bush link to the Kennedy affair lies with George de Mohrenschildt, a rich Russian oilman and long-time CIA agent who lived in Texas and helped Lee

Harvey Oswald settle there after he left the Soviet Union. Shortly before he was due to testify before the House Select Committee on Assassinations, de Mohrenschildt was found dead of an allegedly self-inflicted gunshot wound. His personal address book contained the entry: "Bush, George H. W. (Poppy), 1412 W. Ohio also Zapata Petroleum Midland."

Given this type of security-service background to investigate, it is not surprising that some conspiriologists believe that the then Vice-President Bush was the force behind a conspiracy to assassinate President Ronald Reagan, in 1982, in an attempt to place himself in the White House a few years ahead of schedule. However, perhaps even more worrying are the links that tie the Bush family to that of Osama bin Laden. These are examined more closely in the following entry on George W. Bush, or Dubya.

THE STRANGE PART

The official version of events on 30 March 1982 is that Ronald Reagan was walking to his limousine when John Hinckley, Jr surged forward and opened fire with a pistol. A bullet allegedly ricocheted off the limousine and injured Reagan, but failed to kill him. However, more than one witness reported that at least one shot came from a Secret Service agent who was stationed on the overhang behind Reagan's limousine. As one beneficiary of Reagan's death would have been Bush, conspiracy buffs have made him (or forces controlling him) the prime suspect in the Reagan shooting.

THE USUAL SUSPECTS
The CIA

The traditional bad guys of the conspiracy world have certainly played a big part in the life of George Bush, Sr. It is possible the agency wished to put one of their men into the White House early to help them strengthen their position in the drugs trade and secret wars they were conducting in Central America at the time of the Reagan shooting. The CIA may have already eliminated more than one president – JFK through an assassin's bullet and Nixon by the Watergate scandal – so would have little reason to doubt it could be done again without comeback.

Skull and Bones

It is well known that George Bush was a member of the Skull and Bones – a secret society at Yale college with initiation rites that involve lying naked in a coffin and providing fellow members with a list of blackmail material against you. Members of the Skull and Bones have a tendency to form the ruling elite of America and the society also seems to operate as an unofficial recruiting body for the US intelligence community. No one knows exactly what the true aim of the Skull and Bones is, but placing one of its own in the White House does not sound too unlikely a goal.

THE UNUSUAL SUSPECTS
MJ-12

Allegedly the true ruling power in America and the group behind the cover-up of the existence of UFOs and aliens, MJ-12 may have wanted to eliminate Reagan because he was unstable and could have exposed the group's existence. It is certain that Reagan came close to implying the reality of an alien menace when he made a speech suggesting that the USA and USSR would be forced to unite in a moment if the people of the world discovered that they had a common extra-terrestrial enemy. MJ-12 is rumoured to always include the current Director of the CIA on its controlling committee, which, if true, would have made George Bush a former member of the organization.

Knights of Malta

An allegedly Catholic organization, based around the Knights of the Hospital of St John of Jerusalem, which was created during the Crusades, membership of the Knights of Malta at the time of Reagan's shooting included head of the CIA, William Casey, and Reagan's foreign policy chief, General Alexander Haig. Confusion reigned in the aftermath of the shooting as to who, exactly, was in control of America while Reagan was disabled. When asked about this, Haig said, "I'm in charge now." Were the Knights of Malta behind the shooting as part of a plot to install a president who was an ex-CIA man with close links to certain "Knights"?

MOST CONVINCING EVIDENCE

If you inspect the video footage of the shooting, it is clear that from the position Hinckley was standing in when he opened fire, he would have needed to shoot through a car door to hit Reagan where he did. This impossibility is explained by the "ricochet theory", which is as implausible as the infamous "magic bullet theory" in the JFK shooting.

MOST MYSTERIOUS FACT

Members of the Bush and Hinckley families were very old friends, as both families had made their fortunes in the Texas oil boom. The families shared many connections, and it may be more than just a rather spooky coincidence that George Bush's son Neil was supposed to have had dinner with Scott Hinckley – John Hinckley's brother – the evening that John attempted to shoot President Ronald Reagan.

SCEPTICALLY SPEAKING

Anyone whose hero is Travis Bickle and is obsessed with Jodie Foster deserves the label "nut" and is probably unbalanced enough to attempt the lone assassination of a president. The fact that George Bush is connected to the CIA by a large number of supposed links and secret societies just helps to create the illusion of conspiracy where there is no real evidence for one.

GEORGE W. BUSH

**George W. Bush might not have been born to be president as some
claim, but the moment he decided to run for the job, he was destined to
play a huge role in the theories of many conspiriologists.**

A large section of the public, as well as hardened conspiracy
buffs, sense that there was more to the election of the son of
former President George Bush than the quirky workings of
democracy. Suspicions about how he came to follow in his
father's footsteps are only intensified by the frankly dubious
way in which he triumphed in the presidential election against
Vice-President Al Gore and the strange sense that fighting a
war in Iraq seems to be a bit of a Bush family tradition.

Bush Jr has a conspiracy pedigree second to none. Before
he even became president, his father was suspected of being
involved in the assassination of JFK, Watergate, the Iran–
Contra scandal and the attempted assassination of Ronald
Reagan and also announced the creation of a "New World
Order" on the White House lawn. His grandfather, Prescott
Bush, made a fortune laundering Nazi funds syphoned out
of Germany before the USA enjoined World War II and
his war-time dealings with Nazi Germany per se are still
being investigated under the Trading With the Enemy Act.
As late as 2001, a group of Auschwitz survivors led by Kurt
Goldstein and Peter Gingold pressed a $40-billion class
action against the Bush family fortunes. This suit was rejected
by Judge Rosemary Collyer in 2002, shortly after her being
nominated to take the seat on the bench of the United States
District Court of the District of Columbia, freshly vacated by
none other than George W. Bush!

His father, George Bush, Sr, was from 1998 to 2003
senior advisor to the multi-billion-dollar Carlyle Group,
a Washington-based equity giant in which the bin Laden
family was heavily invested. Most eyebrow-twitching of all
is the fact that the day before the attacks of 9/11 in 2001,
when Osama bin Laden's minions were attacking New York,
Bush, Sr was in a closed meeting in Washington's Ritz-
Carlton Hotel with Osama's brother, Shafig; also present
was Bush's former Secretary of State, James Baker, the man
who orchestrated the fiasco that put Bush, Jr into the White
House. Only after all this became public knowledge in 2003
did Bush step down from his position with Carlyle.

In 1978, George W. set up his own oil company, Arbusto
Energy – his partner being none other than Osama's other
brother, Salem. Three days after the attacks of 9/11 and a
time by which the identity of the orchestrator was open
knowledge, a fleet of black limos was busily rounding
up twenty-four other members of the bin Laden family,
who were resident in the United States, and, without any
interrogation whatsoever, these people were whisked away to
a jet bound for Saudi and safety. Also post-9/11, and when
American ground forces had tracked Osama himself to the
Tora Bora region of Afghanistan, that task-force of a scant 50
men was pitifully small for the size of the region but, despite
the CIA commander's repeated request for at least 800
men, no reinforcements were sent. That commander, Gary
Bernsen, was of the firm opinion that someone back home
simply did not want Osama to be found. His book detailing
his bureaucratically impeded hunt for bin Laden, *Jawbreaker*
(2006), makes for disturbing reading.

Within minutes of announcing his candidacy for
president, conspiracy theorists were speculating online that
the coming election would be fixed for a Bush win, a new
war on Iraq would be started and the government would gain
further powers – all predictions that have been accurately
fulfilled. The only thing they disagreed about was who was
pulling the strings behind the scenes. The assumption was
that a man famous for making statements such as, "I know
the human being and fish can coexist peacefully", and "It's
clearly a budget – it's got a lot of numbers in it", was not the
brains behind any plot to gain control of the White House.

The first prediction of a conspiracy to fix the vote
exploded in a very public way when the Democratic
contender for president, Al Gore, won the national vote
by more than a half-million votes. However, Bush was
installed in the White House due to the result in Florida
– a Republican-controlled state, where his brother, Jeb
Bush, was governor – that swung the Electoral College.
Amid lost votes, faulty voting machines that counted a vote
for Bush, even when a voter selected another candidate,
Bush's chance of becoming president hung in the balance
as his lead dwindled to a few hundred votes in Florida. Al
Gore began pushing for a recount, so Bush supporters in
Miami started to riot. The prospect of spreading violence
helped influence the US Supreme Court to a 5–4 ruling
on stopping a state-wide Florida recount and therefore
making Bush the president. However, it later emerged that
the "Brooks Brothers' Riot" – named after the preppie
style of the protestors' clothes – was led by so-called rioters
who were paid by Bush's election committee. Thus, the
organization spent $1.2 million to fly operatives to Florida

and elsewhere, and a fleet of corporate jets was assembled, including planes owned by Enron, then run by Kenneth Lay, a major backer of Bush. One of the rioters, Matt Schlapp, even ended up as special assistant to the President.

Once in the White House, the conspiracy community, mindful of the words of David Rockefeller that, "We are on the verge of a global transformation. All we need is the right major crises and the nations will accept a New World Order," speculated that something akin to the aborted Operation Northwoods would soon materialize to allow for a war in Iraq and a clampdown on civil liberties.

Northwoods was a secret military plan. It was sanctioned by the joint chiefs of staff but never given presidential clearance to create a public and international climate for an attack on Cuba by hijacking planes, blowing up a US ship and even committing terrorist acts in US cities and then blaming them on Fidel Castro.

THE STRANGE PART

Post-9/11 it was not long before the other elements of the conspiracy theorists' earlier predictions began to take shape. The President – who once said, "There ought to be limits to freedom" – brought in the Homeland Security Act. Among other things, this allows for secret arrest and detention, mandatory vaccinations while giving vaccine manufacturers immunity from prosecution and for the monitoring of all personal communications and financial transactions – even library records. So there was no surprise when the war against Iraq materialized on the basis that Saddam Hussein was readying weapons of mass destruction to attack the Western world.

THE USUAL SUSPECTS
The Skull and Bones

Like father like son, George W. Bush is working on behalf of the Yale-based Skull and Bones secret society. Aside from performing strange rituals akin to esoteric Freemasonry mixed with occult Nazi ceremonies and obtaining blackmail material on all members, their aims remain well hidden. However, with two recent presidents and a host of America's ruling elite coming from within their ranks, their connection to power is obvious.

CIA and American Oil Companies

As the CIA shaped the direction of his father's life and presidency, it is not unreasonable to believe that the CIA and their real paymasters in certain American oil companies are repeating history and pulling the strings of "Dubya". Wars benefiting US oil companies in Afghanistan and Iraq, and more power and money for the CIA have been noticeable outcomes of George II's time in the White House.

THE UNUSUAL SUSPECTS
The British Royal Family

America's position as the most powerful, democratic country ever to have existed in world history is a cleverly constructed illusion. The Bush family is part of a network of bloodlines owing loyalty to the British monarchy who just pretended to lose the American War of Independence. The president's real job is to advocate policies that ensure the continuing success of the secret British Empire and bolster the finances of the House of Windsor.

Reptilian Aliens

George W. Bush is the latest in a line of puppet rulers installed in positions of power by reptilian aliens from the Draco system, who have been secretly running most of the world since 4000BCE.

MOST CONVINCING EVIDENCE

Unofficial recounts by news organizations found that if all the legally cast ballots in Florida had been counted, Al Gore would have won Florida and thus the presidency. American citizens now have less freedom than at any previous time in their history. Despite spending more than $500 million post the second Gulf War on weapon inspection, no evidence that Saddam Hussein had massive stockpiles of weapons of mass destruction and was planning an attack has ever been produced to back up the official reasons for that war.

MOST MYSTERIOUS FACT

"Boy George", as many conspiracy theorists have taken to calling him, was so worried about his past surfacing that he hired a private detective to investigate himself. No details of what the detective found have emerged, apart from the fact that as one person of the Bush campaign team said, "No handcuffs or dwarf orgies were found." However, George Bush's private detective might be a little worried as four other independent investigators looking into his past all died in suspicious or unexplained circumstances.

SCEPTICALLY SPEAKING

"Dubya", his father and grandfather were in Skull and Bones, so the family was bound to attract suspicion. Indeed, it was Dubya's grandfather, Prescott Bush, who dug up Geronimo to pinch his skull for that club and further "augmented" its grim collection by likewise desecrating the grave of the Mexican revolutionary Pancho Villa. This is why Bush, Sr's first oil company was called Zapata Oil – after Emiliano Zapata, Villa's ally!

Add in the fact that all three were stinking rich and in positions of power – which inevitably brought them into contact with some very dubious movers and shakers – and you have a conspiracy dream factory in which you can join up the dots any way you choose.

THE ASSASSINATION OF JFK

Everyone of a certain age today claims to remember exactly where they were and what they were doing when they first heard the reports of the JFK assassination in Dallas on 22 November 1963. Maybe so – but this is one conspiracy theory that, with more than a little justification, refuses to die. And why should it? It has more legs than a millipede. Over 80 per cent of Americans today still believe that Lee Harvey Oswald was a mere patsy who could not possibly have been a "lone wolf" and that JFK had been the target of a conspiracy that ran into corners of the administration that were best kept dark.

President Lincoln was shot in Ford's Theatre. JFK was shot in a Ford Lincoln.

Secret Service agent Clinton Hill attempts to shield the occupants of President Kennedy's limousine.

This was certainly the opinion of the United States House of Representative's Select Committee on Assassinations, which, in 1979, published its conclusion: "The Committee believes, on the basis of the evidence available to it, that President John F. Kennedy was probably assassinated as the result of a conspiracy." Either way, in the light of the October 2017 release of thousands of files relating to the assassination, you can bet your bottom-dollar that the aforementioned figure of 80 per cent is set for a dramatic rise.

The Strange Part

The rifle that Lee Harvey Oswald bought by mail-order in the March of 1963 was undoubtedly an Italian 6.5mm Carcano bolt-action carbine – hardly an assassin's first choice. However, when the first officers to enter the room from which Oswald allegedly fired with stunning accuracy for such an outdated weapon, first used by the Italian Army in 1891, they took into custody a rifle that they all agreed was a 7.65mm Mauser. Deputy Sheriffs Eugene Boone and Roger Craig and Constable Seymour Weitzman, men whose jobs required them to know a bit about guns, all agreed the rifle was a Mauser – apart from anything else, they said, it had "Mauser" stamped into the metal of the breech.

Moments later, US Army Captain Fritz and Lieutenant Day arrived to take into military custody what they *also* agreed was a 7.65mm Mauser rifle. However, by the time the rifle was logged into evidence it had magically morphed into Oswald's 6.5mm Carcano with "MADE IN ITALY" stamped into the stock and "Cal 6.5" stamped into the side of the barrel – something that we are supposed to believe that officers Fritz, Day, Boone, Craig and Weitzman all failed to notice!

All but Craig eventually withdrew their original statements to say sullenly in unison that they were wrong; Craig, who stuck to his original statement and kept making public statements,

was found dead in 1975, having apparently committed suicide by shooting himself through the chest with a rifle. Once again, this was not the best choice of weapon for such a job – especially for a man who had open access to a variety of pistols.

The Usual Suspects
ALLEN DULLES

Whichever path you walk through the web of intrigue woven around the shooting of JFK, sooner or later you will come across the name of Allen Dulles. He was Director of the CIA until he was sacked by JFK for his mishandling of the American-backed invasion of Cuba, which foundered at the Bay of Pigs in 1961. Retreating into the shadows after his sacking, Dulles ran an anti-Kennedy cabal from his home with E. Howard Hunt. This was the man whose later embroilment in the Watergate scandal likely resulted in the assassination of his wife, Dorothy – aka the Watergate Paymistress – who died with a dozen other Watergate suspects when United Airlines Flight 553 inexplicably flew straight into the ground outside of Chicago in December 1972.

A high-ranking member of the CIA himself, Hunt was long suspected of having been one of the so-called "three tramps" or "three vagrants" spotted on the Grassy Knoll. It was from this spot that most believe the real kill-shot emanated and, on his deathbed, Hunt made recorded confessions detailing his own part in the assassination of JFK and implicating Dulles and Lyndon Baines Johnson (LBJ). However, it is Dulles's feathery links to Lee Harvey Oswald that cause the most concern.

Allen Dulles's long-time CIA cohort and lover, Mary Bancroft, was in turn a life-long friend of Ruth Paine-Young, whose son and daughter-in-law, Michael and Ruth Paine of Dallas, were both subversively politically active and under observation. Ruth Paine "accidentally" met up with Lee Harvey Oswald and his Russian wife, Marina, at a party in

February 1963 and latched closely onto them. By September of that same and fateful year, Marina Oswald was living with the Paines, while Lee Harvey was staying at a nearby motel. Meanwhile, the rifle that Oswald would soon allegedly use to kill JFK was stored in the Paines' garage.

On 14 October 1963, Ruth Paine told Lee Harvey Oswald that a neighbour had told her of a job vacancy at the Texas School Book Depository. She further explained that she and Mary Bancroft had already spoken to the depository superintendent, Roy Truly, to make sure that the unemployed Oswald secured the position. That neighbour, Mrs Linnie May Randle, would later tell the Warren Commission – ostensibly set up to investigate the assassination – that despite her brother working at the depository, she had neither been aware of any vacancy nor discussed such with Ruth Paine.

LYNDON BAINES JOHNSON

The finger of suspicion pointing at LBJ's involvement in the killing of JFK is nothing new. However, the files released in October 2017 included intercepted intelligence from Moscow in which the KGB was expressing concern that the whole affair might be laid at their door as an excuse for an American attack on the Soviet Union. These KGB files also discuss LBJ's involvement in the killing, supposedly based on the fact that JFK was to drop him as a running mate in the forthcoming 1964 elections. This notionally meant that LBJ's only shot at the main job was to kill JFK while he was still Vice-President. Of most concern in those Russian files are the repeated and off-hand references to other files containing documented evidence conclusively proving that LBJ had been involved in the assassination.

Without question, no friend or ally of JFK, LBJ certainly had close ties to Dulles, so it is far from impossible that the pair of them were in it together. When he set up the investigative commission a few weeks after the shooting, LBJ bullied the 72-year-old and decidedly "past it" Earl Warren into taking the chair before making sure that six of the other seven seats were occupied by assorted Congressional lightweights. These included the notoriously inept member for Michigan, Gerald Ford, himself destined to stumble into the Oval Office after Nixon got his marching orders. Then, on President Johnson's specific orders, guess which heavyweight, manipulative hawk was put amongst such doves to keep them on the "Oswald was a lone-wolf" line? Our old friend, Allen Dulles.

THE UNUSUAL SUSPECTS
None leap to mind in this case.

THE MOST CONVINCING EVIDENCE

Oswald himself was conveniently assassinated while in police custody shortly after, by Jack Ruby, a man with long-established CIA/Mafia connections. Ruby had nothing to lose, as he was already under the death-sentence of cancer. These events effectively cleared the way for the Warren Commission – or should that be the Dulles Commission – to accept unequivocally the long-ridiculed Single Bullet theory.

Although three shots were fired – with a rapidity that was completely impossible to achieve with a bolt-action carbine – this theory maintained that a single bullet caused all the injuries sustained within the Presidential limo. If we accept that Oswald fired this bullet – with incredible accuracy from his antiquated carbine while it was aimed at a moving target – we are expected to believe that this single bullet inflicted seven separate wounds before finally coming to rest in pristine condition.

The "Dulles Commission" would have us believe that this projectile smashed through Kennedy's head on a downward trajectory before pulling a U-turn to exit his neck. Supposedly, it then continued to plough through the chest of Texas Governor John Connally and smash through his wrists before embedding itself in his thigh. For all this to happen, that bullet would have had to pass through fifteen layers of clothing, seven layers of skin and about eighteen inches of body tissue, while removing a four-inch section of rib-bone and shattering a radius bone before hitting Connally's leg.

However, despite inflicting such terrible damage, the bullet itself was "found" in almost perfect condition on the gurney that was used to wheel Connally into the hospital; with but a couple of minor dents to the nose, the bullet was thus easily proven to have been fired from Oswald's gun – the one that kept morphing from being a 6.5mm Carcano to a 7.65mm Mauser and them back again. And they wonder why so many refuse to believe there was but the one shooter …

MOST MYSTERIOUS FACT

In this decidedly murky pond there are so many dark fish, but the fact that Kennedy's brain went missing from a secure room in the National Archive has understandably attracted more than a little attention. First noted to be missing in the October of 1966 – along with tissue-slides and other autopsy materials – whoever stole it was doubtless anxious to hide from increasingly improving forensics the fact that JFK had indeed been shot from the front by a shooter on the Grassy Knoll and not from behind by any shooter in the Texas School Book Depository.

This would square with the notion held by many that assassins far more deadly and determined than Oswald were in Dallas that sunny day. All they needed to cover their tracks was for Oswald to be at work in the Book Depository, so he could be caught red-handed with his Carcano/Mauser.

SCEPTICALLY SPEAKING

The jury is destined to remain "out" on this one for years to come.

IS TRUMP IN PUTIN'S POCKET?

Both Donald Trump and Vladimir Putin have historic associations with some very shady characters and organisations within Russia, so it was perhaps inevitable that the two would end up scraping hulls somewhere down the line.

In 1984, when Putin was still flexing his muscles in the KGB, a Russian called David Bogatin, an ex-Russian Army pilot of no apparent means, turned up at Trump Tower on New York's Fifth Avenue, to express interest in buying while only a few of the 263 units remained. Unusually, Donald Trump himself took control of the meeting and expressed no surprise when this man-of-no-means hefted onto the table $6m to snap up five of those remaining units. No doubt aware that Russian mobsters were moving into high-end American real-estate as a means of laundering their ill-gotten gains, Trump simply nodded and presided over the closing of the deal.

Three years later, Bogatin was on the run, having been implicated in a massive gas/oil bootlegging scheme orchestrated by the Russian Mob and US authorities confiscated those five apartments in Trump Tower as they were by then known to have been bought with dirty money. Across the past three decades, over a dozen residents of Trump Tower have been identified as having close links to the Russian Mob and Bogatin's brother was revealed a close aide of Semion Mogilevich, the Boss-of-Bosses in the Russian Mafia. In 2005, Alexander Litvinenko, a one-time Russian Intelligence officer, defected to London and began to speak of the strong ties and "good working relationship" that had existed since 1993 between then-President Putin and Mogilevich; this fatal lack of discretion resulting in his being poisoned soon after by agents of the Kremlin.

As for Putin, as President of Russia his last-known official statement of earnings for the year 2015 was declared at 7.7 million rubles, or $137,000, so it is something of a financial miracle that he is directly linked to companies and investments exceeding $2 billion and that his best friend, Sergei Roldugin, a St Petersburg cellist who is also godfather to Putin's daughter, Maria, was recently discovered to be sitting on $100 million for which he volunteered no explanation, despite the Eastern European Organised Crime and Corruption Unit identifying him as the "secret caretaker" of Putin's hidden fortunes.

Getting back to Trump, his first venture into Russia came as early as 1987 when he was flown out – all expenses paid – to discuss high-rolling and reciprocal deals with Russian

Vladimir Putin is pictured with Donald Trump before a photo session of world leaders in Vietnam in November 2017.

oligarchs in both Moscow and Leningrad and, to date, 63 Russians hold significant investments in Trump-branded towers, while the extent of Trump's dealings within Russia is unknown. At a 2017 press conference held on 13 February, Trump stated, "Speaking for myself, I own nothing in Russia. I have no loans in Russia. I have no deals in Russia." Semantically, at least, this could indeed be an accurate statement – but note the careful and personalised use of "*I* own nothing in Russia" – if Donald Trump Inc. holds Russian interests that lie undetected behind a labyrinth of corporate smoke and mirrors then his statement to that press conference would indeed have been accurate in fact, if not truthful in spirit, in that he, Donald Trump, has no personal investment in Russia – but his byzantine empire could be up to its neck in Russian affairs. Either way, few accepted Trump's statement of 13 February as valid.

THE STRANGE PART

One of the first things Trump did on taking office was his initiation of a move to start the dismantling of US sanctions imposed on Russia. These in the main related to Moscow's selling of arms to nations such as North Korea, whilst others had been imposed for its aggressive interventions in the Ukraine and Crimea. Some of these sanctions had been imposed by previous Executive Order, which means that Trump could simply wave them aside – those needing a Congressional vote to be removed he cannot so easily cancel but he does have the power to ensure they are no longer enthusiastically enforced.

THE USUAL SUSPECTS
The Russian Mob

That Trump has connections in Russia dating back some thirty-odd years is a well-established fact but, sticking with the burning question as to whether Kremlin hackers targeted Hillary Clinton to destroy her lead in the 2016 Presidential race and clear the way for a wild-cat Trump victory at the eleventh hour, the answer seems to be a resounding YES!

The so-called Russian Mafia is without doubt the largest and best-connected crime syndicate the world has yet seen, with their largest "market" and money-laundering services to be found in the USA. It is more than possible that the syndicate used Kremlin connections to instigate the Hillary-hack in order to have a man in the White House that they, albeit one-stage-removed, could control remotely by pulling the strings they have attached to highly placed contacts within the Kremlin.

Vladimir Putin

The advantages to Putin of having an American president whose chain he could jerk from time to time need no explanation here. Although denying official involvement, Putin has acknowledged that "patriotic Russian hackers" might have felt moved to produce the massive leaks of e-mails and other sensitive data from the Democratic Party servers and from Hillary Clinton's personal server to boot. Why on earth would "patriotic Russians" strive to put a loose-cannon like Trump in the Oval Office? Hackers from Russia/the Kremlin are known to have been behind cyber-attacks on countless official and commercial institutes in Western Europe and might well have tutored the minions of Putin's puppet in North Korea, which has now been identified as the perpetrator of the recent hack that crippled the British National Health Service.

As early as September of 2015, the FBI was warning the Democratic Party that hacks emanating from Russia were targeting their systems and that at least one server was already compromised. These warnings and up-dates continued right through the Presidential race of 2016 but "inexplicably" ceased upon Trump's surprise victory.

THE UNUSUAL SUSPECTS
The Democratic Party

…or, at least elements therein! This might sound an odd nomination at first but there were factions in violent opposition to their party putting Hillary Clinton up as the runner for the 2016 race. Obviously, it would have been too risky for the anti-Clinton Democrats to "knobble" her themselves – imagine the scandal if that was back-traced! But, if a certain person in the Kremlin could be induced to cry havoc and let slip his cyberdogs of war to trash her run, it could prove a win–win for all involved. The Kremlin could have the fun of overturning an American Presidential election and the Democrats could then call, "Foul!" – have Trump kicked out of office and demand a re-run with Joe Biden as their preferred runner.

MOST CONVINCING EVIDENCE

…of connections between the Russian Mob and Trump Real Estate Inc. Back in 1991, the aforementioned Russian Mob boss, Semion Mogilevich, "bought" a Kremlin pardon for his right-hand man, Vyachelsav Ivankov, then slaving away in a Siberian prison. Upon release, Ivankov went to Trump Plaza on New York's Third Avenue, where he made contact with another Russian "Person of Interest", high-end art dealer Felix Komarov, before establishing himself as the Russian "godfather" of the US, where he set up Mogilevich's "satellite" operation, which would itself grow into a crime giant. The FBI said that tracking Ivankov was like trying to keep tabs on a ghost, but he always made routine visits to the Trump Taj Mahal Casino in Atlantic City with vast amounts of cash. In 2015, that casino was hit with a fine of $10m – the largest Federal penalty ever levied on a gambling-joint – for having spent years "wilfully violating" the money-laundering regulations.

MOST MYSTERIOUS FACT

The FBI tried for years to track down Ivankov's home address – James Moody, the bureau's Chief of Organized Crime, later said, "It may sound silly, but no matter how hard we beat the bushes we simply could not find him. And then we found him – in a luxury condo in [the New York] Trump Tower." Now, just because Ivankov was a neighbour of Donald Trump, does not necessarily say that the two ever so much as met but, against the backdrop of other links between Donald Trump, Donald Trump businesses and Russia, it raised more than a few bureau eyebrows.

SCEPTICALLY SPEAKING

In an organization as massive as Trump's, it is inevitable that its very size will attract money launderers. No one's going to launder $20m through a convenience store and expect it to go unnoticed. It is also unfair to expect Trump, the head of such an octopus, to be aware of everything his tentacles touch. That said, now, as President of the most powerful country, he should, like Caesar's wife, be more concerned with how things appear.

CHAPTER 2:

<u>ORGANIZATIONS</u>

THE CIA

Everyone is suspicious of spy agencies; what would be the point of a covert operations organization that freely admitted what it was doing? In the USA, the CIA is up against a highly liberal Freedom of Information Act – a problem that few of its counterparts in other countries have to deal with. It is the uneasy mix of information and misinformation surrounding the CIA that makes it such a popular target for conspiratorial speculation.

The accusation that most often lands on the Company's doorstep, though, is that it sells drugs to people. Supposedly to Contras and rebels throughout South America in the first instance, to help raise cash for the anti-communist cause and destabilize local countries. Then, Africa was supposed to be the target of drug sales, to help raise independent finance for certain operational budgets that CIA chiefs didn't want Washington to know about even as expenses claims. More recently, the accusation is that the CIA was the force behind the American crack-cocaine explosion of the eighties.

The idea might seem quite a good one – at least to a particularly cynical and sadistic manipulator. Devise a new drug that is extremely addictive, extremely debilitating to the user, and can be sold for large amounts of money, then distribute it to the dealers who service the ghettos and other poor black areas until there's a huge demand economy set up. Once it's firmly entrenched, simply hand over production to the locals, and let them get on with it. The result? Instant internal warfare in those poor quarters.

The overall plan sees the unfortunate citizens in the ghettos so totally distracted by crack – being on it, looking for it, making it, selling it, fighting over its distribution, and finally killing themselves with it – that they wouldn't have any time left to hassle nice middle-class caucasians. Strangely enough, the drugs wars have indeed kept the poor and marginalized more or less out of the way.

Despite the general opinion of the public, amateur and petty criminals such as junkies usually prey on their own social groups. The poor tend to rob other poor people, or better-off people passing through. It normally takes a bolder, more dedicated thief to go into good neighbourhoods and risk the greatly increased police presence, better burglar alarms and other hindrances to easy pickings. Encourage such an addictive drug in the poor areas and, with the police presence differential between bad areas (not many of them around) and good areas (plenty of them around), you keep all those potentially rebellious and troublesome marginal people safely out of the way, busy killing one another.

With its headquarters in rural Virginia, the CIA's operatives are generally known as The Farmboys.

The *San Jose Mercury* published a series, in 1996, detailing supposed CIA involvement in the crack trade. The series was well-researched and carefully thought out, and made some pretty thought-provoking suggestions. The vast bulk of the American press responded with nothing but vitriol for Gary Webb, the reporter who had uncovered the story. The *Washington Post* and the *Los Angeles Times* both conducted thorough investigations of Web's investigation, and found nothing to substantiate his information. Even so, the CIA launched its own "full internal investigation" – described by the *Los Angeles Times* as "the most intensive in their history" – the complete results of which were never published.

THE STRANGE PART

Retired CIA agents who were interviewed as part of the investigation described it as a joke. Duane Clarridge, Chief of Cover Ops for Latin America in the eighties, called the questions "nonsense" and refused to answer. He was interviewed by questionnaire, and returned it blank. Very thorough... Others described the questions as "going through the motions". Former CIA officer Donald Winters said that the interview began with the CIA stating that it held "no substantive evidence that any of the allegations in the *San Jose* article had any basis" – hardly an aggressive questioning stance.

THE USUAL SUSPECTS
WASPs

The people who most consistently feel threatened by poor Afro-Americans are, as everyone knows, the white Anglo-Saxon Protestant middle classes. Many WASPs would do whatever they can to keep the ethnic "minorities" out of sight and out of mind. Many of them certainly wouldn't blink at introducing a new, highly addictive drug to the ghettos.

The Freemasons

It is well known that many members of a Certain Intelligence Agency are also high-level Masons. Some conspiracy theorists believe that the whole CIA is under the control of the Masons and that the drug conspiracy is only part of a larger scheme to keep the world firmly in their control.

The Knights of Malta

Although some claim it to be a purely Christian organization, the Knights of Malta have many highly placed CIA personnel among its ranks. These have included William Casey, head of the CIA at the time of the attempted assassination of Ronald Reagan, and James Jesus Angleton, director of the CIA's counter-intelligence network for more than twenty years. Thought to represent the worst prejudices of certain sections of the white male population, if they wished to conduct a secret race war, the Knights of Malta certainly had access to the powerful people within the agency needed to make it happen.

THE UNUSUAL SUSPECTS
Christian Identity

More of a collection of lunatic sects than a true religion, the Christian Identity movement says that the real descendants of the Biblical Hebrews are actually the white Americans – rather like a US version of the British Israelites. This appeals very much to aggressive, ultra-right-wing, survivalist-style groups. Links have been suggested between Identity members (including Larry Harris, the "Anthrax in Vegas" guy, and Eric Rudolph, accused of the Atlanta Bombing) and the CIA, which is allegedly funding such groups. Could it be that Christian Identity is currently the real faith of the chiefs of the CIA, and their agenda is to wipe out the black American community by any and all means available?

MJ-12

This UFO cover-up organization, alleged to be beyond the control of the US government and to be covertly working with the aliens known as the Greys, always includes top-level CIA men on its committee. Could drug-running by the CIA be a way of bolstering the MJ-12's Black Budget? Reverse-engineering alien flying discs isn't cheap.

MOST CONVINCING EVIDENCE

Even though the CIA refused to publish the full report, they claim that the investigation found no evidence to back up any of the allegations. This is hardly shocking, given that very few figures that were not current CIA agents or retired agents were questioned about the issues. Robert Owen, who had previously provided evidence and called attention to the potential links between the CIA and the drugs trade, wasn't even contacted, let alone questioned.

MOST MYSTERIOUS FACT

A large number of potential CIA whistle-blowers have died in suspicious circumstances, gone missing or "committed suicide". While being in the CIA is obviously a dangerous occupation, the numbers involved are worrying and even include former CIA Director of Intelligence William Colby, who died in a wildly improbable boating accident.

SCEPTICALLY SPEAKING

Such an operation would be very hard to keep hidden; the men and women of the CIA are still just that – men and women. It would take a particularly evil sort of zealot to decide that the best way of dealing with the problem of poverty-stricken black Americans was to infect them with a new drug. While such people do exist, the scale of such an operation would involve a very large number of operatives. Surely someone would have retained enough humanity to leak solid evidence of such a monstrous policy to the press?

NASA

Essentially, NASA was born as a decidedly tarnished phoenix that arose from the ashes of Nazi Germany. In 1945, the Americans, Russians and, to a lesser extent, the British, were all fighting over the reservoir of German scientists and other "specialists" from the darker spheres of Nazi operations.

Walt Disney (left) with Werner von Braun in 1954.

The Russians were furious when the Americans tracked down SS Sturmbannfuhrer Wernher von Braun to his hiding place to include him in their so-called Operation Paperclip, which whitewashed the Nazi past of inductees in order to render them acceptable to the folks back home. They certainly had their work cut out with some that they caught in that net – especially the spies and torturers who were sought by Allen Dulles (yes, him again!).

When it came to the V2 rockets that von Braun had invented, it was thought best not to mention that more people actually died manufacturing them than were killed by their deployment. In Britain, 2,724 people were killed in V2 attacks, while more than 20,000 slave labourers brought in from concentration camps died in the factories that produced them. Nor was it thought "helpful" to make public the fact that the Saturn rocket was basically a re-working of von Braun's A10 Amerika-Rakete, which had been scheduled to take off in 1946 to deliver 2,000lb payloads to New York.

So, throughout the 1950s, the pro-Nazi entertainment mogul Walt Disney was hired by von Braun's shadowy handlers to promote him to the American public. They did this via film and television, depicting von Braun as

everybody's naughty uncle who loved to play with rockets. And it worked!

There was also Dr Hubertus Strughold – promoted by NASA to its adoring public as the Father of Space Medicine; what this man did not know about the effects of radiation, extreme temperature, pressure and vacuum on the human body was not worth knowing. However, what NASA had known all along but had managed to keep from public knowledge was the manner in which Strughold had assimilated all this information. Throughout 1943 and 1944, children from Dachau and the Brandenburg Euthanasia Centre were transferred to Strughold's laboratories in Berlin where, just the right size to fit into his pressure/vacuum/temperature chambers, they suffered unspeakable horrors as Strughold harvested his data. On a lighter note, we have Strughold and von Braun to thank for the countdown to launch – as young men, both had seen Fritz Lang's movie *The Woman in The Moon* (1929) – in which the producer had thought it suspenseful to reverse the count to the rocket launch.

If all the rumours surrounding NASA are to be believed, then it has to be one of the greatest disseminators of misinformation currently active in the world – and the agency most active in the suppression of vital truths: it has got the low-down on everything from alien presence surrounding the globe to a range of useful inventions that it is keeping out of the public grasp. NASA also frequently falsifies mission data in order to justify its huge budgets. Money received is siphoned off for mysterious research projects, conducted away from public scrutiny, using US taxpayers' dollars. No one is accountable, and no one on the outside knows what it is that all this cash is being used for. Alternatively, NASA could just be creaming off huge bonuses for directors, and covering up incompetence.

One particularly paranoid rumour suggests that NASA is in fact building a gigantic tunnel network under the US, code-named Orpheus. This is so deep underground that it can survive a direct strike from a massive meteorite without problems. Geothermal energy supplies heating, lighting, air circulation and microprotein cultures, so the network is self-sufficient. That way, when the big asteroid actually hits, NASA will be well placed to survive with a small military set-up, and be in a position to take control after the disaster.

To make sure all goes smoothly, the approach of this huge meteorite is kept secret so that NASA will be the only organization prepared for the disaster…

One feasible element of this conspiracy is that the moon-landing photographs were faked. They were taken inside a secret warehouse that was made up to look very convincingly like the surface of the moon. There are two possible reasons for this. First, NASA never went to the moon – the launch was faked, radio messages were provided by actors, and the actual landing itself was staged. This might have been to save money for Project Orpheus, or it might have been to provide the US government with a vitally important propaganda victory over Russian cosmonauts.

The second idea is that the moon landing went ahead and the film footage that was broadcast live was genuine. However, the photos that the astronauts took just did not come out, because Kodak underestimated the effect of solar glare on the plates. Faced with massive press demand for stills, NASA considered the financial and PR advantages of selling rights, and the embarrassment of admitting that they took the wrong camera equipment. They decided it was better to bluff it out, and mocked-up a lunar landscape for a photo-session on Earth.

THE STRANGE PART

Evidence keeps on leaking out that NASA knows much more than it releases officially. A former high-level NASA consultant is rumoured to have leaked copies of conversational transcripts from astronauts on the Space Shuttle *Discovery*. In this document, two of the Shuttle pilots are supposed to discuss what appears to be "a huge glowing spacecraft flying around the Earth". Former NASA specialist Dr Hoagland has made claims that NASA not only knows about extra-terrestrials, but also understands hyper-dimensional space and the true origins of human life.

THE USUAL SUSPECTS
The American Government

The most common explanation is that faced with the humiliating prospect of ruining a superb public-relations scoop by having screwed up the photos, the American government told NASA to fake some photos and keep it quiet, or else. If there is a UFO conspiracy, it seems likely that the American government controls NASA's involvement in the suppression of the truth.

The Freemasons

A lot of strange symbolism seems to be involved in NASA's space missions and it appears that astronauts have even been instructed to perform sacred rituals at appointed times, facing in the direction of certain constellations. This is suggestive of the involvement of a secret society with an interest in mystical symbolism – step forward the Masons.

THE UNUSUAL SUSPECTS
Nazis

As previously explained, for the first twenty years of its existence, NASA was essentially driven and directed by an inner-circle of ex-Nazis. It should not be forgotten that these people were, prior to 1945, collectively striving to bring about the destruction of the United States and her allies. Although the original Nazi influx into NASA is now long-gone, there are those who believe that the agency is still being run by a hand-me-down group of neo-Nazis, who continue to drive NASA along the tracks of their predecessors' secret plan.

The Greys

The real reason that none of NASA's UFO sightings have been made public knowledge is that the agency is actually controlled by aliens. Although the Shuttle routinely flew through a ring of different alien craft, the knowledge is kept suppressed by the extra-terrestrials, who are building up slowly to revealing their presence. Gifts of technology keep the US government happy – and, anyway, who better could you have running your space programme?

MOST CONVINCING EVIDENCE

If you look at the shadows of the rocks in the moon landing photos, you'll see that they point in an arc of different directions – sure proof of a point-source of light just off camera. If the illumination was solar, as it would be on the moon, the shadows would all point in the same direction. They would also have higher contrasts to the earth around them, as there is no atmospheric scatter of light on the moon.

MOST MYSTERIOUS FACT

Comments about alien spaceships apart, there is a short, authenticated transcript of an in-flight Shuttle conversation held when the craft was well outside Earth's atmosphere. In this conversation, one astronaut notices an unidentified object outside and asks his partner if he also saw it shoot past then dart off. Whatever it was, it was not a military jet or a weather balloon this time.

SCEPTICALLY SPEAKING

They do say that the only way for two people to keep a secret is for one of them to kill the other. Consequently, the main problem with so many conspiracy theories is the mind-boggling number of people who would have to be involved yet keep their mouths shut. In the case of the moon-landing conspiracy, this would have to include the thousands of scientists, technicians and assorted ground staff who worked on the Apollo project – not to mention the astronauts themselves – and the considerable production team required to build the lunar set on which to film the actors taking part. Assuming for a minute that all these people kept quiet, what about all the staff in the tracking stations around the world who would have been monitoring the moon-shot?

THE BILDERBERG GROUP

They meet once, sometimes twice a year, renting out remote and expensive hotels. The members of this secretive group include the power brokers of the world, from international financiers to heads of state. Their discussions are rumoured to affect everyone on the planet; allegedly, the group chooses the political leaders of countries and just where the next war will erupt, yet the group is answerable to no one.

Their members include such luminaries as David Rockefeller, Henry Kissinger, George W. Bush and Tony Blair. They are the Bilderberg Group and, according to some, they are your masters.

Formed during the paranoid years of the Cold War, the Bilderberg Group was conceived by Joseph Retinger, an American who headed the CIA-bankrolled European Movement, whose contacts included a who's who of global governmental and military powers. Retinger believed in a world where peace would be brokered not by governments but by super-powerful multinational organizations.

After meeting with Prince Bernhard of the Netherlands in 1952, Retinger then proposed a series of meetings to discuss world problems. This idea was well received by other world leaders and the first meeting was held in May 1954, at the Bilderberg Hotel in Oosterbeek, Holland. Since then, the subsequent meetings have retained the name "Bilderberg" as they are moved from one luxurious retreat to another in locations around the globe. The meetings still take place, and usually comprise 120 attendees, drawn from the key elite of the world, with one-third of them being North American, the remainder European. The general makeup of each meeting has two-thirds of the delegates being from the world of business, media and education, with only one-third actually being politicians.

Journalists are not allowed on the premises, let alone allowed to report on the mysterious proceedings. The Bilderberg meetings are held under a complete media blackout, apparently with the complete cooperation of the media itself. So what are the Bilderbergers up to? Are they simply discussing topics on the evening news or are they quietly deciding just what those topics will be?

THE STRANGE PART

When the Bilderberg Group met in Versailles in 2003, just before the start of the Group of Seven (G7) meeting of finance ministers in nearby Paris, French security police were not happy and tried to block the event. Someone within the police was so unhappy that the meeting went ahead on

their patch, that they leaked an internal memo complaining about the vast number of mercenaries privately employed to protect the members. The memo also made it clear that the police believed that the "*conférence privée*" was merely a cover for something much more sinister. When the Bilderbergers have the power to ensure their meetings are not covered by the major international press and can ride roughshod over the wishes of the local security forces, it is clearly more than a talking shop.

THE USUAL SUSPECTS
International Cabal of Greedy Businessmen

The aim of the Bilderberg Group may be nothing more than simple greed. With its concentration of business leaders and insistence on secrecy, the group could merely be fine-tuning economic policy before disseminating it through members' contacts in their respective governments. By ensuring that everyone is singing from a common hymn sheet, the group could simply be making certain that profits stay exactly where they want them – high.

The New World Order

With a high number of members who are bankers and financiers, it's no surprise that Bilderberg favours free trade, an attitude that tends to break down economic barriers and protectionist policies. Free trade has long been seen as a tool for solidifying the grip of the New World Order on an unsuspecting Earth – start by destroying economic barriers, and it's only a short step to destroying any sense of individual nationality.

With an eye to furthering the dream of a New World Order, the Bilderbergers would decide when and where wars would erupt, thus further destroying national borders and making money for those members who choose to finance such conflicts. With a One World government, and attendant World Bank, the Bilderbergers would pick leaders who follow their plans. Clinton was only Governor of Arkansas when he attended a group meeting in 1991, yet became President of the USA two years later.

THE UNUSUAL SUSPECTS
The Greys
This theory has the Greys running the Bilderbergers in much the same way they are rumoured to run other secret societies, all in aid of weakening Earth and making it easier to conquer.

The Illuminati
The Bilderbergers could be nothing but a ruse to draw the suspicions of the media and public while the real decisions are made elsewhere – allegedly by the real group that runs the world, the Illuminati.

MOST CONVINCING EVIDENCE
In 1955, the Bilderberg Group discussed the need to create a tightly bound European market. A year-and-a-half later, the European Common Market was established by the Treaty of Rome.

MOST MYSTERIOUS FACT
Jon Ronson, author of *Them*, investigating the Bilderberg Group for Channel 4 television in the UK, faced some uncharacteristically extreme swearwords from Bilderberg founder Lord Healey when questioning him about the aims of the Bilderbergers. Ronson also sneaked past security to witness a secret Bilderberg summer retreat at Bohemian Grove, where a human effigy was burnt beneath a statue of a 40-foot (12.19-metre) owl.

SCEPTICALLY SPEAKING
The wealthiest people in the world are actually the ones ruling it? Well, fancy that…

Former UK Prime Minister Tony Blair is thought to have attended meetings of the Bilderberg Group.

KGB

For many observers, the true death knell of the Soviet Union was heard in 1991 when an enthusiastic crowd toppled the statue of Felix Dzerzhinsky and the air resounded with the sound of it shattering into hundreds of pieces. For years, his figure had looked across the square that bore his name towards the infamous headquarters of the KGB – the Lubyanka.

Putin is just one of the many Russian politicians who were former agents of the KGB.

Dzerzhinsky was the mastermind behind the Red Terror that allowed the Communists to seize and hold on to power after the overthrow of the Tsar in the 1917 October Revolution. He created the Cheka secret police that over the years mutated into the Committee of State Security – more commonly known by the initials KGB – the most dreaded and pervasive intelligence-gathering network the world has ever seen.

The KGB (Komitet Gosudarstvennoy Bezopasnosti) was responsible for defending the Soviet Communist regime against internal and external enemies. When the statue of its founder was destroyed, it was symbolic of the breaking

of the hold the KGB had on every Soviet citizen, a hold that was maintained from cradle to grave. During the Cold War, wherever there was a hint of conspiracy there was also a rumour of KGB involvement. Some conspiracy buffs believe that the world's largest covert organization did not even owe allegiance to communism, but existed only to serve its own mysterious ends.

In theory, the KGB was responsible to the Soviet Council of Ministers; in practice, it took its orders directly from the USSR's ruling politburo – if it took orders at all. With the collapse of the Soviet Union and the dismantling of the KGB, in 1991, commentators were quick to describe the organization as "lost to history". Some conspiriologists are not so certain that the KGB's awesome, globe-spanning power has been brought to an end.

To many it seemed suspicious that the KGB – which had controlled the Soviet population using fear and an extensive network of secret informers – had allowed the USSR to collapse with barely a pretence of opposition. Particularly as the KGB has a supervisory influence on the Soviet Army. Conspiracy theorists believe that the apparent end of the Soviet Union and the KGB was merely a cover for an insidious KGB plot to consolidate its power and bring about an even stronger Russian empire.

THE STRANGE PART

Since the fall of the Soviet Union, Russia has been sliding into anarchy. One of the main beneficiaries of this has been Vladimir Zhironovsky – leader of the extreme nationalist Liberal Democratic Party. Millions of Russians have agreed with his statement, "What Russia needs now is a dictator, when I come to power I will be that dictator", voting for him in presidential and parliamentary elections.

With links to ultra-right groups in Germany, to the Russian Mafia and even to Saddam Hussein, Zhironovsky is a potential Russian Hitler with a huge arsenal of nuclear weaponry at his disposal – an arsenal he has threatened to use. Perhaps the most worrying fact is that Zhironovsky was a secret KGB agent. Some of his former associates claim he is being prepared for power by the ex-leaders of the allegedly disbanded secret police and espionage agency.

THE USUAL SUSPECTS
Bavarian Illuminati

Even some orthodox historians are beginning to recognize the key role that several secret societies and occult orders had on the creation of Nazi Germany and Hitler. Behind many of these groups is the spectre of the Bavarian Illuminati – whose modus operandi is to stay in the shadows, take control of other clandestine organizations, and then work through them. Could the Illuminati have followed an age-old pattern and subverted the KGB? Given that Zhironovsky has close links to German right-wing groups with fascist origins, it could be that the hand of the Illuminati is controlling the KGB and the Russian Hitler-in-waiting.

Freemasons

It is well established that the KGB infiltrated Masonic organizations as part of its attempt to place its agents in the British government and security services. However, it is suspected that the traffic was two-way and that the Freemasons penetrated deep within the leadership of the Committee of State Security and managed to take control of it. Some conspiracy theorists now feel the KGB and its plans to recreate a Russian Empire are merely part of a larger Masonic plot to achieve world domination.

THE UNUSUAL SUSPECTS
Teutonic Knights

The Germanic protégés of the Knights Templar, the Teutonic Knights once controlled the independent principality Ordensland, which covered Finland, Prussia and large tracts of Russia. Once they lost their powerbase in the fourteenth century, the Teutonic Knights became a secret society determined to regain their lost lands. Some conspiriologists believe that the Teutonic Knights were the hidden power behind the tsars and, that when the Russian Royal Family became hard to control, masterminded the revolution and infiltrated the new secret police. In this conspiracy scenario, the Teutonic Knights staged the disintegration of the USSR and the KGB in order to form a fascist state that would have more popular support and therefore be easier to control.

MOST CONVINCING EVIDENCE

Former president of the Soviet Union Mikhail Gorbachev denies the accusation made by some conspiracy theorists that he instructed the KGB to create Zhironovsky's Liberal Democratic Party. However, he does admit the possibility that the former secret police are controlling Zhironovsky. Gorbachev has stated, "Can the KGB create a whole party? Zhironovsky is a remarkable actor; it is very important to find out who is directing him, who is behind him."

MOST MYSTERIOUS FACT

When Russian voters backed Vladimir Putin as president, they were voting for another KGB creation. While not so extreme as Zhironovsky, he is a former spy who also headed the Federal Security Service – the official successor of the KGB. Often seen on TV practising the martial-art prowess that comes from KGB training, no one has discovered his exact role within the KGB between 1975 and 1989. However, Putin has spoken more than once of the need for a "dictatorship of the law" and some see his rule as being merely a KGB dry run before Zhironovsky is installed.

SCEPTICALLY SPEAKING

There is very little solid evidence of the KGB surviving the disbanding process. History shows that anti-Semitism and severe economic woe are sometimes all the reasons that are needed to explain the rise of a megalomaniac, would-be world dictator.

MI6

MI6 is known across the globe as the British security service responsible for defending the realm from external enemies thanks to its portrayal as the employer of Special Agent 007 in the decades-spanning series of hit Bond movies. However, in the shadows where conspiracy theories thrive, there are many who see MI6's portrayal in the films as a force for good as no more than blatant propaganda. MI6, they feel, is an organization that is secretly dedicated to achieving world domination.

In theory, MI6 is neutral and does not align itself to any particular political party or ideology. Even the most hardened sceptic viewing modern history would have to admit it shows that one thing MI6 could not be accused of is being neutral. There are many established examples of MI6 campaigning against a politician or organization that it feels is too left wing or that does not support the "Special Relationship" between Britain and America. The most famous case is the removal of Prime Minister Harold Wilson from power.

It had long been rumoured that MI6, in conjunction with its sister service MI5, had been behind the sudden resignation of Wilson in 1976. When the government was unable to prevent the publication of ex-MI5 agent Peter Wright's memoirs, the full details of the conspiracy to remove Wilson in a bloodless coup eventually became public knowledge. The devastating allegations point to a treasonable conspiracy undertaken by a cabal of intelligence officers to undermine and bring down the constitutionally elected government of the United Kingdom.

There are also many other cases of MI6 blackmailing,

Several Russian defectors were adamant that Harold Wilson remained a KGB agent while in office.

smearing and recruiting Members of Parliament – not an activity the movies have ever portrayed James Bond undertaking as part of his remit to "defend the realm". One of the key figures seen to be involved with MI6's on-going attempt to subvert its own nation's democracy was director of CIA counter-intelligence, James Jesus Angleton – mastermind of the Italian P2 conspiracy, possible mastermind of the Kennedy assassination and a member of the mysterious Knights of Malta.

Confirmed conspiratorial actions against the British government, undertaken with allies from the American intelligence community, have made many conspiracy theorists wonder just who MI6 actually works for. If MI6 is not loyal to democratically elected British leaders, they feel it may be engaged as a key player in a conspiracy to achieve global domination for a secret Anglo-American cabal.

THE STRANGE PART

There is no doubting that a network of "Atlanticist" groups exist and work behind the scenes of international politics. These round-table groups often share a common membership, which suggests that the American Council on Foreign Relations works closely with British groups such as the Royal Institute of International Affairs. Given that the leadership of MI6 and the CIA plays a prominent role in all of these groups, conspiriologists feel that it is not unfair to suspect the security services are working to a secret agenda on behalf of these organizations.

THE USUAL SUSPECTS
The Royal Family

More than one conspiracy buff has pointed the finger at the Royal Family as the cement that bonds the alleged Anglo-American cabal. They believe that the Royal Family has been working since the nineteenth century to promote the doctrine of "mystical imperialism" and world domination by the two largest English-speaking nations. Early steps in this process included inspiring Cecil Rhodes to set-up round-table groups and the Rhodes Scholarships at Oxford – which would mean the brightest Americans – including President Bill Clinton – received their "education" in England. MI6 swears loyalty to the Crown, so its part in the conspiracy comes from following the direct orders of the Queen.

Rockefeller Family

The Rockefellers are one of the most fabulously wealthy families in the world and seem to be major players in the conspiracies behind international politics. With possible controlling interests in several banks and major corporations – including the Federal Reserve Bank, which controls all money in the US – David Rockefeller is also chairman of both the Trilateral Commission and the Council on Foreign Relations. Some conspiracy theorists believe that the Rockefellers' aim is to create a super-power Anglo-American alliance dedicated to preserving and furthering their financial interests.

THE UNUSUAL SUSPECTS
Rosicrucians

The origins of the Order of the Rose Cross are a matter of heated debate in conspiracy circles. Whether they developed from an ancient Egyptian cult or were the idea of Giordano Bruno – a sixteenth-century philosopher burnt for organizing secret societies and teaching that life existed on other planets – there is no doubting the Rosicrucians are major conspiracy players. Given that they infiltrated British Freemasonry centuries ago, it is not impossible that they are the true controllers of the Anglo-American cabal.

Knights of Malta

Operating out of a small office in the Vatican, the Knights of Malta have included members as diverse as General Reinhard Gehlen, Hitler's Chief of Intelligence, who later worked for the CIA, and General Alexander Haig – the force behind Nixon and Reagan's foreign policy and a friend of the Queen's. Some conspiriologists feel the Knights of Malta secretly control the CIA and via that organization, MI6. Just why the Knights of Malta would want to do this is open to question, but it is known that the Knights Templar regard them as their sworn enemies.

MOST CONVINCING EVIDENCE

People looking for evidence of MI6 trying to establish closer ties between Britain and America, have turned their attention to the British-American Project. Backed by companies such as American Express, Apple Computers, British Airways, Coca-Cola, Monsanto and Philip Morris, it is officially a charitable trust that aims to bring together senior representatives from the intelligence services, business, government, the media and the armed forces from the two countries. However, conspiracy theorists feel MI6's alleged links with the project means that it serves a more sinister purpose.

MOST MYSTERIOUS FACT

Recently disclosed British Government documents show that there were plans to turn the United Kingdom into the fifty-first state of the USA. Was the real reason MI6 chose to remove Harold Wilson from office because he scrapped these plans?

SCEPTICALLY SPEAKING

It seems unlikely that MI6 is competent enough at covert operations to be capable of masterminding an ultra-secret plot to shape world politics. If the organization can't even prevent itself from being publicly exposed as severely compromised by Soviet intelligence, it is doubtful that MI6 has the ability to successfully run a dozen top-level conspiracy organizations and two major governments.

MOSSAD

When the assassins' bullets fly from the smoking gun and change the course of history, it is usually inevitable that within hours both an official version and the conspiracy interpretation of events will be in circulation. However, on 4 November 1995, when Israeli Prime Minister Yitzhak Rabin was shot at a rally in Tel Aviv, it took more than a few hours for the first hints of conspiracy to surface. The reason is Mossad – probably one of the most feared and effective intelligence agencies in the world.

Until recently, Mossad's control over Israeli media was so strong that its very existence, like that of its sister agency the Shaback, was shrouded in secrecy. Everyone knew that the agencies existed, but in Israel none of their activities were ever reported and no one even knew who was in charge.

Mossad's tight reins of censorship may have loosened a little over the last couple of years, but it is certain that they played a strong role in preventing even the mildest hint of there being a conspiracy behind Yitzhak Rabin's death from reaching the Israeli public, for as long as possible. While CNN and even the BBC questioned the official version that the co-winner of the Nobel Peace Prize was not killed by a fanatical, lone gunman, the Israeli security services fought to keep such speculation from its own citizens. Not surprising, since much of that speculation focused on the possible role that Mossad may have played in murdering its own commander-in-chief.

Mossad was formed in 1951 to oversee the intelligence gathering and defence of the recently created nation of Israel, which was surrounded on all sides by hostile countries opposed to its very existence. Over the years, Mossad has developed an impressive track record of counter-terrorist actions, assassinations and covert-operation success stories. Its infiltration of the security services of friends and foes has also meant that Mossad has become the prime suspect in many conspiracy theories. From the killing of media tycoon Robert Maxwell, in 1991, to the death of Princess Diana, and even the attempted assassination of Pope John Paul II, in 1981 – there is no shortage of events in which Mossad may have played a part.

Resourceful, ruthless and fearless – how else could they have abducted Nazi war criminal Adolf Eichmann, stolen a MiG jet from Iraq and smuggled enough weapons-grade plutonium out of America to build a hundred atomic weapons – it seems that nothing is beyond Mossad. For conspiracy theorists, that includes possibly being the shadowy cabal behind Rabin's assassination.

THE STRANGE PART

The Shamgar Commission of Enquiry, which investigated the assassination of Rabin concluded that Ygal Amir was the lone killer of the prime minister. It also concluded that he was acting entirely alone when he shot Rabin twice in the back. In the Commission's opinion, it was those two shots that killed Rabin, while a third shot wounded the PM's body-guard. At his trial, Ygal Amir testified that he loaded his gun clip with nine bullets, yet ballistic tests found eight remaining bullets after security forces seized Amir. This means Amir only had one shot at Rabin. Where did the other shots come from? If there were a conspiracy to assassinate Rabin and subsequently cover up the identity of the killer, it would be impossible for Mossad not to be involved – but why would the agency kill its own leader?

THE USUAL SUSPECTS
The Israeli Right-wing

Rabin had made a historic peace deal with the PLO that gave away Israeli territory and earned the eternal hatred of Israeli right-wing factions in the process. Mossad is not an organization known for its moderate views and many members of the agency have close links to the radical fringe of Zionist politics. The assassination of Rabin would not only be an act of revenge, but would also ensure that the process of returning land to the Palestinians and the cause of peace in the region would both be set back for several years.

Saddam Hussein

The Iraqi dictator had a number of grudges against Israel and Rabin – including one assassination attempt on him, carried out by Mossad for the CIA that had led to the deaths of members of his family. If an Iraqi plot was responsible for the Israeli Prime Minister's death, Mossad would have to cover it up to prevent the possible chemical and nuclear warfare that could have ensued from its exposure. Some even suggest that highly placed members of Mossad were actually in the pay of Saddam.

Israel shows its grief over the death of Yitzhak Rabin.

THE UNUSUAL SUSPECTS
KGB

Although consigned to the pages of history by the majority of commentators after it was officially disbanded in 1991, the KGB is held by many conspiracy buffs to still be playing an active role in covert actions across the world. The aim is to cause as much unrest as possible and so tie up American resources while the KGB attempts to rebuild the former Soviet Empire, unmolested by the attentions of the CIA. It is not impossible that the KGB also infiltrated Mossad in the same way it penetrated the CIA, MI6 and MI5.

CIA

The close links between Mossad and the CIA are well known and many feel that the independence of Israeli security has been compromised by the US. Some people argue that Mossad's attempts to regain its autonomy, by blackmailing President Clinton over the Lewinsky affair, brought about a swift reminder by the CIA of where the balance of power lay. This is considered a wild theory by many, as it is rare for anyone to credit the CIA with the level of competence needed to pull off this type of stunt.

MOST CONVINCING EVIDENCE

Everyone who saw the amateur video footage of Rabin's assassination witnessed the alleged murderer, Ygal Amir, shoot the premier in the back from five feet away. However, Chief Lieutenant Baruch Glatstein, of the Israeli Police's Forensics Laboratory, told a very different story at Amir's trial. Glatstein stated: "In the upper section of the prime minister's jacket, I found a bullet hole to the right of the seam, which, according to my testing of the spread of gunpowder, was caused by a shot from less than 25 centimetres' range."

MOST MYSTERIOUS FACT

Before his death, Rabin was sent a letter stating that an Israeli mathematician had discovered a hidden code in the Bible that appeared to foretell the future, and that the name Yitzhak Rabin was encoded in the Bible, along with the words "assassin that will assassinate".

SCEPTICALLY SPEAKING

The combination of a lone gunman and a major political assassination seems to happen a lot, but surely at least one of them must be exactly what it seems to be, instead of a conspiracy? Maybe the legendary Mossad had an off-day and Ygal Amir was a lone nut who got lucky.

NSA

The National Security Agency is probably the organization most feared by conspiriologists. MJ-12, the Mafia and the Greys are often seen as the most dangerous groups by outsiders but, in fact, it is the NSA that is the most feared, the most suspected.

Will Smith in Enemy of the State (1998), the making of which the NSA tried to disrupt.

The reasons are simple – it is the US spy agency responsible both for external and domestic affairs. The most technologically advanced intelligence agency in the world, these spooks watch American citizens and anyone else they have an interest in.

The NSA is routinely accused of just about everything, from stealing the gold in Fort Knox and replacing it with spray-painted lead, to kidnapping scientists and computer engineers whose ideas could threaten the agency's technological superiority. The sheer secrecy of the organization helps these often-wild rumours to accumulate. However, one of the most persistent accusations to have been levelled at the agency is that it is deeply involved in an attempt to control the global banking system.

The NSA is known for its expertise in cryptography. In the early nineties, the agency was behind the attempts to have a chip known as Clipper accepted as the standard for all computer encryption. This chip carried an in-built weakness, a back door that the NSA could use to decode any data encrypted using the Clipper. Your information would be perfectly safe from anyone, except the government.

The NSA may have succeeded in compromising the banking industry – in the late seventies, a firm called INSLAW (Institute for Law and Social Research) developed an integrated database management system called PROMIS. This allowed huge ranges of databases to be combined into one usable, cross-referenced whole. Law enforcement agencies wanted PROMIS to track national and international crime, and major banking agencies such as the World Bank wanted to use it for an efficient international financial database. The US Department of Justice took the system on board, then refused to pay money owed, driving INSLAW to bankruptcy. Despite court rulings in its favour, the company has still to receive payment for PROMIS.

A journalist named Danny Casolaro claimed to have uncovered evidence that the NSA had modified PROMIS to allow complete access to the contents on the NSA's demand. Apparently, the NSA and Mossad then sold modified copies of the software to banks, foreign governments and law enforcement agencies. The plan was to allow the NSA to spy on the entire legal, governmental and financial systems world-wide. A company called Wackenhut, based outside US jurisdiction on a small Indian Nation reservation in California, carried out this modification.

THE STRANGE PART

Deputy White House Counsellor Vince Foster apparently committed suicide in July 1993. His death was suspicious and he had been a control liaison for a company called Systematics, one of the fronts through which the NSA was selling the compromized PROMIS software. Systematics also laundered profits from covert operations, and gathered back-door information from PROMIS for sifting. A woman was with Foster hours before his death, and her hair colour matched the colour of hairs found in Foster's underwear. Pathologists discovered that Foster had died at the moment of ejaculation. Video-surveillance tapes do not show Foster leaving the building – yet his body was found in a park in Virginia, a short distance from his car.

THE USUAL SUSPECTS
The Freemasons

Harry Truman, a 33rd degree Master Mason, suddenly created the NSA in 1952. It retains its old ties, and its forays into global control of the legal and banking systems are in fact carried out on behalf of the Freemasons. It was they who organized the murders of Foster and Calosaro, to hide their mastery of international banking.

THE UNUSUAL SUSPECTS
The Greys

It has been suggested that the NSA's power over cryptography comes, not from putting back doors into computer programs, but from a mastery of advanced mathematics given to the agency by the Greys in return for a quota of US citizens that they can take and use for experiments every year.

MOST CONVINCING EVIDENCE

In Bob Woodward's book, *VEIL: The Secret Wars of the CIA, 1981–1987*, on page 386, former CIA Director William Casey claims of his time in office: "There was penetration of the international banking system, allowing a steady flow of data from the real, secret sets of books kept by many foreign banks, that showed some hidden investing by the Soviet Union."

MOST MYSTERIOUS FACT

Journalist Danny Casolaro was murdered on the same night that he mentioned having discovered evidence to support his story, as was Alan Standorf, the NSA agent supposed to have passed him documents. Twelve days before his death, Foster's secret Swiss bank account was mysteriously emptied of its $2.7 million contents without his knowledge.

SCEPTICALLY SPEAKING

Why drive INSLAW to bankruptcy? It seems likely that it would have been easier just to pay a licence fee as the contract required, and then negotiate the rights to sell the software on to other parties, keeping everything discreet.

THE ROYAL FAMILY

The dramatic, ever-changing story of the Royal Family is perhaps the longest-running and most enjoyed soap opera the world has ever known. Watched and adored by millions around the globe, the everyday routines of the British royals have become the stuff of dreams and form the material for endless discussion.

When a major life event occurs in the Royal Family, whether it's a wedding or a birth, it becomes an excuse for international celebration. They are the Royal Family, and their lives take precedence over the perceived mundanity in the lives of their fans.

In its current incarnation, the British Royal Family stems from the House of Windsor, a family tree that can trace its roots to Germany. Under the stern eye of Queen Elizabeth II, the Royal Family has endured much in the past few years, but the death of Diana, Princess of Wales, in 1997, put the spotlight on the family with a white-hot glare not seen before. A world mourning the loss of Diana, its most beloved princess, watched to see how the family would react. But even as the memorial flowers that had mounted against the security fences surrounding royal homes were finally swept away, the story continued to unfold. Images of Diana and other members of the Royal Family are sold on everything from books and videos to commemorative tea towels.

But behind the smiles and waving hands, behind the castle gates and power of British tradition, just what is the Royal Family truly up to? What dark secrets lay hidden in their palatial closets? Are they really just nostalgic figureheads or, like their plotting, politically vicious predecessors, are they busy planning to seize power and create a renewed and glorious British Empire?

THE STRANGE PART
When the Queen dramatically stopped the trial of Paul Burrell (Princess Diana's butler, who was charged with theft of her possessions), she created a scandal that more than rivalled any toe-sucking or lurid phone-sex headlines caused by more junior members of her family. After it emerged that she had conveniently forgotten to tell police that Burrell was innocent until a few minutes before he was to take the stand, it also came to light that after Diana's death, the Queen had told Burrell to beware of "dark forces" operating in the country.

THE USUAL SUSPECTS
The Virginia Company
Some theorists believe that the Royal Family heads the

mysterious Virginia Company – an organization that aims to run the world. The fall from grace of the Royal Family could have been a cleverly orchestrated public relations campaign to disguise their plans for world domination – which is nothing short of a re-establishment of the glory days of the British Empire. While they continue to project an image of reserved dignity and eccentricity, the royals secretly manage all major banking institutions and top-level security forces such as the KGB. There are even rumours that the Royal Family planned the American Revolution, and that, to this day, they still rule sovereign over America's shores.

British Shadow Government
The current Royal Family may be nothing more than it seems – an ongoing media circus. The constant engagements of royalty opening paint factories, giving speeches, or grabbing space in newspapers as they play polo may be designed to distract media and public attention from the activities of the British Shadow Government, an elite backroom conspiracy headed by ex-members of M16. As their forces quietly pass legislation in the House of Commons or test weaponry that will facilitate the coming of the New World Order, the evening news pacifies the populace by showing Prince Harry getting his knee scraped on a games field.

THE UNUSUAL SUSPECTS
Impostors
The current House of Windsor could be a family of impostors who lacked the apparently essential secret Bloodline of Christ. They orchestrated the murder of Diana because, as a Stuart, she alone possessed the true remnants of the Bloodline. Thought at first to be easily malleable to the policies of the Royal Family, Diana's strong spirit proved to be too much of a liability, and she was removed in a badly managed assassination before she could inflict any more damage to the Windsors' plans.

MOST CONVINCING EVIDENCE
Queen Elizabeth II is among the richest women in the world, and is still head of the British Commonwealth, a glaring anachronism in the days of blurring national boundaries

and international culture. Instead of being relegated to a secondary position of nostalgic tradition, she still exerts a considerable amount of power, but uses it discreetly, thus proving that there's more to the Royal Family than they would have us believe.

THE MOST MYSTERIOUS FACT

To suggest that the present occupants of Buckingham Palace are a bunch of impostors is perhaps a bit strong. However, there is a glaring question mark over their right to that occupancy and, by extension, their entitlement to all the power and wealth that goes with it. That question mark is provided by the questionable parentage of Queen Victoria, whose birth would, according to present medical and scientific knowledge, break the bloodline by which the present Windsors claim their rights.

Both haemophilia and porphyria are genetically inherited conditions – the latter suffered by Victoria's grandfather, "Mad" George III. However, after the birth of Victoria, this condition magically disappears from the Windsor line. Conversely, haemophilia suddenly appears to manifest

itself in the Russian royal household, care of Victoria's granddaughter, Alexandra, who married Tsar Nicholas II. Medically speaking, both these genetic "flukes" are impossible unless, of course, Victoria was illegitimate.

Queen Victoria's mother, Princess Victoria, was known to have been carrying on with her personal secretary, Sir John Conroy. Indeed, the Duke of Wellington is on record as stating that the young Victoria once caught them engaged in what he diplomatically termed "some familiarities". At the height of a succession crisis, Queen Victoria's parents married in 1818, with her father already aged 50 and his wife 20 years his junior. This resulted in a marriage that nobody could really describe as one of history's great passions. Thus, when the baby Victoria arrived, everyone was so relieved that there was at last an heir to carry on the bloodline that none dared to question the issue – unlike many prominent geneticists today.

SCEPTICALLY SPEAKING

The fact that *Coronation Street* is still broadcast suggests royal intervention on a grand scale – but nothing else does.

The wreckage of the most famous car crash of all time. Many theorists believe that the Royal Family was behind the death of Princess Diana.

THE VATICAN

A veritable vipers' nest of murder, lust and intrigue since its very inception, the Vatican's considerable power and influence was first threatened by the Unification of Italy in 1871, when the new civil authorities confiscated most of the papal territories across the newly formed Italy.

In a state of "Mexican standoff", no pope then left the confines of the Vatican for the following sixty years and no Italian official was allowed to visit. It was during this period of isolation that the Vatican extended and cemented its initially tenuous links to the Mafia, which, to be fair, was not then the kind of organization it is today. With its name meaning something akin to bold and swashbuckling, the Mafia has its roots in the groups of resistance fighters that were formed to combat the Saracen invasion of Sicily in the ninth century. However, by the nineteenth century it had morphed into a pan-Italian network of small clans that were dedicated to protecting the locals from oppressive landlords and corrupt officials – for a price, of course. Either way, the early-modern Mafia became the Vatican's eyes and ears throughout Italy.

This standoff between the Vatican and Italy came to a close in 1929, when it signed the Lateran Treaty with Mussolini, who promised the Vatican would be recognized as a separate state within Italy and would receive compensation for those aforementioned confiscated territories. Thus began the Vatican links to the darker political forces on the rise in Europe. By this time, the Mafia had become completely criminalized but, with its bonds already too strong to break, the Vatican remained content to drift downstream with its clandestine affiliate, studiously turning a blind eye to the Mafia's less appetizing activities.

In the lead-up to World War II, the Vatican cozied up to the pro-Nazi Spanish leader General Franco. By way of reciprocation, Franco then turned a blind eye to the theft of over 300,000 babies from his own country by Catholic priests and nuns, who, telling the mothers that the babies were still-born, filled the Vatican coffers by selling them on the international "baby market". All this was achieved through established Mafia connections, so it is safe to say that by the mid-late 1930s, the Folks on the Hill were nothing if not criminal themselves. When World War II finally erupted, the notoriously anti-Semitic Pope Pius XII conducted himself and the Vatican in such a manner that he soon earned the epithet of Hitler's Pope. Then, after the war and mainly under the guiding hand of Bishop Alois Hudal, elements within the Vatican ran rat-lines to spirit away fleeing Nazis, including the likes of Eduard Roschmann (aka "the Butcher

of Riga" and the man fictionalized in Frederick Forsyth's *The Odessa File*), as well as the notorious war criminals Josef Mengele and Adolf Eichmann.

In more recent times, certain Popes have demonstrated a willingness to confront such issues as Vatican profiteering from the hoarding of Nazi loot and the laundering of Mafia funds. One in particular – Pope John Paul I – most likely paid for such interference in the status quo with his life.

THE STRANGE PART

Having made no secret of his intention to dig into the dark corners of Vatican activity, on the night of 28 September 1978, John Paul – aka "the Smiling Pope" – retired to bed to leaf through papers relating to Vatican dealings with the Mafia. He also read about the shady deal between Archbishop Paul Marcinkus and Roberto Calvi, by which the former, President of the Vatican Bank, had facilitated the takeover of Venetian Catholic Bank by the latter's Banco Ambrosiano. At 5:30a.m. the following morning, Pope John Paul was found dead and the papers missing; he had only been pontiff for 33 days!

The Vatican doctor, Renato Buzzonetti, arrived on the scene with suspicious speed. Without ever having examined John Paul or asking anything of the symptoms, with nervous haste he pronounced the cause of death to have been a massive myocardial infarction. However, no cardiac event so violent would have left the victim lying in a state of composed peace such as John Paul displayed. No autopsy was performed as the embalmers began their work at 7:00p.m. – despite Italian law dictating that a period of 24 hours must elapse before such intervention. Also, despite it being normal practice for the internal organs to be removed before embalming, no such steps were taken in this case, perhaps to make sure there was nothing left for any forensic examination.

THE USUAL SUSPECTS
The Mafia

Mafia influences had long been suspected of playing a key role in many aspects of the Vatican. This alleged influence came under close scrutiny following the death of Pope John Paul I. Assuming the mantle of pontiff, the popular Pope almost certainly began to uncover deep levels of corruption

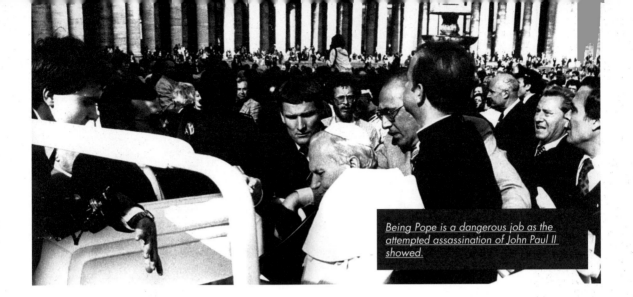

within the Vatican, including direct ties to the Mob through the Vatican Bank. To prevent him taking action to end the corruption, the Mafia and their men in the Vatican may have murdered the Pope.

Ultra-Conservative Catholics

John Paul I was set to revolutionize the Catholic faith by allowing birth control and instigating moves to redistribute some of the Church's enormous wealth. These two moves were enough to upset staunch conservatives and insiders within the Holy See. After he was found dead in his bed on 28 September 1978, a new Pope was chosen – one who, not surprisingly, was far more conservative than his predecessor.

THE UNUSUAL SUSPECTS
P2 Masonic Lodge

When the body of the head of the Vatican Bank, Roberto Calvi, was found hanging from Blackfriars Bridge in London, in 1982, it blew the lid off many sordid dealings within the Vatican. The incident also brought to light the power of the P2 Masonic lodge. With members of the Mob, archbishops and top Italian politicians all involved with a group banned by the Catholic Church, many wondered if P2 had been involved in John Paul I's death. An investigation into their activities would have been disastrous for them and, with a membership that included CIA agents, planning and carrying out a conspiracy was well within the ability and power.

Aliens

Rumours have surfaced that the Vatican has a direct line to the Hubble space telescope, and was aware that the Hale Bopp comet carried a "companion", thought to be an alien spacecraft. Connections between the Vatican and this spacecraft are pure speculation but, reportedly, the Pope was directly involved in the situation, receiving up-to-date emails on the subject. One of the reasons for such concern about life elsewhere is the Vatican's worries over whether the symbolic significance of the death of Christ – which absolved all humanity from the taint of original sin – would also apply to aliens. Members of the Pope's staff have already considered converting any aliens discovered to Catholicism.

MOST CONVINCING EVIDENCE

But conspiracies within the Vatican did not stop with the death of John Paul I. His successor faced two assassination attempts displaying worrying links to the Stasi – the secret police of East Germany. In 1998, a member of the Swiss Guard murdered his superior and his wife. Dismissed by the Vatican as purely an unfortunate case of madness, the murdered man – Alois Esterman – was rumoured to have links to the Stasi. What is even more interesting is that he had saved the Pope in 1981 by blocking the line of fire. So was Esterman killed by the Vatican – or someone connected to the assassination attempt to prevent those potentially embarrassing ties becoming public?

MOST MYSTERIOUS FACT

As some suspect that John Paul I was murdered by a dose of digitalis added to his night-time coffee, it is suspicious in the extreme that the cup was the first thing to be whisked out of the room. One would have thought that with a newly elected and dead Pope on their hands, those in attendance that morning would have more pressing matters on their minds than doing the washing-up.

SCEPTICALLY SPEAKING

Jesus Christ once explained the relationship between wealthy men, camels, needles and the entrance to Heaven. With all the wealth in the Vatican, from its library and bank, to the untold treasures secure in its vaults, it's apparent that they missed that particular Sunday-school lesson.

CHAPTER 3:

SECRET
SOCIETIES

AL QAEDA

It has become a sad fact of human history that major civilizations and powers seem to need to define themselves through conflict by those who oppose them. With the end of the Soviet Union, it seemed as if Western democracies – especially the United States – lacked any opposition. Some academics even talked of an "end of history" and the era of the unchallenged Western power. All of that changed on the morning of 11 September 2001.

Within the hour between the first plane hitting the World Trade Center at 8:46a.m. and the hijacked American Airline Flight 77 crashing into the heart of American military power at the Pentagon, world history was forever changed and the USA had a new and deadly enemy to confront. Even before the twin towers of the World Trade Center had fallen to the ground, the terror network al Qaeda was already being mentioned by many informed commentators as the prime suspect behind the most devastating terrorist attack to have been launched in American history.

Over the next few days, the public worldwide came to recognize and to dread the previously obscure al Qaeda and the face of its leader – Osama bin Laden. It soon became apparent that there was a vast terror network at large in the world with access to huge financial resources that was able to mount highly sophisticated terrorist strikes right in the heart of US economic and military power. It was also apparent that al Qaeda and bin Laden had been known about by the US intelligence agencies for several years. This was not least because they had played a role in funding them and training them to fight since the early eighties when al Qaeda was at the forefront of frustrating the Soviet Union's occupation of Afghanistan.

The previous strong links between the CIA and the terrorists, especially the detailed knowledge held on members of its leadership, should have allowed the Secret Service an inside track on tackling al Qaeda. This campaign should have been in high gear after the US blamed al Qaeda for turning on them with its bombing of the American embassy in Yemen and an attack on the USS *Cole*. Many were surprised to find so little had been done to combat the growing menace of bin Laden and his gang between 1998 and 2001. Known supporters – including oil companies in which the Bush family had interests – were able to invest in US companies and al Qaeda members were even allowed to indulge in fund-raising activities while in America. It can certainly be argued that either al Qaeda was the cleverest terror outfit of all time or they were receiving support from

forces with enough power to smooth their operations right under the noses of the US authorities.

THE STRANGE PART

Italian newspaper journalists managed to discover that Osama bin Laden received treatment for a longstanding kidney condition at an American hospital in Dubai on 1 July 2001. They also obtained statements from witnesses who claimed that while in hospital, bin Laden received several American visitors, including one known to have strong links with companies operating as CIA front-organizations in the strategic Gulf state. Given that he was already wanted by the US security services for his role in terrorist activities against them in Yemen and the Gulf, why did they not use this opportunity to seize him?

THE USUAL SUSPECTS
The CIA

Since the death of Osama bin Laden, it can be argued that there is no longer such an organization as al Qaeda. Now under the leadership of the Egyptian-born Ayman al-Zawahiri, al Qaeda is instead a convenient umbrella-name for various disparate groups with broadly the same objectives – and one to give the public a named demon on which to focus their ire. The term was first used by the CIA to describe the considerable force of Mujahedeen fighters that they trained, armed and funded to combat the Russians in Afghanistan in the 1980s. Therefore, due to that fact alone, it can be stated quite categorically that al Qaeda is yet another monster created by the CIA. It was former British Foreign Secretary Robin Cook who, in a moment that was either unguarded or one that was quite calculated, first revealed to the public exactly what the name "al Qaeda" meant, further describing the organization itself as "a product of a monumental miscalculation by western security agencies". If the CIA insist on creating their own dogs of war, perhaps they would be well advised to invent a stronger leash.

Major oil companies

Many of al Qaeda's original backers in the fight against Soviet forces in Afghanistan were from US oil-company backgrounds. Later, al Qaeda invested much of the money it made from the opium trade in Afghanistan back into US oil companies. Given the impact that war on terrorism has had on oil prices, possibly al Qaeda and its corporate backers real motive is something as simple as profit.

Saudi Arabia

Osama bin Laden comes from a dominant and well-connected Saudi family and there is strong evidence to suggest that even post-9/11, powerful members of the Saudi Royal Family used their influence and wealth to protect al Qaeda members across the globe. Despite the kingdom historically being a US ally, al Qaeda may be a Saudi creation to extend their power under the guise of religious extremism.

THE UNUSUAL SUSPECTS
European Union

Whenever you start a close examination of al Qaeda, you begin to find a host of links between the terror network and individuals, companies and security organizations based in the countries that make up the European Union – especially Germany. The possibility that al Qaeda is part of a shadowy EU agenda to destabilize its major Atlantic rival for global power should not be totally dismissed.

China

Worried about the problems created by growing Islamic nationalism in its outer provinces and wanting to take US eyes off its growing military and economic power, the Chinese Secret Service could have infiltrated al Qaeda and turned it into an anti-American organization. While its two enemies fight a protracted and costly war, China can continue unmolested with its quest for global supremacy.

MOST CONVINCING EVIDENCE

There is little doubt that al Qaeda and those related to the family of bin Laden held a lot of sway in certain circles in the US. On 13 September – a day when all civilian air traffic in the United States was grounded – a charter flight left Florida, containing not only members of the Saudi Royal Family, but also members of bin Laden's family. The plane left an airport run by a defence contracting company with close links to the US military, and bin Laden's family was accompanied by ex-security service agents. This suggests that far from being seen as enemies, bin Laden's people were treated as important and valued allies by someone with enough power in government

to get them out of the US before the authorities – especially the FBI – caught up with them.

MOST MYSTERIOUS FACT

Before 11 September, former FBI Deputy Director and Head of Anti-terrorism Agent John O'Neill claimed that elements of the Bush administration were illegally negotiating with the al Qaeda-backed Taliban administration of Afghanistan. O'Neill resigned when nothing was done over his report that a giant American oil company was trying to obtain permission to build a pipeline through Afghanistan to transport the large oil reserves of land-locked Kazakhstan. Sadly, he was killed in the 9/11 attacks in New York City.

SCEPTICALLY SPEAKING

What is more unbelievable? – (1) The world is full of religious fanatics, some of whom have a hate for America in their hearts, or (2) there was a plot to create an enemy for the only superpower left just so the Marines had an excuse to go to foreign countries and kick butt? Hmm …

Six-times married Osama bin Laden – the billionaire terrorist.

FREEMASONS

Knock three times . . . The Masonic Rites underpin one of the oldest and certainly by far the most successful of the secret societies.

Do they keep an eye on us all from the back of every $1 bill?

Potential candidates – those who would like to be admitted – have to find a known Mason and ask, on three separate occasions, to be considered for membership. Only after the third request is the Mason allowed to acknowledge having heard the plea. Admission to the Masons is rigorously policed, and while any member is free to admit their own membership, they may not reveal any other member's name, or any ritual or decision internal to the craft. In this way, the Masonic Rites have, for centuries, made sure that only the right people get in – but what sort of people are considered to be right?

Certain groups maintain that Masonry is working to take over the world. There is no doubt that many important or influential people – politicians, policemen, lawyers, cardinals and bishops, media tycoons, celebrities and so

on – are Freemasons. In many cases, it is a matter of public record. Before his death, Bill Cooper, a major conspiracy writer, claimed (perhaps somewhat enthusiastically) that, "The Masons are major players in the struggle for world domination." He went on to say that the infamous Italian P2 lodge, implicated in the murder of Roberto Calvi (discussed elsewhere), has connections with the Vatican and with the CIA. He also claimed that P2 persuaded Pope John Paul II to admit Freemasons to the higher ranks of Vatican officials.

Many of his beliefs were based on fully provable links between the CIA, the Mafia, the Vatican, the British Royal Family and Freemasonry. He also claimed it was possible to trace Masonic influence in the selection of political leaders of various ruling parties across the globe.

THE STRANGE PART

It may or may not be significant that the Masonic term for non-Masons is "Profanes", implying that the rest of us are less sanctified, or less holy, than they are. It seems a strangely intolerant term for what is a supposedly benevolent organisation.

THE USUAL SUSPECTS
The Illuminati

The mystery traditions in general, to which Masonry traces many rituals, frequently used the term "Illuminated" to refer to a person who was a member. This has been taken to signify a link to Adam Weishaupt's Illuminati, who were officially announced to the world on 1 May 1776 in Bavaria. The Illuminati were supposedly controlling world events for hundreds of years before that date, and are still in power now. Could the Masons be under the control of the Illuminati?

The New World Order

Because their numbers include so many powerful people, the Masons are suspected by some theorists of being lynchpins in the New World Order, the movement towards a unified, global population with no religion, a centralized government and limited technology.

THE UNUSUAL SUSPECTS
Satan

The most popular accusation levelled at Masons is that they are in league with the Devil. The hidden nature of their rituals, along with the occult imagery employed, has led many Christian groups to denounce Freemasonry as working for the forces of Evil.

Of course, it is easy to laugh at such a notion; however, the demonic aspect of the dark creatures and gargoyles used by Masons to "decorate" the external walls of churches and cathedrals must be considered – as well as other decidedly non-Christian rituals observed during the construction of assorted places of worship.

The very early Masons most certainly used to mix the blood of human sacrifice with their mortar to guarantee the validity of whatever building they were working on. Although the vast majority of ground-breaking and foundation-laying rituals enacted by earlier Masons involved animal sacrifice instead, the odd human corpse still found its way into church walls and foundations right up to the eighteenth century.

Human remains have been discovered in, for example, the parish church at Kirkcudbright in Scotland, Holsworthy parish church in Devon and the foundations of Wickenby parish church in Lincolnshire.

MOST CONVINCING EVIDENCE

Former 33rd-degree Freemason Jim Shaw revealed in his book, *The Deadly Deception*, that even the supposed highest level of Freemasonry is just a lower rung for another Freemason controlled pyramid-based power structure. Through his time as a high-ranking Mason, Shaw was able to gather convincing evidence that, at the levels kept secret from even Masons who think they are in control of the Brotherhood, is a powerful group who have "gone higher" and really pull the strings of the secret society.

MOST MYSTERIOUS FACT

Despite the fact that some Masons claim the origins of the Brotherhood go back to ancient Egypt, there can be no doubt that the ceremonies of Knights Templar had a huge impact on most of the rituals conducted within Freemasonry. However, the elements of Masonic ritual designed to allow a Freemason to control his emotions and energies to perform magical feats do seem to hark back to an even older period of history.

SCEPTICALLY SPEAKING

The great majority of Freemasons are respectable, upstanding professionals and business people with busy careers and family lives, and every year the Masonic lodges donate a fortune to charity and charitable work. Many priests and vicars are Freemasons, and the order is open to all religions. It seems unlikely that so many decent people are in fact working for Satan, and it is certainly hard to imagine exactly how helping to organize a school jumble sale is playing straight into the hands of Evil Forces. Apart from anything else, Masons have no reason to support the Dark Side in the hope of gaining favour – most of them are already successful before they join. Not only are the Masons probably one of the oldest and most successful secret societies, they are also the most-blamed by conspiracy theorists, which seems a little unfair given that they are ostensibly an organization devoted to charity, brotherhood and the search for truth. But then, you don't know whether I'm a Mason or not . . . do you?

THE BAVARIAN ILLUMINATI

Adam Weishaupt was born in Ingolstadt, Germany on 6 February 1748. Educated by the Jesuits, he became Professor of Natural and Canon Law at the University of Ingolstadt in 1775, aged 27, and was initiated into the Masonic Lodge "Theodore of Good Council" in Munich, in 1777.

Weishaupt was a cosmopolitan man who despised the bigoted superstition of the priests of his time. He decided to establish an enlightened – or Illuminated – society to oppose injustice and this he did, forming the order that would become "The Illuminati of Bavaria" 1 May 1776.

Originally called "The Order of the Perfectibilists", its object was to allow its members to team up in order to "attain the highest possible degree of morality and virtue, and to lay the foundation for the reformation of the world by the association of good men to oppose the progress of moral evil".

In collaboration with a range of other influential figures, including Baron Von Knigge, Xavier Zwack and Baron Bassus, Weishaupt developed an order that became extremely popular. Before long, some 2,000 people had enrolled as members. Lodges of the Illuminati were located in France, Italy, Poland, Hungary, Sweden, Denmark, Belgium and Holland. The Bavarian authorities issued a suppressive Edict concerning the order on 22 June 1784, which was repeated the following year in March and again in August. That same year, 1785, Weishaupt was stripped of his professorship and exiled from Bavaria.

Once it began to experience attempts at suppression, the order started to go into public decline and by the end of the century it had apparently vanished completely. The authorities illegally raided Xavier Zwack's home in 1786 and the documents that were seized were used to help suppress the order.

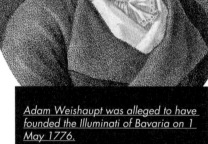

Adam Weishaupt was alleged to have founded the Illuminati of Bavaria on 1 May 1776.

Most serious commentators take this decline at face value. The *Encyclopaedia Britannica* barely mentions the Illuminati, and the vast majority of historical sources follow suit, judging the order to be insignificant. Others feel that the Illuminati disbanded into Masonry, a movement that was infiltrated in much the same way as cancer takes over a healthy body. Since that time, they allege, the Illuminati have stayed within the Masons, seizing power and manipulating the whole order.

THE STRANGE PART

In 1906, the British Museum in London received a copy of a manuscript called The Illuminati Protocols. These first appeared in Bavaria in the late-eighteenth century, and Joly used parts in an 1864 play. The copy the British Museum received was written in Russian. It is also interesting that both Adam Smith's capitalist treatise *The Wealth of Nations* and that great democratic treatise the American Declaration of Independence were written in 1776. It has been suggested that Weishaupt may have been the mysterious Black-Cloaked Man who presented Washington with the text of the declaration. It is also rumoured that the raid on Zwack's house was spurred on by the chance interception in 1784 by the authorities of a document telling the head of the French Illuminati, Robespierre, how to orchestrate the French Revolution in 1789. Warnings were ignored, and the revolution happened on schedule.

THE USUAL SUSPECTS
Freemasons
To achieve their goal, the Masons knew their real target – overthrowing all world government and organized religion in order to allow peace and liberty to prevail – had to remain concealed. So, in order to avoid promoting hysteria against themselves, and as a way of dealing with criticism and exposé, the Masons created the Illuminati as a front organization to take the blame for any perceived misdeeds or shortcomings. It is a strategy that has worked brilliantly for two centuries.

THE UNUSUAL SUSPECTS
Robert Shea and Robert Anton Wilson
In the seventies, Robert Shea and Robert Anton Wilson published a cult set of books called *The Illuminatus! Trilogy*. This was a novel masquerading as the largest conspiracy theory ever seen, disguised as a grand exposé of the Illuminati. It is this book that has set the Illuminati back in the public mind. Of course, no one claims that the trilogy is anything other than a good work of fiction – or that Robert Anton Wilson is the current chief of the Illuminati . . . do they?

MOST CONVINCING EVIDENCE
In 1902, the Freemason William Westcott records receiving membership in the Order of the Perfectibilists from Theodor Reuss. Similarly, the occultist Eliphas Levi strongly connected the Bavarian Illuminati with Freemasonry in 1913.

MOST MYSTERIOUS FACT
Among the list of notable members of the Illuminati is the name Marquis Saint Germain de Constanzo. This seems likely to be the Marquis de Saint Germain, the man most commonly suspected of being the only true immortal known in the world. He has cropped up as a sorcerer, an alchemist and a wise man throughout medieval history. Who better to help found the world's most successful secret society?

SCEPTICALLY SPEAKING
There is, when you get down to it, no real evidence whatsoever to suggest that the Illuminati were anything other than a short-lived Bavarian secret society – just a lot of hearsay. If it hadn't been for *The Illuminatus! Trilogy* the Bavarian Illuminati would still be an obscure sect lost in the footnotes of history.

Das

verbesserte System

der

Illuminaten

mit allen

seinen Graden und Einrichtungen.

Herausgegeben von

Adam Weishaupt

Herzoglich Sachs. Goth. Hofrath.

Hic situs est Phaeton, currus auriga paterni:
Quem si non tenuit; magnis tamen excidit ausis.
Ovid. Met. B. 2.

Neue und vermehrte Auflage.

Frankfurt und Leipzig,
in der Grattenauerischen Buchhandlung. 1788.

An early recruitment poster advertising for new members.

THE KU KLUX KLAN

This group of pointy-hatted pranksters was founded on Christmas Eve 1865 in Pulaski, Tennessee, by a small group of disgruntled Confederate officers after the American Civil War.

Largely of Scottish heritage and classically educated, these men based their name on the Greek "*kyklos*", meaning a band or a circle, adding "klan" as a reference to their origins. Although their infamous burning cross has been hailed a blasphemy of Christian tradition, it was in fact nothing of the sort. Rather, it was an invocation of the so-called "Fiery Cross", as was anciently carried through the Scottish Highlands to summon the clans to fight a common enemy.

The standard version of their history has the Ku Klux Klan, or "KKK", rising in power towards the close of the 1920s after which, and mainly due to the Great Depression, it went into a rapid decline – but did it really? No; finally realizing that dressing up in silly costumes to dance round a burning cross in the middle of nowhere was all a bit *infra dig*, the Klan entered the most sinister and frightening stage of its evolution. People with such opinions don't simply evaporate just because their "klub" goes into a decline; on the contrary, the new and insidious face of the Klan became that of smiling respectability in a nice suit.

Throughout the 1920s and '30s, the likes of Senior Senator Robert C. Byrd was a leading Klansman, rejoicing in the silly title of Exalted Cyclops, as was Supreme Court Justice Hugo Black. Other Klansmen in government included Senators Theodore G. Bilbo (Mississippi), Rice W. Means (Colorado), George Gordon (Tennessee), John Tyler Morgan (Alabama), Edmund Pettus (Alabama) and John Brown Gordon (Georgia). Higher up the ladder were State Governors Edward L. Jackson (Indiana), Clarence Morley (Colorado), Bibb Graves (Alabama) and Clifford Walker (Georgia); all the above being better known on their home turf as the Grand Wizard, or some similar title. More alarming still are the ever-persistent and not unfounded speculations that Presidents Warren Harding, Harry S. Truman and "Silent" Calvin Coolidge were also member of the new and faceless Klan.

During the late 1930s and early 1940s, the Klan forged alliances with both Berlin and Nazi elements within the US, their main contact being Berlin's Special Envoy to America, the delightfully named Heinz Spanknobel. Conspiriologists maintain – and with more than a little justification – that the KKK and the German American Bund putting pressure on the likes of the abovementioned politicians was instrumental in delaying American involvement in World War II. Nor is this trend yet dead. David Ernest Duke (b. 1950), variously Senator, State Representative and Governor of Louisiana, ran in the Democratic Presidential Primaries of 1988 and, switching sides, the Republican Primaries of 1992. When he took control of the KKK network in the mid-1970s, he said he did not wish to be known as the Grand anything but rather as the National Director, reminding all that it was high time the Klan "got out of the cow-pasture and into hotel meeting rooms".

THE STRANGE PART

As one might expect, defenders of President Calvin Coolidge deny he was ever a member of the KKK and, to be fair, many of his statements square with such defence. However, there again, such statements could well have been for public consumption only. If Coolidge was not a Klansman, why, in 1925, did he commission Gutzon Borglum to sculpt the massive faces of Presidents Washington, Lincoln, Jefferson and Teddy Roosevelt into Mount Rushmore? It was common knowledge that Borglum had sculpted Stone Mountain in Georgia, the setting for the formation of The Second Klan in 1915, as inspired by the advent that year of W. G. Griffith's pro-Klan film, *The Birth of a Nation*. It was also common knowledge that Borglum had agreed to carve a massive KKK altar into Stone Mountain and, given that he was in 1925 one of the six Knights sitting on the Klan's Imperial Koncilium (can't these guys spell?), why didn't Coolidge think that Borglum's involvement would put an indelible stain on such a national monument?

THE USUAL SUSPECTS
The CIA and the FBI

The Klan has been implicated in the murders of popular black political leaders Martin Luther King and Malcolm X, apparently acting because both men posed a threat to the Klan's vision of America – a vision allegedly shared by many in the CIA and in the FBI. King's vision of peaceful racial integration was unpalatable, as was Malcolm X's more contentious view that blacks were superior to the white man in every respect. For refusing to conform to the Klan's ideal of a black man, both men were killed. In the case of King, Klan and FBI involvement seem particularly strong, since the FBI openly recruited Klan members before King's death.

Black Ops Race War

The KKK may be part of a race war directed against blacks and Jews, playing a role in the creation and distribution of the AIDS virus along with black-ops government agencies. The Klan is also suspected of spreading false conspiracy rumours about ZOG (the Zionist Occupation Government), a purported Jewish plan to take over the US. Such rumours help deflect attention from America's true enemy – the Shadow Government and its black-ops agents.

THE UNUSUAL SUSPECTS
The New World Order

The Klan may be a front for the NWO, secretly furthering the aims of the New World Order while openly pretending to fight its influence on every level. This would include Klan involvement in the phenomenon of black helicopters, which, it is alleged, the Klan uses to incite panic in the populace which, the Klan hopes, will provide an environment in which it is easy to stir up racial tensions.

The US Government

Despite the recent liberalism of the US Government, many leaders in corporate, government and military circles still favour a more conservative outlook, a viewpoint shared by the Klan. Funds could be diverted to the Klan, as well as weaponry and clandestine political support. This would explain David Duke's political career after he left the Klan.

Also suspected: the Bavarian Illuminati; the Order of the Green Dragon.

MOST CONVINCING EVIDENCE

The continued existence of the Klan in an age where hate groups are not tolerated suggests some high-level connection with the US government. The American Constitution's guarantee of free speech as the right of every American is a guarantee that the US government has shown in the past it will ignore as it sees fit (in the McCarthy Era, for example). The Klan persists, and in the modern world, that poses the question of just who is looking out for its interests.

MOST MYSTERIOUS FACT

President Woodrow Wilson has also long stood accused of being a Klan member – or at least one of its most highly placed fellow travellers. In 1915 and at Wilson's personal insistence, W. G. Griffith's *The Birth of a Nation* became the first film ever shown in the White House. A glorification of the nocturnal excesses of the Klan, the film was based on *The Clansman* (1905), a novel in the same vein penned by Wilson's close personal friend and political ally, Thomas Dixon. Griffith's silent "epic" included a still presenting a quote from Wilson that his defenders would rather we all forgot: "The white men were roused by a mere instinct of self-preservation until at last there had sprung into existence a great Ku Klux Klan, a veritable Empire of the South, to protect the southern country." So, the tentacles of the Klan were then all-pervasive – as indeed they remain.

SCEPTICALLY SPEAKING

You don't need a conspiracy to explain the ignorance that lies behind race hatred. Anthropology classes probably would not be a hit with the Klan as the strong possibility that all humanity shares a common black ancestry might put a dampener on cross-burning activities.

The burning crosses and hooded members of the KKK strike fear into minority groups across America.

THE MAFIA

Since the start of the twentieth century, the Mafia has constituted a significant part of the organized crime underground in the US. In addition to its American operations, the Mafia is currently active in Italy, Southern France, Germany and Russia.

The facts of the Mafia's presence and its wide range of criminal activities – from prostitution and illegal gambling through to drugs distribution, contract assassination and slavery – are undisputed. What is less well known is the extent to which the Mafia is one unified organization.

The Mafia was first formed in the ninth century AD, in Sicily. The original Mafia valued loyalty above all and respected culture, family and heritage. Membership was only open to Sicilians and the organization's aim was to protect the interests of its members. As the centuries passed, the Mafia evolved the belief that justice, vengeance and honour were matters for the individual to look after, and not responsibilities that should be delegated to the current government – which was often put in place by invaders anyway. Secrecy was maintained through the tradition of *Omerta*, which said that betrayal of the society's trust was repayable by death.

Early in the eighteenth century, the Mafia started to become openly criminal. Money was extorted from wealthy Sicilians, who would receive a picture of a black hand. If cash were not forthcoming, arson, kidnappings and murder would follow.

The Mafia has been active in the US since the early nineteenth century, particularly in New Orleans. Word soon good back to Sicily that a lot of money could be made in the New World, and the organisation grew swiftly. In 1924, Mussolini cracked down on the Mafia in Italy and Sicily, and many members fled to the US. Ever since its super-profitable days of Prohibition, the Mafia has been spreading its influence throughout American political, legal and financial institutions, creaming off vast amounts of money in the process.

THE STRANGE PART

The Mafia in the US is commonly thought to be a collection of rival gangs, clans that are organized on a family structure and have little but hatred for each other. However, this may be far from the truth. While the different gangs do certainly compete, the heads of the 24 families regularly meet in a cartel called the Commission. At these meetings, they settle territorial and business disputes, and decide policy for the coming months. It is possible that the Commission may also negotiate with government agencies, particularly the CIA, on areas of activity where mutual benefit can be derived.

THE USUAL SUSPECTS
The Network

Major world crime organizations are teaming up to maximize profits. Just like any legitimate big business, crime empires that merge activities can improve profitability. The Mafia has joined forces with the Triads, with the Yakuza and with drugs cartels. This alliance, known as the Network, also accepts junior members such as Jamaican Yardies and Algerian slave traders. Because different groups control different resources, they have much to offer each other. The American Mafia, for example, can provide access to the US banking industry, law enforcement and justice systems as required.

Established Government

To what extent are government and organized crime actually different? Paying tax or protection money amounts to much the same thing, and few criminal organizations have caused as much public death as the US did courtesy of Vietnam, or Russia did in Chechnya. Some conspiriologists believe that established governments actually control the Mafia as a way of having authority on the otherwise impossible-to-govern world of crime.

THE UNUSUAL SUSPECTS
The Freemasons

The Mafia has long held strong ties to Masonry through the shadowy Vatican lodge P2, that is said to be the most powerful Masonic lodge in Europe. When Pope John Paul I determined to clear the Masons out of the Vatican – having discovered over 100 among the priesthood – he was killed, supposedly by the Mafia. Could the Masons be the power driving the Mafia's relentless advance over the years? Certainly both groups own a lot of judges and policemen.

MOST CONVINCING EVIDENCE

The spread of the Mafia is truly staggering. In the US, the Mafia and officials from the government were maintaining an Illinois-based bank as a criminal enterprise, laundering money. The bank was run by an alleged Mafia associate, the Catholic

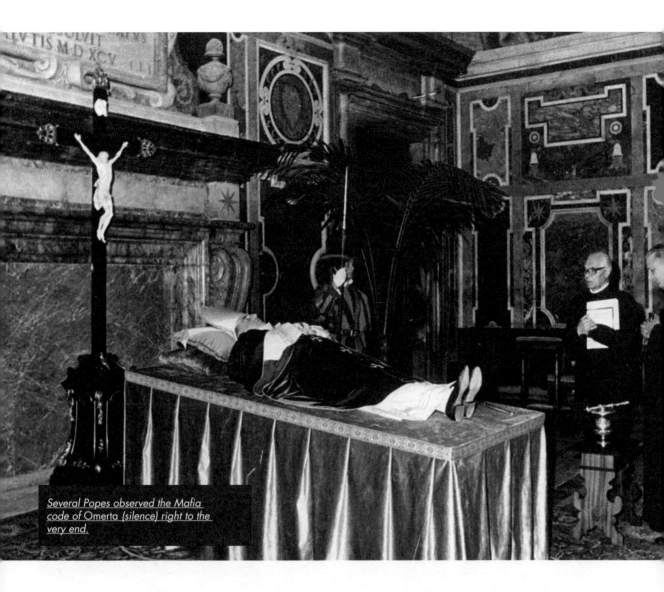

Several Popes observed the Mafia code of Omerta (silence) right to the very end.

Bishop of Cicero Paul Marcinkus, head of the Vatican Bank until 1991 working in association with a Congressman who was a controller of the CIA's Black Ops budget.

A documentary detailing this was made, but before the programme could be broadcast, State law enforcement officers threatened the makers, families were harassed, and one was falsely arrested.

MOST MYSTERIOUS FACT

The Mafia believes deeply in conspiracy theories. Some Mafia members even claim that the organization was originally

formed to fight the mysterious "*potere occulto*" or hidden power they believe is rife in the world.

SCEPTICALLY SPEAKING

Organized crime is just that – organized crime. The last thing it wants to do, surely, is to take over the irritating trivia of everyday government, something that isn't necessary anyway, given the number of politicians already in the pay of Mafia Dons.

MJ-12

In 1947, the now-famous crash of an alien spacecraft at Roswell, New Mexico, allegedly left the US military in possession of a partly destroyed alien craft, along with several alien corpses.

Evidence for UFOs keeps on cropping up. Is MJ-12 covering up the truth about alien activity on Earth?

The Roswell Air Force base announced the discovery in the world's press. The story was retracted three days later, when the President, Harry S. Truman, suppressed the information in the national interest, remembering the panic caused by Orson Welles's famous radio broadcast *The War of the Worlds*. He assembled a group of 12 military, strategic and scientific advisors to conduct a thorough investigation of the wreckage. This group was given security classifications above "Top Secret", and named the Majestic Twelve, or MJ-12 for short. The craft was taken to the top secret Nevada test area called Watertown, now known as Area 51.

From here, MJ-12 oversaw a number of different projects. In 1953 and 1954, President Dwight D. Eisenhower instituted Project Grudge under the auspices of Majority Agency for Joint Intelligence, or MAJI. Grudge was given a security clearance of MAJIC (MAJI Clearance), the highest security classification of all.

The work of MJ-12 is alleged to have led to the US government signing a treaty with aliens to allow them to perform tests on animals and humans in return for technological information. MJ-12 also agreed to suppress all information regarding the alien presence, and cover up the evidence of their tests, an operation known as Project Garnet. A further operation, Project Delta, was set up for this purpose, and employs personnel to suppress, by any means necessary, evidence of alien presence. Project Delta provides the so-called Men in Black.

THE STRANGE PART

When an undeveloped film containing images of files purporting to be a Presidential Briefing concerning MJ-12 turned up out of the blue in the post-box of a prominent UFO researcher, many people were quick to dismiss the documents as fakes. However, as more investigation was made into the claims of the so-called "MJ-12 documents" it became harder to dismiss them, as they identified the only days possible when all the 12 original members could have met for meetings – a level of detail unlikely in a hoax.

THE USUAL SUSPECTS
The US Military

Always known for being pragmatic, the military supports MJ-12 recognizing that although the aliens may not be a good thing, there is little that can be done to change matters. While research into weapons with which to fight the aliens continues, MJ-12 can only stick to its end of the bargain in order to prevent the invaders taking matters into their own hands. Better a few missing abductees and a few murdered UFO investigators than the human race enslaved.

MAJESTY

MJ-12 is not in control at all. That dubious distinction falls to the MAJI committee, also known as MAJESTY – a combined council of the heads of the intelligence agencies, along with the President. MJ-12 is a group of consultants to MAJESTY, and has never known the whole truth. Information on MJ-12 has been released in order to muddy the waters, and obscure the truth about MAJESTY and the MAJI committee, the groups that really run Project Grudge.

THE UNUSUAL SUSPECTS
The Elder Race

MJ-12 and the UFO story is only a cleverly constructed decoy story to divert attention away from the real source of mankind's advances in science over recent years – technology recovered from the ruins of an advanced Elder Race that was wiped out by a massive, global catastrophe. Those behind the conspiracy want to hide the truth – both of humanity's origins and the fact that we may also one day share the fate of the Elder Race.

MOST CONVINCING EVIDENCE

Defense Secretary James Forrestal was allegedly one of the original members of MJ-12. Shortly after Roswell, he appeared to have a mental breakdown, though few conspiriologists believe that he leapt through a window to his death from the sixteenth floor of a hospital, as was officially claimed. Especially as his personal journals – which were seized by the government – are still classified above "Top Secret" after 50 years.

MOST MYSTERIOUS FACT

The aliens who allegedly signed a treaty with MJ-12 claim that they have been genetically tinkering with humanity for millennia. They created Jesus Christ and have used a tachyon scanner that can view images from any time in history, to show his crucifixion. This time-movie has been recorded on to video, and the aliens hold its release in reserve, should they want to cause spiritual chaos.

SCEPTICALLY SPEAKING

While occasional documents have been found to back up the information regarding MJ-12 and its various projects, almost all this evidence includes errors. The people who suggest that the documents were deliberately made to look suspicious when first created, in order to minimize damage if they were leaked, are forgetting the fact that when first written, the supposed authors would have had no reason to know that such an elaborate conspiracy would ever be necessary.

THE ODESSA

The popular belief, reinforced by countless war movies and other forms of corporate-controlled media, is that the Allied Forces at the end World War II soundly defeated the Nazi Party.

The evil had been vanquished, never to rise again. Or did many Nazis not only escape the grasp of the Allies, but also actually receive help from them? Could the Third Reich still be exerting influence over the world? Yes, according to the theories surrounding the Odessa.

Mid-way through World War II, sensing the way the wind was blowing, many Nazis (among them Otto Skorzeny, Reinhard Gehlen and Martin Bormann) began to take steps to ensure their own survival. This metaphorical lifeboat was called the Odessa.

The Odessa splits into three divisions. The first division, headed by Skorzeny, developed a system for smuggling important members of the Nazi Party to safe havens across the world, including places like Indonesia and South America. The second division, the brainchild of Gehlen, (who had been head of Nazi Intelligence during World War II) was an organization of Nazi spies, that would set up shop in Munich and in time call itself "the Org". The third division handled perhaps the most crucial element in Nazi survival: the transport of money and gold, stolen from Nazi victims, out of a fallen Germany. This was also the work of Skorzeny.

But such grandiose plans, no matter how clever and ruthless the perpetrators, would not have succeeded without help. And here the tale of the Odessa takes a much darker turn – it appears that this help came from the US. In fact, it can be argued that without Nazi intervention, the CIA would never have existed and NASA would never have made it to the Moon. Perhaps the Nazi dream did not die – it may have simply changed address.

THE STRANGE PART

Captured by Allied forces, Otto Skorzeny did not face a war crimes tribunal, as would have befitted a Nazi war criminal. Instead, the Americans released him in 1947.

THE USUAL SUSPECTS
The OSS/CIA

Following the war, Allen Dulles of the OSS (Office of Strategic Services) in the US contracted the spy services of Gehlen, blatantly ignoring the US law that made the employment of Nazis illegal. Using American tax dollars, (rumoured to be around $200 million), Gehlen polished

his ring of Nazi spies into the Org. Then, working alongside Dulles, who later became head of the newly-formed CIA in 1947, Gehlen was in a position to manipulate American domestic and foreign policy.

The US government

Under the notorious Project Paperclip, in which the US government tried to snag German scientists of the Reich for its own programs, several acts of subterfuge and moral laxity were committed. One of the chief beneficiaries of this breaking of American law was NASA, which acquired the services of Werner von Braun, a force behind the dreaded V-2 rocket, to work on its space program.

THE UNUSUAL SUSPECTS
The New World Order

The Nazi Regime may have been the forerunner of the New World Order, with Hitler set to conquer the world with the aid of several corporations. But as Hitler proved too unstable, he was removed from his position of power through an inglorious suicide and the Reich was dramatically dismantled. As the dark forces behind the NWO settle down to wait for another opportunity to realize their dream, they took steps to ensure that their more loyal servants would still be available to continue the work.

MOST CONVINCING EVIDENCE

After being caught by American forces, Gehlen bargained for his freedom by offering microfilm copies of everything that his Nazi intelligence service had gleaned about Russia. The US made a deal with Gehlen for the microfilm and removed his name from the lists of Nazi POWs in American hands.

MOST MYSTERIOUS FACT

Allen Dulles's older brother, John Foster Dulles, besides being Secretary of State in the Eisenhower Administration, also acted as American liaison to IG Farben, a chemical company that not only supported the Nazi Party, but even had a plant in Auschwitz itself. Farben made the Zyklon-B crystals that were used in Auschwitz's gas chambers.

SCEPTICALLY SPEAKING

Nazis escaping post-war retribution had no need of their own organization – they were getting all the help they needed from the Russians, the Americans, the British and elements within the Vatican. Besides, would they really call their "secret society" by a name translating as "Organization of Former SS Members"?

Most are of the opinion that Odessa was largely a figment of self-styled Nazi-hunter Simon Wiesenthal's imagination; a bogeyman invented by the old fraud to keep the donations rolling in. Claiming to have tracked down over 1,200 Nazi criminals, Wiesenthal's real tally was close to a dozen – and all of those were but minor players in Hitler's grotesque circus.

Let's put it this way: in 2007, when the British World War II historian Guy Walters was researching his *Hunting Evil* (2009), the Simon Wiesenthal Centre had Erna Wallisch at Number 7 on its Most Wanted List; Walters simply looked up the one-time Ravensbruck guard in the Vienna phonebook and popped round to interview her over coffee. Her name and flat number was even included in the residents' listings posted in the foyer of her apartment block.

104 German rocket scientists at Fort Bliss, Texas. The group includes Werner von Braun and Ludwig Roth.

THE TEMPLARS

The Knights Templar was a monastic order that came into being some time around 1120 in Jerusalem in order to provide protection to the pilgrims from Europe visiting the Holy Land.

Founded by a group of nine French knights, the order's full title was the Poor Knights of Christ and of the Temple of Solomon. Within a few decades, the group grew substantially and became an officially sanctioned Christian order backed by the Pope and by the combined Monarchs of Europe.

The order's sponsor, and the man who drew up the codes of conduct and oaths of poverty that the members followed, was Cistercian Abbott St Bernard of Clairveux, the chief spokesman of united Christendom, often called "the Second Pope". Because of their members' vows of poverty and the donations they took from the wealthy pilgrims they escorted, the Templars quickly became rich. With wealth came power, and back in Europe after the Crusades, the influence of the Knights Templar grew. Pope Innocent II had exempted the Templars from all authority other than that of the papacy, so they were exempt from law. This same immunity allowed them to practise usury – lending of money for interest – and they became major financiers to European kings. In the process, they created a structure that would later become the banking and finance industry.

Perhaps making use of their legal immunities, the Templars held secret meetings and rituals at which the business of the Order was conducted. The truth of what went on at these meetings has long been debated, but whether it was Satanic worship or financial strategic discussions, the end was the same. By the start of the fourteenth century, King Philip "the Fair" of France was deeply in debt to the Templars. Rather than repay them, he chose to conspire with the Pope, Clement V, who resented Templar influence. On 13 October 1307, Philip had the Templars arrested for Heresy, which allowed him to seize all their funds and torture the knights into confessing to a variety of bad deeds, including demon-worship, possession of occult powers, trampling the Cross, and sodomy. On 22 March 1312, the Order was formally dissolved by Clement V's Papal Bull entitled "Vox In Excelso".

THE STRANGE PART

It has long been held that Freemasonry was formed from the dying embers of the Knights Templar. Many Templars fled from Europe to Scotland, where the Order was not suppressed. It is suspected that the Order survives to the present day, both within Freemasonry and separate to it as an individual organization. Long used to manipulating governments and finance, the Templars have kept light hold on the reins of power, and still sit in the background of Western society, waiting for the right moment to reveal themselves again.

THE USUAL SUSPECTS
The Freemasons

Several Masonic degrees and rites draw explicitly on Templar imagery, and even use Templar titles. Given that the Order fled to Scotland and that there is a Scottish Rite (or branch; the three Rites are theoretically separate organizations) of Freemasonry, the Templars could well have become the Freemasons, which would leave them still in power at the beginning of the twenty-first century.

THE UNUSUAL SUSPECTS
The Assassins

The famed Assassins of the Middle East were the fighting force of the Ismaeli Sect of Islam – ruled today by the Aga Khan. Known to work via infiltration, the Assassins may have compromised the Knights Templar during the Crusades as a way of gaining a foothold in the Western world – a foothold on which they have been building ever since.

MOST CONVINCING EVIDENCE

One of the most compelling pieces of evidence for the continued exist-ence of the Templars is the existence of the Templar Research Institute, part of a mysterious group known as CIRCES International Inc., a non-profit-based fraternal charity. According to its charter, the Templar Research Institute is dedicated to chivalry, but conspiracy theorists – as usual – have their doubts.

MOST MYSTERIOUS FACT

On 19 March 1314, the last Grand Master of the Knights Templar, Jacques de Molay, was burnt at the stake. As he died, he cursed King Philip and Pope Clement, telling them that they would join him within the year. The Pope died within five weeks of the prediction, and Philip died within eight months.

SCEPTICALLY SPEAKING

A greedy King and an unscrupulous Pope wanted to get rid of their enemies, so they trumped up a load of charges and tortured the Templars for confessions, then shut the order down.

THE TRIADS

Triads have one of the longest pedigrees of all the crime organizations with their roots in a precursor, imaginatively named "the Red Eyebrows", that was founded during the first century BC to overthrow the Han Dynasty.

The first proper Triad organization – that is, the first one that can be traced directly through to the current day – was the Hung League, which arose during the seventeenth century. Also called The Heaven and Earth Society, it was supposedly founded by five monks for the purpose of rebelling against the Chi'ing dynasty and returning power to the Ming dynasty.

In modern China and Hong Kong, the Triads are extremely active, but are more often visible as small-scale gangs rather than large entities run by criminal masterminds. They provide muscle and expertise at street level, running small extortion rings, prostitution, forgery, fencing stolen goods and distributing drugs on a day-to-day basis. Before a major government clampdown in 1956, the Triads had been much more organized, with a comparatively rigid control structure, treaties and some degree of co-operation.

Emigration from Hong Kong and Taiwan allowed the Triads to set up in the United Kingdom and in America. Government reports have assessed that, although much of the crime in the Asian communities in both countries is linked to the Triads, they are not controlled from Hong Kong or China. However, such findings might well be prompted by vested interests – neither the British nor the American governments want to admit to yet another powerful, organized crime body operating on their territory, and it is also in the interests of the Triads that they should be severely underestimated.

THE STRANGE PART
Despite protestations that there is little central organization, there is a serious Triad-related problem across the UK and US with forged credit cards. It appears that Triad members terrorize vulnerable waiters in Chinese restaurants into copying credit card details from customers paying for a meal. These card details are then shipped to a central source and passed back to the Far East, where forged credit cards are manufactured in bulk using the stolen details and then passed for worldwide distribution. This sort of co-ordination would be tricky to achieve if the Triads were as fragmented and as preoccupied with infighting as government reports suggest they are.

THE USUAL SUSPECTS
The Network
It is feared that following the hand-over of Hong Kong to China, the Triads have moved out into the world at large. It is thought that from their new operational HQs in Australia, the Triads have joined with the Yakuza, the Tongs, the Mafia and the IRA to extort money on a grand scale from governments and major corporations, partly through electronic terrorism such as viruses and hacker scares.

THE UNUSUAL SUSPECTS
Japan
When the Japanese invaded China in the thirties, they paid the Triads to work for them. Even though the Communists under Mao Tse Tung eventually won, the Japanese government paid the Triads in Hong Kong (through an organization called the Lee Yuen Company) to police the residents and suppress any anti-Japanese activity. The Japanese government may still be the force behind Triad activity today.

MOST CONVINCING EVIDENCE
Although the theft and re-distribution of fake credit cards is well documented in England, the extent can be quite shocking. One restaurant in Birmingham was found to be the source of 19 incidents of credit-card duplication (with subsequent fraudulent transactions) in the Far East in just 14 days, which suggests a very well-polished organizational structure.

MOST MYSTERIOUS FACT
In one well-publicized interview of a notorious Triad enforcer, known as BC, by the journalist Terry Gould, several allegations were made about the scope of gang activities. BC revealed that there is a large Triad organization called the Big Circle, and said that it consisted of several sections. There is a degree of debate as to whether the Big Circle was just a large Triad, like the 14K, which is known to have several subsidiary groups, or whether it was an over-arching unificatory power, dictating policy and action.

SCEPTICALLY SPEAKING
Although the case for central organization is quite persuasive, given the endemic violence between rival Triad groups, it seems more likely that the apparent co-operation is merely one small skein of mutual interest. In most matters, on a day-to-day basis, the Triads remain a collection of petty gangs, operating under a common name purely because of the fear the Triad name can cause.

CHAPTER 4:

HISTORICAL

THE GUNPOWDER PLOT

Given that the Gunpowder Plot was exposed before it was successfully completed, there is a tendency to view it as a failed conspiracy – one that has been fully investigated, resolved and consigned to the pages of dusty history books.

Bates — Robert Winter — Christopher Wright — Iohn Wright — Thomas Percy — Guido Fawkes — Robert Catesby — Thomas Winter

"No! You were supposed to bring the matches!"

However, some conspiriologists have nagging doubts over the whole matter and feel that the Gunpowder Plot as taught to British school children is only the visible tip of a much larger conspiracy.

The bare facts of the plot are well known. Guy Fawkes was caught red-handed in a cellar underneath the Houses of Parliament the night before King James was due to preside over the State Opening of Parliament. His fellow conspirators were soon hunted down. Those who did not die resisting arrest were tried, found guilty of treason and sentenced to death. Within a week of their trial they had all been hanged, drawn and quartered.

The accepted theory – usually the one you need to be deeply suspicious of – is that a small group of Catholic fanatics, working alone, planned to kill King James I. They hoped that in the confusion after his death they would be able to put a Catholic on the throne of England. That Fawkes and his associates were conspiring to blow up the House of Lords while the king was in attendance is beyond question: but who was pulling the strings; who was the hidden puppet-master?

And where did they get all that gunpowder – equivalent in volume to about a quarter of the national reserve? Given that they had about 5,000lb of the stuff packed into thirty-six barrels, how on earth did they transport it onto site undetected? Are we really expected to believe that a known group of Catholic activists could rent a cellar directly under the House of Lords and make repeated journeys thereto with something close to two-and-a-half tons of gunpowder? Surely they would have attracted at least the passing interest of Robert Cecil, 1st Earl of Salisbury, one of the most insidiously efficient spymasters England has ever produced?

THE STRANGE PART

In 1601, Robert Catesby, leader of the 1605 Gunpowder Plot, was involved in the rebellion led by the Earl of Essex against Elizabeth I. Wounded and captured, he fell into the hands of Robert Cecil, but, strangely, was released instead of executed. It was at this point that most suspect Cecil "turned" the Catholic militant to his own devious use. To say that Cecil instigated the Gunpowder Plot is untenable, but it is almost a certainty that, having become aware of such a plot, he decided to encourage and "oversee" it to draw out as many Catholic activists as possible.

On his deathbed and making his final confession, Catesby's squire reiterated what he had said all along – that a few weeks before 5 November 1605, he had inadvertently walked in on a meeting between his boss and Robert Cecil and overheard the visitor promising to ensure that "the cellar" would be made available for rent.

The plot was "uncovered" in the nick of time, thanks to an anonymous letter sent to the Catholic Lord Monteagle, by coincidence (yes, of course …) related to one Francis Tresham. He was one of the conspirators, and the letter warned not to attend the House on 5 November, as it was then to receive "a terrible blow". Others present at the time of the letter's delivery recalled their surprise at Monteagle's insistence that his secretary should read the letter aloud, as the contents could have related to any number of personal or confidential matters. On the other hand, such a move would have made perfect sense had Monteagle been expecting just such a letter and had been keen for others to witness its content. Either way, Monteagle took himself and the letter off to Robert Cecil, who, in all likelihood, was the author of the same and in need of some "trigger" to activate his search.

THE USUAL SUSPECTS
Robert Cecil, Earl of Salisbury
Once made aware that a terror plot is afoot, spymasters have often been inclined to let it run its course in order to cast their net wider – and then step in as the avenging angel at the eleventh hour. Cecil certainly benefitted from his "discovery" of Fawkes in the cellar in the early hours of 5 November; his standing in the king's eyes dramatically increased to leave him nicely positioned to implement the crack-down on Catholics that he had so long desired. It is also evident from surviving paperwork that Cecil not only had Monteagle's name removed from most, if not all, of the trial documents but he also supressed letters that Monteagle had written in vilification of James I. He also "doctored" the transcripts of the collective confessions of the accused to ensure the removal of certain names and mention of certain events. Notionally, this was an effort to "simplify the procedure" for the court – much as today the CIA redact their own files when one of their "tame" terrorists is dragged out into the light.

The English Nobility
When James was crowned King of England in 1603, he united two countries that had been at war far more often than they had been at peace. It is inconceivable that this unification could happen without upsetting plenty of people – as soon as James arrived in London he began appointing Scottish nobles to positions of power. Among the displaced English nobles were members of the mystical order known as Meonia – including Sir Walter Raleigh – who were known to have links with some Gunpowder Plot conspirators, including Robert Catesby and Thomas Wyntour.

THE UNUSUAL SUSPECTS
The Tobacco Lobby
Sir Walter Raleigh had first introduced tobacco from the New World a generation earlier and the fashion for smoking it had spread like wildfire throughout England – making some merchants who dealt in tobacco very rich indeed. There was a rumour that the King was intending to introduce a series of punitive taxes on tobacco to raise some much-needed cash. These taxes would have seriously damaged the financial interests of several powerful people in England and Virginia, so the Gunpowder Plot may have been one of the first times that big business decided to flex its muscles.

The Scottish Nobility
James I of England was also James VI of Scotland, and Scotland, at this point in history, was as torn apart with plots and treason as any soap-opera plot could ever become. Plots, conspiracies and assassinations were commonplace and one of the most favoured ways of disposing of an enemy or rival was death by explosion. James I's father had been killed by this method and the King himself had ordered the destruction of his enemies be carried out with explosives. James had plenty of enemies in his home country who wanted him out of the way and would not have minded the Catholics taking the blame.

MOST CONVINCING EVIDENCE
Two of the other major plots exposed during James I's reign that led to the downfall of Sir Walter Raleigh – the Main Plot and the Bye Plot – shared certain common elements with the Gunpowder Plot. They both failed, they were both uncovered at the last minute thanks to Cecil, and they both left the establishment and the King stronger and more firmly in place.

MOST MYSTERIOUS FACT
On 28 December 1604, King James I attended the society wedding of the Earl of Montgomery to Robert Cecil's niece. Bizarrely, among the other guests attending this glittering social function was Guy Fawkes. If Guy Fawkes was the Catholic fanatic painted by many historians, with a burning desire to murder James I, then why did he not simply bring a knife to the wedding and attempt a more straightforward assassination?

SCEPTICALLY SPEAKING
Sometimes the official explanation is not only obvious but also correct. Catholic countries, such as France and Spain, certainly had an interest in destabilizing England and were known to work via underground networks of priests to ferment unrest. Maybe this is one conspiracy that really is as simple as it seems.

HITLER

Nobody is in any doubt that Adolf Hitler, leader of the Nazi party, was one of the most evil and dangerous men to have come to power in all of human history.

The legacy of death and suffering that he left behind him is staggering. Approximately six million Jews were slaughtered, primarily in death camps, as part of his "Final Solution" – almost two thirds of their world population. It is also important to remember he murdered a large proportion of Europe's population of gypsies, Seventh Day Adventists, Jehovah's Witnesses and Socialists.

During World War II, some sixty million soldiers were mobilized across Europe, the Americas, Russia and the Far East. Almost a third of them were killed. The total death toll for the war has been estimated around 52 million people – 18 million soldiers, 16 million civilians killed in military action, and 18 million people murdered in the death camps. Hitler lurked behind all this death, the lynchpin of the entire war. These facts are horrific enough that surely no conspiracy can compete – but there are suggestions that Hitler's ultimate goal was not to unite Europe under his rule at all, but simply to cause widespread death and destruction to appease his Satanic masters.

The Brotherhood of Death is the name given to a rumoured world-wide coalition of primarily Satanic organizations. Each organization has, as its logo, the skull and two crossed bones, the emblem we most commonly associate with pirates. The German branch of the Brotherhood of Death was allegedly the Thule Gesellschaft, or Thule Society. Centred on a semi-mythical land from ancient times, the legend of Thule shares certain features with that of Atlantis. The land of Thule is supposed to have been the cradle of the Aryan race.

In 1919, disgusted by the way that the German government had "thrown away" World War I, Hitler joined the Thule Society, which at that time was led by Dietrich Eckhardt. When the Brotherhood of Death began their ambitious plan to reshape society in a more controllable form, their end goal was the surveillance and monitoring of an increasingly isolated and malleable population. Europe was identified as a potential flashpoint for a useful war. Germany, having just lost a major war, was ripe for destabilization, and Hitler, whom Eckhardt believed to be the Antichrist, was chosen as the obvious leader to initiate the gigantic conflict and death required. This would scar the human psyche so deeply that people would become paranoid and withdrawn, and once isolated they could be

manipulated into giving up autonomy to the Brotherhood and its evil masters.

The Brotherhood of Death believed firmly that contact with ancient powers of spiritual evil – the Devil – was not only attainable but very desirable, and that by following the dictates of their master, they could achieve great earthly power. They used sexual perversions and practices to fuel their magical operations, which made their spells and rituals phenomenally powerful and opened channels of communication to the forces of evil.

By tapping the power of evil, the Thule Society was able to manipulate the consciousness of the German people and bring the Nazi party to prominence. By appealing to the basic human psychological programmes of hatred, fear and greed, the Nazi party was able to divert the current of evil into the minds of usually decent people, and foster the political climate that led to Hitler's rise. Once he was in power, it was frighteningly simple to steer the world into a gigantic war, with the death camps providing the incredible amounts of magical energy needed to change human consciousness forever.

THE STRANGE PART

Eckhardt's final act was said to be Hitler's initiation through an astonishingly sadistic black-magic ritual that left the Nazi leader impotent. From then on, Hitler was forced to seek sexual fulfilment through sadomasochistic release, and it was this blow that forced him into becoming the greatest monster we have seen this century.

THE USUAL SUSPECTS
Satan

If ancient powers of spiritual evil are behind the Brotherhood of Death and the Thule Gesellschaft, then that rather implies the Devil. Given the Devil's well-known propensity for misdirection, it seems likely that in the event that his plans succeed, the Brotherhood will lose out along with everyone else.

Bavarian Illuminati

This age-old German secret society is often thought to control everyone from the Mafia to the Knights Templar. The Illuminati were the power behind many occult orders in pre-

Adolf Hitler, Chancellor of Germany, is welcomed by supporters at Nuremberg in 1933.

war Germany and may have been Hitler's ultimate puppet-master. It is recorded that Heinrich Himmler was closely involved with societies linked to the Illuminati.

THE UNUSUAL SUSPECTS
The Elders of Zion
The least credible and perhaps most offensive theory is that the Elders of Zion were responsible for the actions of the Nazi Party. By causing a massive depopulation of Jews, the England-based group would have less difficulty in claiming to be the inheritors of Moses' wisdom. The horrors of the Holocaust would also breed sympathy for all causes even tangentially related to Judaism.

MOST CONVINCING EVIDENCE
On his deathbed, Dietrich Eckhardt is said to have announced: "Follow Hitler; he will dance, but it is I who have called the tune. I have initiated him into the Secret Doctrine, opened his centres of vision, and given him the means to communicate with the powers." Given that

society continues to get more fragmented, violent and subjugated by television, despite the fact that it is in no one's interests, not even those of the world governments, the Brotherhood of Death could be said to be doing a particularly effective job.

MOST MYSTERIOUS FACT
The USA too has a society with the logo of the Brotherhood of Death – Yale's Skull and Bones society, rumoured to have been started in the 1800s as a US lodge of a German university-based society. President George Bush, Sr belonged to this group, as did many important figures in American society and political circles.

SCEPTICALLY SPEAKING
To dismiss the Holocaust and the evils of the Nazi empire as a simple tool for generating magical energy seems somewhat offensive to those who died. In addition, the circumstances surrounding the rise of the Nazi Party are well understood in sociological terms – tragic, but hardly mysterious.

THE MAN IN THE IRON MASK

The mystery of the Man in the Iron Mask has been a focal point for doe-eyed romantics and for serious historians since the seventeenth century, generating countless theories about the identity of the masked prisoner.

But the world is still no closer to discovering who this tragic figure was and, as the years pass, the chances of discovering his (or her) true identity continue to fade.

Little is known about the prisoner. What little information that exists in French official documents paints a deliberately sketchy picture: he was arrested in 1669, and was imprisoned first in Pignerol, a fortress high in the French Alps. He was transferred in 1681 to Exiles, which lay close to Pignerol, and in 1687 he was moved yet again to the southern French coastal island of Saint Marguerite. His stay on the island lasted 11 years, until he was sent to the Bastille in Paris. Finally, the prisoner died in 1703, an undoubtedly welcome release.

Throughout his entire imprisonment, there were reportedly only two instances of witnesses who were not prison officials actually seeing the prisoner. During his move from Exiles to Saint Marguerite, the prisoner was seen wearing a steel mask. With the move to the Bastille, this cumbersome disguise was replaced with a more humane mask of black velvet. It has also been discovered, through official correspondence between a government minister and Saint Mars (the prisoner's jailer) that the prisoner was not to be allowed to communicate with anyone, by spoken or by written word. If he did, he was to be executed on the spot.

What terrible secret could this man have possessed that demanded such secrecy? Historians have wondered why he was even kept alive: if the knowledge he held was of such danger to the King and government, wouldn't it have been politically safer simply to kill him? And why such a concern over people seeing his face? Did he resemble someone well known to the French populace, which would have to make him very famous indeed, bearing in mind the primitive state of print media during the seventeenth century? Once again, simply killing him – an option not in disuse in the French court of the time – would have made more sense.

The mystery of the Man in the Iron Mask is as unfathomable now as it was three hundred years ago. What is known is that a man paid a horrible price for an alleged crime – or deadly secret – that history can only guess at.

THE STRANGE PART

Saint Mars, the man appointed to jail the mysterious prisoner, held that position from the first day of his incarceration until the prisoner breathed his last in 1703. With the turnstile approach to political appointments of the day, this constancy is intriguing.

THE USUAL SUSPECTS
Louis XIV

Many fingers point towards the King of France. The masked prisoner could have been the twin brother of Louis, rumoured to have been conceived at the same time but unfortunately born last. He didn't know his own true identity and, to clear up any messy succession issues, Louis imprisoned his brother. Other theories suggest that he could have been an elder brother, the result of an extramarital affair of Louis' mother. Another theory states that the prisoner was a doctor who attended Louis XIII's autopsy and unfortunately discovered the late king incapable of siring children, thus endangering Louis XIV's right to the throne. Following the same thread, the prisoner could have been the true father of Louis XIV, recruited on account of Louis XIII's inability in the bedroom.

Count Antonio Matthioli

He may have been the prisoner, wearing the mask for the most pointless of reasons – because it was the fashionable thing to do in Italy at the time.

Louis Oldendorff

A Lorraine nobleman, Oldendorff was the leader of the Secret Order of the Temple. The rules of this society would not allow them to replace him while he still lived. After he died, another man was made to wear the mask, thus maintaining the illusion of Oldendorff's imprisonment, and keeping the Order from selecting a new leader.

Also suspected to be the prisoner: Richard Cromwell; the Duke of Monmouth; Vivien de Bulonde.

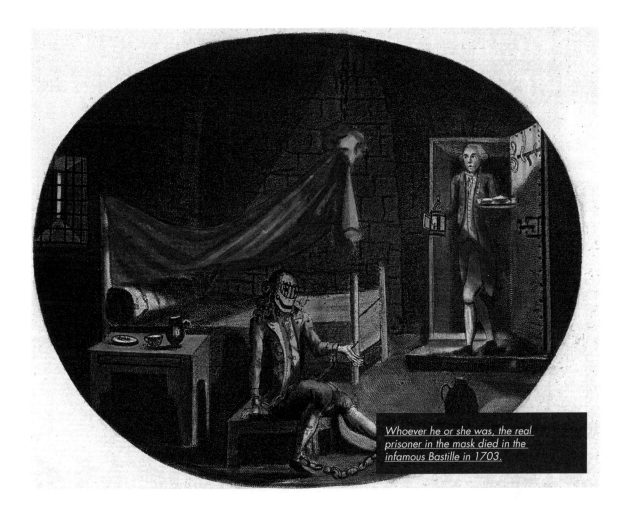

Whoever he or she was, the real prisoner in the mask died in the infamous Bastille in 1703.

THE UNUSUAL SUSPECTS
Hidden Daughter of Louis XIII and Anne

Terrified of not having a son, the elder Louis may have hidden away his newborn daughter and replaced her with an infant boy changeling. When she grew up and discovered her identity, Louis XIV (the changeling) had her imprisoned.

Molière

As beloved as the playwright was both by the French public and by Louis XIV, Molière made many enemies because of his lack of religious beliefs and general disdain for the French establishment. He especially angered the Company of the Holy Sacrament, a strong and influential Catholic group. The theory follows that Molière's death was staged in 1673, with the playwright becoming the Man in the Iron Mask as punishment.

Nicholas Fouquet

Fouquet was allegedly imprisoned for discovering hidden knowledge that Christ didn't die on the cross, but survived, leading to a secret bloodline of direct ancestors.

MOST CONVINCING EVIDENCE

The fact that the prisoner wasn't simply killed indicates that there must have been a royal connection. Anyone else would have been garotted and left to an unmarked grave.

MOST MYSTERIOUS FACT

Despite the backstabbing of French politics, the gains that could be made by revealing who this prisoner was, and the methodical examination of records, there is no indication of who the prisoner was. It was a universally kept secret, by all parties involved.

SCEPTICALLY SPEAKING

The identity of the Man in the Iron Mask is so well hidden, one can surmise it's simply because he didn't exist at all. The vision of such a figure would go far towards quelling any dissidence to the King's rule. The prospect of lifelong imprisonment does that sort of thing…

THE MURDER OF CHRISTOPHER MARLOWE

Fate can play cruel tricks on the gifted, and Christopher Marlowe (1564–93) was undoubtedly gifted. At one time he was England's leading playwright, thanks to such works as _Doctor Faustus._

There was a lot more to Christopher Marlowe than merely his talent with a pen. In his short but tempestuous life, he tasted the extremes of wealth and poverty. In 1589, he was even imprisoned for his part in a swordfight in which one William Bradley, a notorious thug and bully, was killed. Although Marlowe is often said to have been Bradley's killer, he was not. During the fight, Bradley soon knocked Marlowe unconscious, and it was in fact Marlowe's friend and fellow poet, Thomas Watson, who despatched the thug. However, both men were held until it was established that Bradley had instigated the affray. Be that as it may, Marlowe certainly met with a violent end himself on 30 May 1593. His demise occurred not in a bawdy tavern, as myth-history would have us believe, but rather in the Deptford home of one Mrs Eleanor Bull, who rented out rooms for private dinner parties.

Few have ever accepted the official verdict that Marlowe was fatally stabbed though the eye during a row with his fellow guests over who should pay for what when the bill for dinner arrived. This is mainly because Marlowe was a spy, as indeed were the other members of his small private party – Nicholas Skeres, Robert Poley and, most interesting of all, Ingram Frizer. All four men were attached to the web of intrigue spun by the Elizabethan spymasters, Thomas and Francis Walsingham.

England in the sixteenth century was a turbulent place. The country was troubled by enemies at home and abroad. The defeat of the Spanish Armada had ended the King of Spain's plans for a purely military conquest of the country, so he turned to espionage and began attacking England by more subtle means. The internal threat centred on religion. For many years there had been conflict between Protestants and Catholics, with prominent figures on both sides dying at the stake. Although the official attitude in 1593 was toleration, there was an active and dangerous Catholic underground with strong links to foreign powers.

To counter these threats it was necessary for the English crown to operate an efficient counter-espionage system. Elizabeth I's spymaster was Francis Walsingham, who recruited Marlowe at Cambridge University. Marlowe's public profile and wide network of connections made him a useful, if somewhat unreliable, agent. He infiltrated many secret societies and organizations while performing this role.

Given his secret life, his murder may not have been the simple affair it has been portrayed as.

THE STRANGE PART

At the time of his murder, Marlowe was in residence at Scadbury Manor, the home of Thomas Walsingham, which stood nine miles from Deptford. When not conspiring to espionage, this Walsingham was an avid supporter of the arts and a sponsor of Marlowe's writing career. Frizer – the man who actually pushed the dagger into Marlowe's eye – was also in residence at the manor as he was Walsingham's right-hand man, and it was he who suggested that Marlowe accompany him to Mrs Bull's establishment for a night of drinking and dining. Frizer was acquitted at his trial of 1 June 1593, backed by the perjured testimony of Skeres and Poley, both of whom gave suspiciously identical accounts of how Marlowe had attacked Frizer with a dagger leaving him no option but to defend himself. Further, at Thomas Walsingham's intervention, Frizer then received a royal pardon from Elizabeth I on 28 June. This was a very hurried sequence of events for the time.

THE USUAL SUSPECTS
Sir Thomas Walsingham

Late in May 1593, the Privy Council – but one of Robert Poley's paymasters – decided to issue a warrant for the arrest of Marlowe. This decision was due to Marlowe's notorious habit of making public jokes and comments that most deemed blasphemous and heretical. Had this happened, Walsingham stood to lose all of his estates and wealth to the Crown – despite his elevated position – as the sponsor of a convicted heretic whom he was keeping under his own roof. Tipped off by Poley as to this imminent eventuality, Walsingham could well have given the nod to Frizer to eliminate the problem, making it clear to his minion that his cushy life would also come to a shuddering halt if he, Walsingham, met with such catastrophe. Goaded by the stick of his own financial ruin and the carrot of Walsingham's promise of protection in the aftermath, Frizer did his boss's bidding.

Dr John Dee

After the sudden death of Sir Francis Walsingham, in 1590, his position as spymaster-in-chief to Elizabeth I was filled by Dr John Dee. When not running England's cloak-and-dagger activity, Dee dabbled in astrology, necromancy, contacting angels and alchemy. The transmuting of base metals into gold is a neat way of explaining the funds that passed through his hands and were provided by various paymasters. The good doctor was not a man overburdened with scruples and had he felt that Marlowe, due to his impending arrest for heresy, had become a liability or perhaps suspected him of being a double agent, then he would have had no qualms himself over instructing Frizer to "take out the trash".

THE UNUSUAL SUSPECTS
William Shakespeare

The theatre of the sixteenth century was a cutthroat environment – there was no funding from any Arts Council and playwrights had to find sponsorship where they could or starve. Both Shakespeare and Marlowe were members of the so-called School of Night, a raggle-taggle group of writers, theatricals and assorted shady characters. On occasion, the latter group included Edward de Vere, the semi-renegade 17th Earl of Oxford. It has been suggested that somehow, Marlowe got wind of the fact that de Vere – no mean playwright himself – was in fact the author of the plays paraded under Shakespeare's name. This is a suspicion that persists to this day. Fearing public disgrace and ridicule, could Shakespeare have slipped Frizer, who he knew through Marlowe, a "fistful of groats" to do the business?

The Masons

Among the many secret societies that were flourishing in Elizabethan England were the Freemasons. It has long been suspected that Marlowe drew on Masonic imagery in his plays and was almost certainly a member of the order. While being a Mason probably helped to advance his career as a playwright, it would also have given him access to insider information in his role of spy. Marlowe may have made the foolish mistake of breaking his oath of secrecy to the organization, which retaliated by hiring his own associate, Frizer, to enact the ritual retribution of stabbing Marlowe through the eye. (Bear in mind that, as already stated, this is a far from conventional method of despatch!) In short, the murder of Christopher Marlowe may have been

the dire consequence of his underestimation of just how much Masons then valued their own version of the Mafia's "*omerta*", or vow of secrecy.

MOST MYSTERIOUS FACT

This has to be the strange despatch of Marlowe by stabbing him through the right eye which, like many other such ritualistic killings, would tend to indicate that someone somewhere was sending a message. The "All-Seeing Eye" is a prime symbol of the Masons and one intended to remind all within the organization that God is watching and judging our actions at all times. Thomas Walsingham was definitely a Mason, as was Frizer who, having been given the "green light" on Marlowe, might have decided to complete his task with a ritualistic flourish?

MOST CONVINCING EVIDENCE

Sir Thomas Walsingham had two strong motivations for unleashing Frizer on Marlowe, the second of more importance than any threat to his estates and wealth. While feigning loyalty to Elizabeth I, both he and his wife, Lady Audrey, were closet-supporters of the Catholic James VI of Scotland, son of Mary, Queen of Scots, recently executed by Elizabeth. Both were engaged in coded correspondence with James and conspiring to oust Elizabeth and install James on the English throne. If Marlowe, as seems likely, had been convicted of heresy – then regarded as treason – Walsingham would be tainted by association and banished from the court he so desperately needed to attend in order to harvest intelligence to send back to Scotland.

SCEPTICALLY SPEAKING

There is not much to say here: four of Walsingham's spies went into a closed room for a meal and only three came out. Whoever he was acting for, Frizer never denied the killing, simply claiming to have acted in self-defence after Marlowe, in a fury, had slashed him about the top of his head as he sat at the table. Claiming these wounds to have been over a quarter of an inch deep – hard to believe, given the shallow depth of the flesh on the pate – these wounds had all miraculously healed in the 24 hours before Frizer's arrest. However, nobody thought all this this worthy of question at his trial. Marlowe was definitely murdered by Frizer, but we shall never know the true identity of the puppet-master behind the action, nor his actual motivation.

WOLFGANG AMADEUS MOZART

Genius may bring its blessings, but it also brings its fair share of enemies. No one knew this more than the brilliant composer Wolfgang Amadeus Mozart. A child prodigy by the age of five, his musical gifts brought him more pain than joy. While his work is heralded today as the finest that classical music can offer, in his time he was openly reviled, with several of his contemporaries plotting his destruction.

History may have given him fame but in his lifetime he knew no such comfort. Mozart, perhaps the greatest composer ever to have lived, died penniless, his remains buried unceremoniously in a common grave in Vienna.

Born in Salzburg, Austria, in January 1756, Mozart quickly displayed his musical gifts: by the age of four, his father had arranged harpsichord lessons for him; by five, he was composing his own music; by the time he was six, his father took the young Mozart on a performance tour of Vienna and Munich. By the time he was 15, he was concertmaster of the Archbishop of Salzburg's orchestra. The future seemed to belong to the extremely gifted young man.

But there were personality conflicts between the Archbishop and Mozart – the fact that Mozart wasn't paid for three years may have been one reason. In 1781, he left the prestigious (but poorly paid) position and went to seek his fortune in Vienna. There, the poor relationship he had had with the Salzburg court continued with the Viennese composers. This became so bad that Mozart's father complained to Emperor Joseph II that the other composers were deliberately ensuring that a composition of his son's was not being performed.

Yet Mozart persevered, despite his difficulty in getting paid and his inability to spend money wisely. His marriage to Constanze Weber was fraught with financial difficulties and tragedy – of their six children, only two survived past childhood. Mozart was not a favourite with the Viennese court, and his work received lukewarm response from the public, if it was played at all. By 1791, Mozart was not in the best of health, but his mounting debts left him no option but to accept a commission from the Count Franz von Walsegg, who wanted a requiem to commemorate the recent passing of his young wife, Anna. However, Mozart himself died on 5 December that same year, aged just 35, with the work unfinished. Left on her own and in dire need of the sum promised by Walsegg, Constanze turned to Mozart's friend, the composer Franz Süssmayr, to complete the piece and deliver it to the owner.

THE STRANGE PART

For reasons unfathomable, since the identity of *Requiem's* commissioner is well documented, some have tried to weave a conspiratorial cloak about its composition with talk of a black-clad figure who periodically darkened Mozart's door to chivvy him into its completion. In the wildly inaccurate but most enjoyable film *Amadeus* (1984), that anonymous spectre is presented as Mozart's alleged jealous rival, Antonio Salieri, who supposedly strove to drive Mozart into his grave. Mind you, that same film, from which most of us glean our perception of the relationship between the two men, also perpetuates the notion that Mozart was poisoned by Salieri; Mozart was certainly poisoned, but not by any human hand.

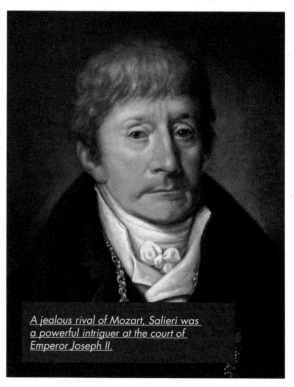

A jealous rival of Mozart, Salieri was a powerful intriguer at the court of Emperor Joseph II.

THE USUAL SUSPECTS
Antonio Salieri

In the Vienna of the day, there were two distinct musical lobbies – the German and the Italian – with Mozart and Salieri their respective leading lights. There was, as one might expect, a broad rivalry between them. However, there were most certainly no personal vendettas between Mozart and Salieri, who were on cordial terms throughout their time together in Vienna. It was Mozart himself who started all the rumours of his having been poisoned by his "enemies", while he was in a delirious state towards the end of his life. With Salieri the undisputed leader of the musical "opposition" in Vienna, silly rumours quickly circulated the city. Mozart's widow Constanze was completely hostile to the suggestion, later sending her son, Franz Mozart, to be tutored by Salieri – something she would hardly do had she the slightest suspicion that this was the man who had poisoned the boy's father. Nevertheless, in terms of the rumours, the damage was done – and muffled sniggering weighed heavy on Salieri's mind.

Salieri was hospitalized with dementia in 1823 and could oft be seen wandering the facility either naked or in his nightshirt, screaming that he was the man who killed Mozart. No doubt thinking "that'll do nicely", the Russian playwright Alexander Pushkin wrote a melodrama entitled *Mozart and Salieri* (1830), presenting this as historical fact. In turn, Pushkin's play was taken as the foundation of the Peter Shaffer play, *Amadeus* (1979), made into a film in 1984 – and there you go!

Count von Walsegg zu Stuppach

It has been suggested that, when von Walsegg recognized the genius of *Requiem*, he did away with Mozart himself to keep secret the fact that the work was not of his own hand. Although it is true that von Walsegg – a wannabe composer – was known to secretly commission works from various composers and then pass the pieces off as his own, it is unlikely he would have desecrated the memory of his beloved Anna with such a charade. Deeply in love with her and only 28 years old himself at the time of her death, von Walsegg never remarried nor sought female company. Besides, Mozart was already dead by the time that von Walsegg received the composition and everybody already knew that the work had been commissioned.

THE UNUSUAL SUSPECTS
The Masons

A Freemason himself for the last seven years of his life, Mozart was known to have been an acute embarrassment to the Viennese lodges. Musical genius he may have been, but he was also possessed of a decidedly scatological sense of humour; let's just say that the same mind that conjured forth *Requiem* was also responsible for other less well-known works such as the six-voice canon in b-flat that rejoices in the title of *Lick Me in*

the Arse (Mozart catalogue number 231). He also wrote other pieces in similar vein with titles best not translated here, and *The Magic Flute* is known to have also ruffled Masonic feathers for its hinting at too many of their secrets. Either way, it has been suggested that, tiring of such embarrassment, the Masons themselves might have removed its source.

Disgruntled Black Magician in the Court of Emperor Joseph

A story survives of an army general in Joseph's court complaining about Mozart's lack of court decorum to the Emperor. The Emperor replied that he could get a general any time he wished, but he would never get another Mozart. This could have led to someone in the court using black magic to kill Mozart, leading to the confusion among doctors concerning his death.

MOST CONVINCING EVIDENCE

As previously stated, Mozart was not poisoned by any human hand – he was bumped off by a pig!

His rapid decline began on 20 November and, fifteen days later, Mozart was dead. No poison of the day took such a time to act nor did any produce the symptoms presented by Mozart who, filling the house with the stench of putrefaction, was at the end so bloated that he was unrecognizable as a human being. Mozart was notoriously fond of pork and his well-documented symptoms match exactly what one would expect of someone who had ingested the parasitic trichinella nematode, so often found in pork, and which can easily survive inadequate cooking. Given that trichinella was not identified until 1860, Mozart's doctors would have known nothing of this nematode and, even if they did, no medicine of the day would have been able to combat its ravages.

MOST MYSTERIOUS FACT

Mozart was initiated into a Viennese Masonic Lodge at the age of 18, with his father joining shortly thereafter. Curiously, despite the connection, Mozart was denied membership to the Viennese Society of Musicians. Also interesting to note was that his last public performance was a cantata for the dedication of his Masonic Lodge's new temple.

SCEPTICALLY SPEAKING

At the end of the day, Mozart was, health-wise, a dead man walking; he had already endured the debilitating effects of syphilis, bronchitis, smallpox, typhoid, pneumonia and at least three bouts of rheumatic fever – so perhaps the question to ask is not why he died when he did but how did he manage to last so long? Be that as it may, far from being murdered by some envious rival, the genius that was Mozart was actually laid low by a pork chop.

RASPUTIN

There most certainly was a conspiracy behind the slaying of Rasputin, but not the one that most know – or think they know. Firstly, it is essential to set the backdrop of the stage that Rasputin walked onto in November of 1905 to place himself front-and-centre of the Russian Royal Court.

Russia in the opening years of the twentieth century was still basically a medieval country; the feudal system so long abandoned by the rest of Europe had only just been dismantled and the occupants of the Court at St Petersburg, isolated in their opulence, were obsessed with the occult. They wished to find the authentic "Wolshebnik", or "Miracle-Worker", to serve as their hotline to God, whom the Tsar was convinced spoke truths to man through the mouths of lunatics.

As a result of this strange belief, the Tsar hauled into court a succession of bizarre characters such as Matrona the Barefooted One who, when not running through the palace wailing, advised the Tsar on matters of domestic and foreign policy. When the American magician and escapologist Harry Houdini put on a show for the court in mid-1905 the Tsar, ignoring Houdini's insistence that all was trickery, proclaimed him the true Wolshebnik and demanded he stay with them in that capacity. Later explaining that he feared he was about to be detained as some sort of performing "pet", Houdini fled to leave the vacuum that was so quickly filled by Grigori Efimovich, better known by his nickname of Rasputin, which translates appropriately enough as "The Debauchee".

Rasputin is of course best remembered for seeming to have the ability to assuage the distressing bouts of haemophiliac bleeding that afflicted the Tsar's son. Some maintained that his success was attributable to his use of hypnotism or mystical healing, but there is no evidence for either. More likely is the fact that Rasputin insisted the boy be locked in a room with him while he prayed, as this kept the Court doctors at bay. They would probably have dosed the boy with their new wonder-drug aspirin – now a recognized anti-coagulant, which would have been the worst thing to give a haemophiliac. So, albeit by default, Rasputin did have a beneficial effect on the Tsar's son, which meant that in the eyes of the Tsar and Tsarina he could do no wrong. However, like all charlatans throughout history, Rasputin pushed his game too far.

In 1915, Rasputin was making overtures to Berlin, presenting himself as an undercover peace-broker who could persuade the Tsar to pull out of World War I – for a price, of course. Given the green light from Berlin, Rasputin began ear-bashing the Tsar to withdraw from the conflict and return Russia to a state of isolation from Europe and all its woes. As far as the British were concerned, this would result in 350,000 German troops being stood-down from the Eastern Front and thus free to join their comrades on the Western Front, where such an injection of numbers would undoubtedly tip the war in Germany's favour. It really was that serious; so as far as British Intelligence was concerned, the Mad Monk Rasputin had to go!

A young intelligence officer named Captain Oswald Rayner was ordered to re-establish contact with Prince Felix Yusupov, a flamboyant transvestite who had been Rayner's lover when the pair studied together at Cambridge. More importantly, Yusupov was known to be very much in favour of a dead Rasputin, as indeed were so many of the Russian elite. By October 1916, Rayner was in close contact with Yusupov, to set the stage for the impending assassination of 30 December 1916.

THE STRANGE PART

According to Rasputin's daughter, Maria, on the morning of the day in question, her father received an anonymous phone call informing him that he was about to be killed. This might suggest that there was a leak in the plotters' camp; alternatively, as Rasputin received many such anonymous calls and letters, perhaps it was just a coincidence. Not wishing to trust her own life to "coincidence", after her father's death Maria fled to a succession of European countries before ending up in America, where she first toured with a circus as a lion-tamer – as you do. Badly mauled by a bear in 1935, she left the circus to work as a welder in a US Navy dockyard before dying in Los Angeles in 1977.

The Yusupovs also ended up in America, where their daughter, Irina, eventually befriended Tatyana, the daughter of Maria. In 1932, the Yusupovs successfully sued MGM over their representation in *Rasputin and the Empress*. The enormous settlement that they received led to the now-familiar inclusion in films of the disclaimer that all persons are fictional.

THE USUAL SUSPECTS
Prince Felix Yusupov and Friends

Yusupov's version of events has been told so many times that most people accept it as truth – hell; even Yusupov himself ended up believing it! Allegedly, he had invited Rasputin to his Moika Palace on the night of 30 December 1916 having previously laced all the nibbles and wine with enough cyanide to kill a regiment. However, his alarm and distress approached hysteria as the happy "victim" sat gorging himself on the hors d'oeuvres and drinking the wine like there was no tomorrow which, for him of course, there was not. Tired of watching this inhuman monster enjoying himself, Yusupov shot Rasputin through the heart a couple of times; however, this only made Rasputin angry – as you might expect.

Now under attack from the walking dead, Yusupov was joined by other conspirators, who stabbed Rasputin, shot him again, beat him with iron bars, whipped him with chains and stamped on his throat. At last presuming him dead, they left the room to get a carpet in which to wrap the body and dump it in the nearby and freezing River Neva. However, in their absence, the "dead" Rasputin had escaped, to be seen running across the courtyard, yelling that he would tell all to the Tsar and Tsarina. So Yusupov and his cronies shot him again and took turns once more with the iron bars and chains; you name it, they did it – but Rasputin was still alive and snarling when they shoved him through a hole in the ice on the Neva. Clearly, he was the devil incarnate!

However, all this was actually an elaborate fantasy woven by Yusupov. He presented himself to the Tsar and Tsarina as a man who had saved Mother Russia from the malevolent influence of a man who was so clearly demonic, while hiding the fact that he had involved the agents of a foreign power in internal affairs.

THE UNUSUAL SUSPECTS
British Military Intelligence

Pivotal to the organization of the "party" of 30 December 1916, Captain Rayner – who would later make no secret in his role in the death of Rasputin – had arrived at the Moika long before Rasputin to lie in wait in an adjacent room with two other Intelligence officers, Captains Stephen Alley and John Scale. When Rasputin arrived, a gramophone was put on to play Yankee Doodle at full volume, in order to obscure any inadvertent noise that Rayner & Co. might make to alarm the "guest". Charlatan he might have been, but Rasputin was also very street-wise and canny – and, bearing in mind his anonymous call that morning, he smelt a rat. As Rasputin made to leave, Yusupov shot him with a .22, which, inflicting but a minor wound, brought Rayner into the room to shoot Rasputin straight between the eyes with his service pistol. No slavering devil refusing to die; just bang – you're dead – and down Rasputin went like a house of cards.

As Yusupov descended into a force-10 flap, Rayner, Alley and Scale calmly rolled the body into a rug and dumped it in the River Neva before leaving.

MOST CONVINCING EVIDENCE

Not only do we have Rayner's word for his involvement in the death of Rasputin, but the log of his driver in St Petersburg lists the numerous visits to the Moika – the penultimate one on the night of the killing and the last the day after. Additionally, the autopsy on Rasputin conducted by Professor Dimitri Kossorotov states there was no cyanide in the body – and he was specifically looking for it having heard Yusupov's version of events. Instead, he listed the cause of death to have been a single shot through the forehead from a heavy calibre pistol. This autopsy was reviewed in 1993 by Dr Vladimir Zharov and again in 2005 by Derrick Pounder, Professor of Forensics at the University of Dundee, with neither finding fault with the original. The Firearms Department of the Imperial War Museum also went over the forensic photographs taken at the time to agree that the entry wound in the head was typical of that inflicted by a Webley .445 British officer's pistol, which was unique in its day for still using the old-style unjacketed and heavy lead slug.

MOST MYSTERIOUS FACT

In the end, Rasputin was to prove more far-rangingly dangerous dead than he was alive. Furious that the British had killed their best hope of Russian withdrawal from the war, the following February the Germans focused their attentions on Vladimir Lenin, who was then sulking in exile in Switzerland. The Red Revolution had started, but it was disjointed and chaotic. Consequently, the Germans put Lenin in their infamous Sealed Train with 50 million gold marks and whisked him into Petrograd to take control, give the revolution cohesion and keep Russia too busy with internal affairs to bother about any war in Europe. And it worked! Thanks to Rasputin – or perhaps we should just blame Harry Houdini – Russia signed the Treaty of Brest-Litovsk with Germany to leave itself free to concentrate on its capitalist-funded Communist revolution. Of course, this was a contradiction in terms if ever there was one – but Germany got its money's worth and we all caught the Cold War.

SCEPTICALLY SPEAKING

Rasputin was not a mystic; he was not a healer; he had no hypnotic skills. He was just a randy old peasant on the make who, in the right place at the right moment, hit the big time thanks to the aforementioned gullibility of the St Petersburg Court. Invited into such a hen-house, a canny fox like Rasputin had little problem promoting himself as a mystic to such an audience; all he had to do was keep uttering existentialist guff that sounded like a couplet from a Bob Dylan song, knowing that no one would risk appearing stupid by calling his bluff with an indignant, "You what?"

JACK THE RIPPER

The mystery surrounding the Jack The Ripper murders in 1888 has fascinated and tantalized criminologists, conspiracy buffs and Hollywood producers for more than a hundred years.

Theories and counter-theories have arisen, mutually exclusive "authentic" diaries, confessions and notebooks have been discovered and published. It is doubtful whether anyone will ever be able to provide a definite answer.

On Friday, 31 August 1888, Polly Nichols was murdered. Her death was followed by that of Annie Chapman on Saturday, 8 September, then by Catharine Eddowes and Elizabeth Stride on Sunday 30 September, and Mary Kelly on Friday, 9 November. Their throats were cut and their bodies mutilated; the internal organs were often removed with surgical precision and carried away from the scene of the crime. Mary Kelly, who was three months pregnant, was found naked, with her clothes piled tidily on a chair nearby. It is also possible that there was an earlier victim –

What part did Prince Albert Victor play in the Ripper conspiracy?

Martha Tabram, who was murdered on Tuesday, 7 August. Elizabeth Stride may not have been killed by the Ripper. All six women were prostitutes in the East End of London. Some commentators add three more women to this total.

The Ripper used a fairly consistent modus operandi. When the victim lifted her skirts she was grabbed and throttled to unconsciousness, then laid on the ground. Once the woman was lying down, her throat was cut, and in most cases one of the victim's internal organs was removed, presumably as a trophy. The degree of precision exhibited in this procedure suggests that the Ripper had medical training; in one instance, a kidney was removed frontally, without damaging any of the other organs. This would require some skill in an operating theatre, and would be very hard indeed at night, in the dark, under the pressure of being in a public place with the corpse of someone you have just murdered.

Scotland Yard's files show that two notes were received by the Central News Agency from a person claiming to be the Ripper, one entitled "Dear Boss", and the other "from Hell". Both were strangely written, and took a boastfully gloating tone. Most researchers into the matter doubt that either were actually written by the murderer. A chunk of diseased kidney was also sent to a Whitechapel vigilance committee with a letter that claimed the organ was from Katharine Eddowes. While there was no way of knowing for certain, the damage to the kidney was consistent with the effects of the particular disease from which Eddowes suffered.

THE STRANGE PART

On the night of 30 September, police officers found a piece of Catharine Eddowes' apron that the Ripper had used to wipe his knife. This was very close to a doorway over which the message "The Juwes are the men That Will not be blamed for nothing" had been written. Senior police officers felt this would spark anti-Semitic riots and erased the message. The odd phraseology and strange spelling has sparked suggestions that it was actually a Masonic message, and the police erased it to hide the fact.

THE USUAL SUSPECTS
Prince Albert Victor

The grandson of Queen Victoria, Prince Albert Victor (known as "Eddy") was a mentally subnormal youth, described by one royal commentator at the time as "a gleaming goldfish in a crystal bowl". Eddy seems likely to have been an occasional homosexual – a criminal offence in Britain at the time – and died in 1892. Rumours suggested the cause of death was syphilis. His madness is supposed to have been the spur that led him to murder prostitutes, and fear of scandal led to a conspiracy hushing up the Prince's guilt. An alternative theory suggests that he may have got one of the prostitutes pregnant. When she tried to blackmail the government, she and her friends were killed by royal agents in a manner that would distract investigators from the real reason for the deaths.

Dr Francis Tumblety

An American doctor, Tumblety was strongly suspected by John Littlechild, head of the Secret Department at Scotland Yard during the investigations. The doctor fled back to the USA, and Scotland Yard sent detectives to interview him.

THE UNUSUAL SUSPECTS
Dr Roslyn D'onston Stephenson

A heavy-drinking occultist who went to the police with his own theory to explain the Ripper and his murders, the doctor ended up becoming a suspect himself in some theorists' eyes due to the discovery made by author Mabel Collins in 1890 while cohabiting with Stephenson. She claims to have found seven blood-stained ties used in the murders. This possible evidence ended up with England's most famous occultist Aleister Crowley after he obtained them from Mabel's lover, Victoria Cremers.

Inter-dimensional Invader

Victorian London was also plagued with another notorious Jack – Spring-Heeled Jack. This strange figure, wearing armour, cloak and a helmet, could allegedly jump over buildings. He was seen by hundreds of witnesses and hunted for by a vigilante force led by none other than England's most famous soldier Wellington. Some feel that Spring-Heeled Jack was an inter-dimensional invader and the true Ripper.

MOST CONVINCING EVIDENCE

In 1970, Dr Thomas Stowell claimed to have found documents that showed Prince Albert Victor's doctor

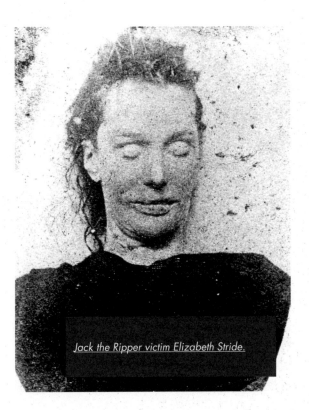

Jack the Ripper victim Elizabeth Stride.

William Gull was seen more than once in the Whitechapel area on the nights of the murders. They also detailed how policemen and a medium had visited Gull to make enquiries and that Gull had confessed. Stowell believed this was a brave attempt to protect the real Ripper – the insane, syphilitic Prince Albert Victor.

MOST MYSTERIOUS FACT

When Stowell's claim found widespread attention, he tried to retract his evidence and denied that he had implicated Prince Albert. However, Stowell died before his retraction could be printed and his family immediately burnt his notes and papers before his claims could be verified. They also burnt all evidence relating to Stowell's career as a Freemason. It may be a coincidence, but he died on 9 November 1970, the anniversary of Mary Kelly's death.

SCEPTICALLY SPEAKING

Jack the Ripper has become an archetypal nightmare figure and moved beyond the realms of unexplained murderer into Legend of the Night. A whole myth-making industry has grown up around the case, which is served by distorting the facts and lengthening the shadows. Given this, it is not surprising that conspiracy theories continue to proliferate and yet still fail to find a truly convincing solution.

CHAPTER 5:

TRAGEDIES

AIDS

Known in medical circles of the time as GRID – Gay-Related-Immune-Deficiency – AIDS/HIV was first identified in 1982 by the French virologist, Luc Montagnier. As it was also known more judgementally as the "Gay Plague", virologists looked for it within the gay sub-culture and, finding it there in abundance, wrongly presumed it to be a condition exclusively linked to male homosexual activity.

Religious protestors opposite St Patrick's Cathedral in New York City during a Gay Pride march in 1985.

At the time, virologists were unaware that the prevalence of HIV/AIDS within that group was due in the main to the promiscuity of members and the internal lesions caused by their preferred form of intercourse, which so effectively facilitated the efficient transfer of the virus. They were quite unaware that countless women too were walking about with the same ticking bomb. They were also unaware that the syndrome was rampant in its true birthplace of Africa where it was known as the Thin Disease due to the tissue wastage.

It was this blinkered gay-focus that promoted group studies of the early 1980s, looking for HIV/AIDS in the prominent gay subculture of California, where, of course, they again found what they set out to find; they also managed by mistake to brand one particular patient, a Canadian flight attendant called Gaetan Dugas, as The Man Who Gave Us AIDS. Because Dugas was from outside the study area and only an occasional visitor due the nature of his work, he was meant to be tagged Patient O, as in O for "outside", but a clerical error imposed the typo of Patient 0, as in zero, leaving people to believe him the progenitor. Naturally, with HIV/AIDS first identified in the 1980s, everyone presumed it to be a virus of that decade – until a retrospective testing on the tissue samples retained from the autopsy of the otherwise puzzling case of the 16-year-old Robert Rayford of St Louis, Missouri. Deceased 1969, Rayford presented such a concatenation of symptoms and manifestations that stunned and puzzled any and all who treated him. It transpired that he too had died of HIV/AIDS. None yet suspected that HIV was a mutant strain of the simian SIV, which had been stupidly and cynically ushered across the species barrier in Africa during a series of "experiments" of the late 1920s/early 1930s, these conducted with a secret agendum that almost beggars belief.

THE USUAL SUSPECTS
GOD
The immediate knee-jerk reaction from many TV-evangelist preachers was to proclaim that the condition was a divine visitation on gays to punish them for their sinful ways. It was proclaimed to be the Wrath of God pouring down on the depraved heads of all gays. As recently as 2014, Pastor Steven Anderson of Arizona's Faithful Word Baptist Church called for the execution of all HIV/AIDS patients as a means of purging the condition from the sacred soil of America.

THE CIA
Some conspiracy theorists have traced the escape of AIDS into the world's populations to the CIA's biological activities against Cuban soldiers fighting in Africa. An attempt to infect Cuban troops with a more orthodox biological agent may have backfired when it mutated into the disease we now call AIDS and spread much further than its intended Cuban targets.

THE UNUSUAL SUSPECTS
The Kremlin
Blame for HIV/AIDS can arguably be laid at the feet of Josef Stalin, who, in 1926, dispatched the Russian animal-hybridization specialist Ilya Ivanov to Africa, to continue his experiments into the creation of what he called the humanzee. Setting up his laboratory in Conakry, in what was then called French New Guinea, Ivanov was soon busy trying to effect the successful insemination of African women with simian sperm. The women, all of them local prostitutes attracted by the participation fee, were never told the true nature of the procedures inflicted upon them and, with all such cross-fertilizations unsuccessful, they were returned to their normal lives.

By 1927, French administrators of the area were getting wind of what Ivanov was up to, including rumours of his having recruited African men, paid to attempt the impregnation of female monkeys by the more traditional method, shall we say. He was invited to leave the country without delay. Although he returned to Russia to continue his Freakensteinian experiments in Stalin's native Georgia, all came to naught – but the world would soon be paying dear for the for the legacy he left behind in Africa.

MOST CONVINCING EVIDENCE
Now hailed by many as the Father of AIDS, Ivanov and his profoundly disturbing programme seems to have facilitated the transfer of SIV, the simian progenitor of AIDS which, present in simians for centuries, suddenly leapt across to humans at the same time that Ivanov was up to his monkey-business. Significantly, the first accepted case of HIV/AIDS was that of a woman in Cameroon, also in West Africa, in 1931.

MOST MYSTERIOUS FACT
Why on earth did Stalin sanction such an off-the-wall experimental programme? Some say it was because he relished the prospect of a new breed of slavishly obedient soldiers or uber-strong labourers. Others say it was his desire to prove wrong both Darwin and the Church in their notions as to the creation and development of the species by conjuring forth a new strain of humanoid at the drop of a hat. But, we shall never know the answer to that one.

SCEPTICALLY SPEAKING
Not only does the chronology detailed above quash any possibility of HIV/AIDS having been a manufactured bioweapon of the 1980s but also the syndrome profile does not fit that of any such weapon. The incubation period is far too long to be of any interest to the military and, with human sexual behaviour being what it is, once released the originators would have had no control over the direction of its spread or who it infected. A bioweapon rampaging through the home population of the originators does not make sense on any level.

THE CHALLENGER EXPLOSION

It was 28 January 1986, when the *Challenger* blasted off on a voyage that was the centre of media attention. On board was a civilian teacher, Christa McAuliffe, who was destined to become the first teacher in outer space. McAuliffe had been specially chosen by NASA officials for the honour; and with her good looks and upbeat spirit, she quickly became a darling of the media.

The shockwaves from this disaster reverberated around the world.

But 73 seconds after takeoff, America watched in horror as McAuliffe's dream ended in a massive explosion. As the smoke from the destroyed shuttle craft billowed across the sky, throwing debris down into the Atlantic Ocean, a stunned shock fell across the nation. Something had gone terribly, terribly wrong. Seven crew members had met horrible deaths in the destruction of *Challenger*.

This was not the first time NASA had lost crew members.

Three astronauts had died on what would have been the Apollo One mission. But that was in the early days, and by the time of the *Challenger* disaster, NASA had hoped that such tragedies – and public relations disasters – were things of the past. The optimism that had surrounded the space programme, enveloping it almost like a protective shield, was rent asunder by the *Challenger* explosion. NASA's dreams of further space exploration ground to a virtual halt for almost two years.

THE STRANGE PART

In the investigations that followed, blame for the explosion was placed on an O-ring, a simple rubber seal, positioned between the solid rocket boosters, which gave the shuttle the power to escape Earth's gravity. The reason for the O-ring's failure? The weather on the day of the *Challenger* launch was uncharacteristically cold for Florida at that time of year, around 28.5 degrees Fahrenheit. The O-rings were not designed to operate under such chilly conditions, and as a result, were unable to restrain hot gases from igniting the main liquid fuel tank. This glaringly obvious mechanical problem, obvious to the technicians of NASA, led to the explosion.

THE USUAL SUSPECTS
NASA

NASA's apparent laziness and arrogance is the root cause of the disaster, according to some theorists. Riding high on public approval over the success of the shuttle missions, NASA had become proud and complacent. In the excitement of the *Challenger* launch, with the attendant swirl of cameras and television coverage, the problem of the O-rings may have been overlooked as inconsequential. Engineers at the agency knew full well that the O-rings were not designed to function in the unusually cold weather, but decided to go ahead with the launch anyway, even though the launch manual expressly forbade such action. Even more disturbingly, this wasn't the first time NASA had experienced performance faults with O-rings – erosion of the rings had been discovered after flights five years previously, but nothing had been done to correct the problem.

Parts Manufacturer

In 1977, the parts manufacturer and engineering company that designed the O-ring apparently became aware of the defect the equipment experienced in cold weather. The company went as far as reporting its findings to the commission that had appointed the company to design a new rocket. Again, nothing was done. In the case of *Challenger*, NASA had allegedly put pressure on the company to provide a waiver concerning the functionality of the O-rings in cold weather, a waiver that would allow the launch to proceed. Faced with the prospect of angering one of its most lucrative contracts, the company agreed.

THE UNUSUAL SUSPECTS
MJ–12

It makes sense that the agency with the most knowledge about UFOs and extra-terrestrials would have operatives within NASA and, according to one theory, it was these MJ-12 controlled operatives that engineered the *Challenger* explosion. Increasingly concerned that space exploration would reveal evidence of alien life, they were instructed to slow down NASA efforts to establish a greater role for man in the solar system. By destroying the shuttle, not only did they bring the agency into disrepute, which led to a massive shake-up of personnel, they also managed to stall its operations long enough to ensure that the next time a shuttle went into space they had the whole of NASA under their control.

The Great Galactic Ghoul

Several attempts to explore space, American and Soviet, have met with mysterious problems and setbacks that baffle technicians. Missions to Mars have been affected particularly badly, but relatively simple trips into Earth's orbit have also had problems. The rash of problems has been nervously blamed on the Ghoul, a mysterious force that could be the Greys or something as yet unidentified, which is apparently determined to maintain a glass ceiling around the Earth.

Also suspected: Fundamentalist Christians; secret factions of NASA controlled by MJ-12.

MOST CONVINCING EVIDENCE

Huge sums of money (reportedly running into the millions) were granted to the bereaved families of the *Challenger* explosion by the US government and the Morton Thiokol company. The speed with which the money was handed over might imply a guilty conscience as well as a need to brush the entire incident under the carpet as quickly as possible. In many government legal cases, civilian plaintiffs are subjected to ridicule and forced to navigate a costly path through a jungle populated by lawyers determined to break them down, emotionally and financially. Not this time.

MOST MYSTERIOUS FACT

To lose one Shuttle could be seen as a disaster, to lose a second … Well, maybe there is something to the conspiracies. When seven astronauts died after the space Shuttle *Columbia* disintegrated on re-entering the earth's atmosphere on 1 February 2003, it was the worst space disaster since *Challenger* was lost. Officially blamed on a compromised heat shield, many of the questions and theories first raised about *Challenger* could spookily be applied to *Columbia*. However, some have seen a grim significance in the fact that the debris from a Shuttle carrying an Israeli astronaut rained down over an area of Texas called Palestine.

SCEPTICALLY SPEAKING

Want to get away with murder? Call your victims heroes and have the President of the United States read a nice poem about them. There is little evidence of conspiracy but sure signs that our governments are often indifferent to the cost of human life.

SARS

<u>When Lia Jianlin, a 64-year-old medical professor from Guangdong Province in Southern China, made a trip to a relative's wedding in Hong Kong in March 2003, he had no inkling that within a few weeks he would be dead. Or that he would be accused of being the Angel of Death responsible for the spread of the killer virus SARS.</u>

Severe Acute Respiratory Syndrome (SARS) became the first pandemic of the twenty-first century. A viral, pneumonia-like illness, it spread quickly to more than 30 countries across almost every inhabited continent, infected thousands and killed at least 10 per cent of those who caught it. The great difficulty in breathing caused by the disease meant that the majority of the deaths were drawn-out and painful. While at first many were reassured that the number of SARS cases was small when compared to the world population, panic began to grow as scientists placed it among the ranks of mysteriously mutating "super-germs". They also voiced concerns that it could be the "Big One" – an influenza virus that would produce a super flu that would kill billions of people, as the "Spanish flu" did between 1918–19.

The World Health Organisation (WHO) began to advise against travel to cities such as Toronto, where SARS had broken out and the economic impact of the disease began to rise into multi-billion figures. As scientists the globe over began to study it, the origin of SARS was traced back to Guangdong and its movement out of China to the visit of one unfortunate wedding guest. Scientists also discovered that the SARS coronavirus arose when the genes of an animal and human virus swapped genes and that there was no known cure.

When it became established that the Chinese military had known about SARS and had covered up its existence since November 2002, the virus caused political as well as medical havoc. China's health minister and the Mayor of Beijing were forced to resign. Prime Minister Wen Jaibao, along with President Hu Jintao, criticized the military for its non-co-operation and initial cover-up. This allowed them to make veiled criticism of former president Jiang Zemin, who had refused to relinquish chairmanship of the Central Military Commission.

Surprisingly, a retired Chinese military doctor, who helped reveal the SARS cover-up in Beijing, was not silenced and even given unprecedented coverage in the Chinese official media. This may mean that the whole exposé was part of a set-up engineered by Chinese President Hu Jintao as part of his power struggle against opponents controlling elements of the military. It has also been suggested that Hu Jintao also encouraged rumours of Western plots to create SARS

to attack China to focus anger about SARS away from government cover-ups and mishandling of the SARS crisis.

As SARS was seemingly brought under control, a barrage of explanations from authorities across the globe came out, trying to convince the world that the virus had its origins in the animal markets of Guangdong province. However, the official version left a lot of questions unanswered

THE STRANGE PART

Many scientists in Russia believe that SARS is manmade. Nikolai Filatov, head of Moscow's epidemiological services, made the initial claims over this idea and was soon backed up by Professor Sergei Kolesnikov, whose research showed the virus could only be produced in laboratory conditions. The Siberian bio-weapon expert also believes that SARS probably came from an accidental leak from a laboratory somewhere in China.

THE USUAL SUSPECTS
Chinese Military

Given that China's most important bio-weapon research centre is based in Guandong, the province where SARS originated, it is not surprising that the finger of suspicion has turned towards Chinese bio-weapon scientists and their bosses in the Chinese military. This is only heightened by the fact that the virus started to spread out from China's military hospitals. It is conceivable that hard-liners in the military hoped that SARS would isolate the country, bring about martial law and give them an excuse to reverse China's liberalization policies.

Medical Establishment

While SARS cost more than $16 billion alone to the Chinese economy, one group certainly benefited financially from its trail of death – the medical sector. SARS led to a huge boost in the budgets of medical, pharmaceutical and companies involved in virus research. It also benefited those involved in security and law enforcement. Would certain sections of the scientific establishment have been amoral enough to create and release SARS, and then play up its potential danger to enhance their profits?

Actually, the SARS coronavirus is so small that it goes straight through surgical masks.

Anglo-American Cabal

The height of panic over SARS occurred at exactly the same time that Anglo-American military forces were invading Iraq. An Anglo-American Cabal may have created a deployed of interests SARS to provide not only a global media distraction to the war but to harm the interest of China – one of the most important countries to oppose their invasion and one of their most powerful economic rivals.

THE UNUSUAL SUSPECTS
Al Qaeda

Al Qaeda are well known to be investigating the use of bio-weapons in their campaign of terror. SARS could be an early test of their potential, not only against the West, but also against communist China, which has earned their wrath for the crack down in the activities of Islamic separatist factions in some of its remoter provinces.

World Health Organization

SARS was a minor virus released by the WHO as part of a mass social experiment to see how a virus could spread and people react ahead of the "Big One" – a biological agent that will wipe out up to half the Earth's population.

The Bilderberg Group

Some of the more paranoid conspiracy researchers believe that global industrialists and members of the ultra-rich, who regularly come together under the guise of the Bilderberg Group, released SARS as a test-run for a population control programme. And the ultimate aim? To reduce the number of poor people, who use up shrinking global resources, and consolidate their control of those who remain.

MOST CONVINCING EVIDENCE

Peter Rottier of Utrecht University in the Netherlands led a team of Dutch scientists who transformed a coronavirus that was lethal to cats into one that infected mouse cells by replacing a single gene from a mouse coronavirus. He admitted that his work strengthened the idea that the SARS coronavirus might have arisen when an animal and human virus had been engineered to meet and swap genes. Michael Lai of the University of Southern California confirmed this, "It's a very plausible explanation; coronaviruses are unusual in that their genes can be reshuffled easily."

MOST MYSTERIOUS FACT

Some heavyweight scientists, including Professor Chandra Wickramasinghe of Cardiff University, believe that the only explanation for some of the odd characteristics of SARS is that it has an extra-terrestrial origin via cosmic dust. Given that scientists only go in for extra-terrestrial theories when their backs are really up against the wall to come up with a simpler explanation, it is fairly obvious that the truth behind SARS has the global scientific community stumped.

SCEPTICALLY SPEAKING

If there is one thing that travels faster than a new virus across the globe, it is a conspiracy theory about the virus. Stupid and risible stories about super-bugs almost certainly pose a danger to those who take them seriously and to the pocket-linings of anyone making surgical masks or creating quack cures. Of course, they do not harm certain governments who are all too happy to see the conspiracy theories run amuck, helping deflect some of the anger that should rightly be aimed at their national leadership.

THE JONESTOWN MASSACRE

The images coming from Jonestown in 1978 were ghastly. Bloating in the sweltering heat of the South American sun lay the bodies of hundreds of people, the result of an apparent mass suicide. Some of the bodies had their arms linked around friends, as if they had gone to face the afterlife together. All were members of a religious cult called the "People's Temple".

Allegedly, they had been convinced to drink cyanide-laced Kool-Aid by their charismatic leader, an American religious leader and sometime-faith-healer called Jim Jones. His body was also found among the dead, but Jones had opted out of taking cyanide like his followers, dying instead of an apparent self-inflicted gunshot wound.

The events leading up to this massive loss of life (later estimated at over 900 fatalities) were equally strange. Jones, the son of a member of the racially intolerant Ku Klux Klan, surprisingly preached a doctrine that called for a better world where there was harmony between the races. He dreamt of building a version of Utopia. Considering himself the reincarnation of not only Jesus Christ but also Vladimir Lenin, Jones founded his People's Temple in Ukiah,

California. His followers, who were mostly black, were kept in line by Jones' own security force, who relieved the cult members of all the money they had, which generally arrived in the form of government assistance cheques.

Reports that followers who tried to leave his Temple were abused and sometimes died, prompted Jones to move to the more anonymous San Francisco, where he was able to expand his Temple. As the media continued to hound him, in 1977, Jones decided on a spot deep in the jungles of South America as the location for his "Utopia". Without question, his followers moved with him, and he was able set up the infamous "Jonestown", a community in which he was the only law.

But still the reports of abuse continued. By 1978, the furore was so loud that it prompted US Congressman Leo

Just some of the deluded disciples who followed Jones' orders to the bitter end.

Ryan to fly down to Guyana to look into the problem for himself. On 18 November 1978, Ryan entered Jonestown, along with a few curious reporters and the deputy chief of the US mission to Guyana, Richard Dwyer. As they were preparing to return to the US from a nearby airfield, the entire investigative party, with the mysterious exception of Dwyer, was shot dead.

Shortly after the killings took place on the airfield – or perhaps as he gave the order that lead to the deaths of the investigators – Jones issued his suicide order. Within hours, the People's Temple turned into a charnel house. Jonestown, as an example of the lethal power of religious cult leaders, was disturbing enough. But as time passed, it became clear that there was more to Jonestown than simple religious mania. Soon, the highest levels of the US Government were implicated, adding a new dimension of horror to an already sickening tragedy.

THE STRANGE PART
Even though Jones's body was found in Jonestown, dead from a self-inflicted gunshot wound, the apparent suicide weapon was found 200 feet from the body. This would indicate that either Jones was murdered himself, or it wasn't Jones at all. Close examination of the corpse revealed that it lacked Jones's tattoos . . .

THE USUAL SUSPECTS
Jim Jones
Jones' history reveals he was more than a simple faith healer. He was a fundraiser for politicians, including the impeached President Richard Nixon. While he professed grandiose ideals of Utopia, he was a strong supporter of the Republican Party. In 1961, he worked for a year in Brazil, rumoured to be doing work for the CIA. It was this work, or rather the $10,000 he earned from it, that allowed him to set up his first Temple in Ukiah. While in Jonestown, his followers were numbed with drugs, fed next to nothing, worked as slave labour and were forced to run through practice "suicide drills". Jones may have been running a massive mind-control experiment in Jonestown, with the help of the CIA. When it became apparent that the news would be released after Ryan's visit. Jones simply erased the evidence.

The CIA
There are several links with the CIA and Jones. Aside from his work in Brazil, Jones's associates included a member of UNITA, the CIA-sponsored Angolan army, and Dan Mitrione, who worked for another CIA-bankrolled outfit, the International Police Academy. Jones's mind-control experiments in Guyana could easily have been an extension of the CIA's MK-Ultra work, undertaken in a location far from the prying media. In fact, drugs used in MK-Ultra were also found in Jonestown. It's also interesting to note that

Dwyer, the sole survivor of Ryan's party, was listed in the book *Who's Who in the CIA*.

The US Government
The US Embassy helped Jones move his temple into Guyana, and when its was reported that cult members had been shot, not poisoned, it was discovered that a group of American Green Berets had been in the area. Green Berets are valued for their skill in covert killing, and were a favourite tool of the military in Vietnam. A cover up was suspected, especially with the US government's reluctance to return bodies of the dead to their families. Many bodies were "accidentally" cremated.

UNUSUAL SUSPECTS
Worldvision
A worldwide evangelical order, Worldvision has been long suspected of working with the CIA. After the Jonestown deaths, Worldvision repopulated the village with ex-CIA Laotian mercenaries. Ex-Worldvision employees include John Hinckley, Jr (would-be assassin of Reagan) and Mark David Chapman (assassin of John Lennon). Both assassins, according to some theorists, were under the influence of mind-control when they acted.

The Process
New evidence has emerged linking Jones's early time in California with members of the English religious group known as the Process Church – a cult that emerged from Scientology, mixing "brain-cleansing" techniques with Gnostic beliefs. Although Process had melted away from the scene by the time of Jonestown, its influence on Jones may not have been entirely positive, just as its involvement with Charles Manson may not have been entirely beneficial to Sharon Tate.

MOST CONVINCING EVIDENCE
When coroner C. Leslie Mootoo suggested that the Jonestown deaths were murder, not suicide, thus warranting investigation, the US Army disagreed. The bodies were left to rot in the sun.

MOST MYSTERIOUS FACT
Several people who could explain the truth about Jonestown, including ex-Jones aide Michael Prokes, and authors Jeanie and Al Mills, have been found murdered.

SCEPTICALLY SPEAKING
Given that Jones chose to pick most of his followers from the ranks of the poor and minority groups, it is no surprise that so little fuss was kicked up. The mass suicide of a cult is tragic, but hardly unexpected. It happened before Jonestown, it has happened plenty of times since and it will continue to happen while figures such as Jones only come to the attention of authorities when it is far too late to save anyone.

THE OKLAHOMA BOMBING

On 19 April 1995, a massive explosion in Oklahoma City, Oklahoma, destroyed a huge part of a Federal office building, killing many of the people inside.

The other face of terror – Timothy McVeigh convicted of the Oklahoma bombing.

Until that moment, America considered itself immune to terrorist attack, lulling itself into a false sense of security by glossing over terrorist attacks such as the bombing of the World Trade Center. The Oklahoma bombing was high-profile however, and, as well as killing and injuring a lot of people, it also inflicted some nasty wounds on the US national psyche.

Timothy McVeigh, a Gulf War veteran, was convicted of the bombing. Certainly, there is plenty of evidence that he was peculiar enough to have carried it out. He sent a series of letters to his sister some considerable time before the bombing took place, in which he wrote about his "anger and alienation". These letters included comments about committing suicide, about dropping out of society and into hiding, and about the government of the "Evil King". The letters were so disturbing that McVeigh's family suspected him of being the Oklahoma bomber almost immediately. His sister believes that McVeigh's mania against the government stemmed from the army's insistence that he repay them $1,000 that he had been overpaid.

McVeigh had applied for Special Forces training, and had failed the assessment course. He claimed in one of his letters that his assessment at Fort Bragg had revealed that he would be in line for performing several unsavoury duties should he make the grade. Special Forces operatives, he alleged, could be required to work with civilian police, silencing – killing – people who were considered a security risk. They would also be expected to help "the CIA fly drugs into the USA to fund covert operations". It was the evil nature of these assignments that turned McVeigh against the US government.

But is McVeigh actually? There is some evidence to suggest Middle Eastern terrorist involvement in the bombing. Investigative journalist Kelly Patricia O'Meara discovered that Timothy McVeigh's convicted co-conspirator, Terry Nichols, attended a meeting in the early nineties on the island of Mindanao in the Philippines – a hotbed of fundamentalist activities – at which Ramzi Yousef was present. The themes of the meeting were Bombing activities, providing firearms and ammunition, training in making and handling bombs. Later, Yousef came to prominence as one of those involved in the World Trade Center bombing in 1993.

Many eyewitnesses saw individuals identified as being of Middle Eastern extraction speeding away from the Murrah Federal Building just before the blast in a pick-up truck. It has also emerged that McVeigh was seen in the company of at least one Iraqi refugee, who had been brought to live in Oklahoma City as part of President Clinton's programme to bring several thousand Iraqis into the US for resettlement.

THE STRANGE PART

Rather than looking objectively at Jayna Davis's excellent research, virtually all of the Oklahoma City and national media adopted the Bill Clinton-Janet Reno thesis that the OKC bombing was a domestic "right-wing" attack and rejected out of hand any evidence of foreign ties to the bombing. A careful review of Davis's extensive evidence and our own parallel investigation quickly convinced this writer that Davis was on solid ground. Of the thousands of Justice Department and FBI agents involved in the investigation, none ever interviewed the Iraqi community in Oklahoma or pursued some of McVeigh's associates in the spook field.

THE USUAL SUSPECTS
The CIA

A large amount of evidence has emerged over the last few years to suggest that a cabal of senior military and security officers were planning a coup to remove President Clinton

from office due to their disgust at his alleged political and financial corruption. Two days before the bombing a plane carrying many members of this cabal crashed in Alabama. It is believed by some that the CIA created the disaster in Oklahoma as a diversion to prevent investigation into the planned coup and a focus for national unity at a time when the Presidency could have been jeopardized by further military revolt.

The Ku Klux Klan

A local major Grand Wizard in the Oklahoma Ku Klux Klan and local leader of the White Aryan Resistance had met McVeigh and was an associate of Terry Nichols. The leader – banned from entering Canada and the United Kingdom and classified by Interpol as a terrorist – was never even questioned. This has forced some to the unsettling conclusion that the KKK may not only have been involved in the bombing, but may have also received some form of Secret Service support.

THE UNUSUAL SUSPECTS
Christian Identity

This is the American version of the British Israelite movement. It claims that white Americans are the true descendants of Moses. Certainly, the Identity is very popular with right-wing maniacs and it may have been involved in the bombing. There have been suggestions that McVeigh was acting on the instructions of a powerful Christian Identity leader to help fulfil the prophecies leading to the return of Christ.

MOST CONVINCING EVIDENCE

The failure of the FBI to conduct even cursory interviews with obvious suspects and to pursue potentially interesting leads is unsettling in the extreme. Either it was criminal neglect of duty or part of a deliberate effort to ensure they got a suspect who fitted the theory that it was a simple attack by domestic right-wing elements.

MOST MYSTERIOUS FACT

In 2002, it emerged that certain Pentagon officials believed that Timothy McVeigh was working in conjunction with Iraqis due to the fact that he was in possession of Iraqi telephone numbers. However, this revelation may have been a smokescreen to throw investigators off the track since it emerged that Chandra Levy's disappearance may have been related to McVeigh's execution.

SCEPTICALLY SPEAKING

To believe that there is more to the Oklahoma bombing than we have officially been told implies some degree of authority collusion in the deaths of scores of innocent government workers. At the very least it means the authorities were not interested in getting the real culprits – surely too big a leap into the darkness on the basis of the facts currently available.

WACO

On Sunday, 28 February 1993, at around 9:30a.m., the US Bureau of Alcohol, Tobacco and Firearms (BATF) attempted to enforce a search warrant at premises occupied by a religious cult – the Mount Carmel stronghold in Waco, Texas. Besides wanting to search the compound occupied by the apocalyptic Branch Davidians for a suspected illegal stockpile of explosives and firearms, the agents also carried an arrest warrant for the charismatic leader of the cult, David Koresh.

Something went terribly wrong. A gun battle erupted between the agents and members of the Branch Davidians, leaving four agents dead and 16 wounded. Several Branch Davidians were also killed or wounded. Pulling back, the BATF initiated a siege of the Mount Carmel compound that lasted 51 days. It involved the FBI, the Attorney General, Janet Reno and President Bill Clinton. It ended in a mysterious fire, with Mount Carmel burning to the ground – an event that was broadcast live on CNN. In the ashes, investigators found the bodies of 17 children and over 60 adults, among them the body of Koresh himself.

Questions quickly surfaced as to how the standoff could spin out of control so rapidly after 50 days of relatively peaceful negotiations. As the FBI propelled tear gas into the compound from combat engineering vehicles (CEVs), they also knocked down walls with the machines, possibly killing children inside the compound – children that the government repeatedly told the media it was trying to protect. The sudden fire later that day is also questioned, with both sides blaming the other for starting it.

Since that fateful day in 1993, Waco has become a symbol of many things – from the cost of fervent religious belief, to the ruthlessness of a government trying to cover up its own mistakes.

THE STRANGE PART

As a justification for sending tear gas into Mount Carmel, Janet Reno, the newly appointed Attorney General, stated that the Branch Davidians were beating babies inside the compound. Janet Reno relied upon the FBI for her information, and the FBI later admitted that there was no proof to confirm the truth of the assertion she had been led to make.

THE USUAL SUSPECTS
The BATF and FBI

There is still some question as to who actually fired first at the start of the siege, and there are rumours that the BATF may have been either a little gun-happy or ill-prepared for the raid on the compound. In Congressional hearings that followed the grisly end to the siege, BATF agents, not surprisingly, claimed that the Branch Davidians fired first. Directly after the raid, however, one agent claimed to have fired first – killing a dog. He later retracted that story. The Branch Davidians stand by their claim that they only fired when fired upon. The BATF also claimed that Koresh's people were manufacturing methamphetamines – another assertion, later shown to be a lie.

The FBI also did its part to inflame the situation. One team of agents deliberately harassed the Davidians by playing loud music (such as Tibetan chants and Christmas tunes) through the night, directing blinding spotlights into the compound, and shutting off their electricity. The team of negotiators felt these activities weakened their attempts to end the siege peacefully. The FBI wasn't entirely truthful in its reports to Janet Reno. Reportedly, Reno was apprehensive about an attack on the compound, but quickly changed her mind when a FBI agent remarked about the possibility of child abuse – a possibility that was never substantiated. A simple desire by the BATF for revenge could also have played a significant part.

David Koresh

Koresh believed himself to be the reincarnation of Jesus Christ, and the siege of his compound would have given reality to his apocalyptic visions. He was fascinated by the Book of Revelations, and throughout the siege, talked about writing a manuscript to explain the meaning of the Seven Seals. He claimed to be in contact with God, who reportedly gave him advice throughout the ordeal. The FBI also endured several rambling sermons over the phone from Koresh. The burning of the compound would be a fitting end in Koresh's Messianic eyes, since his beloved Revelations spoke of the world itself ending in fire. This may explain why the Davidians displayed signs that read "Flames Await".

Bill Clinton

While Clinton professed concern about the children inside the compound, he also made it clear that the decision to gas the compound was Janet Reno's alone. Having washed his hands of blame, Clinton could have been using the Waco tragedy as a way of improving his political image – as a no-nonsense President.

THE UNUSUAL SUSPECTS
The New World Order

A favourite theory of the Far Right is that Waco was evidence of a United Nations plot to disarm everyday Americans in preparation for the imminent implementation of a One World Government, the dreaded New World Order. Why else raid a compound for guns in a state like Texas, where everyone owns at least one gun?

Neo-Nazi Conspiracy

David Koresh and the Branch Davidians may have been agents of a global Nazi conspiracy, dedicated to resurrecting the Third Reich and giving Hitler's public image a more positive spin. Other members of this conspiracy include right-wing conservatives like Pat Buchanan, and racist skinheads everywhere. "Remember Waco" has become a battle cry for neo Nazis in the States, apparently.

Gun Control Advocates

Waco may have been orchestrated by gun control advocates, possibly working in conjunction with Clinton's Democratic Party, as a way of demonstrating the dangers of allowing just about anyone to own a gun.

MOST CONVINCING EVIDENCE

In his controversial documentary, filmmaker Mike McNulty showed helicopter machine-guns firing into the compound. The documentary also showed a tank attack and the presence of a Delta force military unit. Muzzle flashes captured on film suggest government forces are shooting into the compound – all of which seems to undercut government claims that its force was fired on first and only engaged only in defensive fire.

MOST MYSTERIOUS FACT

Shortly before his tragically early death from cancer, comedian and major conspiracy buff, Bill Hicks, had obtained video evidence that seemed to disprove many of the FBI's claims about the last hours at the compound. In his routines, Hicks always joked that if you knew the truth, you were next in line for the magic bullet.

SCEPTICALLY SPEAKING

If Koresh had had his own television show and dressed in a bad suit, he'd not only have been left alone, but called a pillar of the community.

The Branch Davidian compound engulfed by the fire in which David Koresh and 75 of his followers perished.

GULF WAR SYNDROME

The 1991 Gulf War was considered a success by the media and the US government: the Iraqi forces, led by Saddam Hussein, were driven out of Kuwait by the superior military strength of the United States and the coalition forces. But while George W. Bush and Colin Powell still bask in the glow from that military victory, a more malignant reminder plagues thousands of soldiers involved in the war. It is an insidious disease that has puzzled doctors and destroys the lives of those it affects – it is called GWS or, more commonly, Gulf War Syndrome.

A list of the symptoms of Gulf War Syndrome illustrates how debilitating it can be: night sweats, disturbances of the nervous system, tumors, drastic weight loss, diarrhoea, insomnia, chronic fatigue, intense joint discomfort, bizarre rashes, disturbing personality changes, and loss of mental faculties. There have also been reports of extensive blood loss. GWS is a vicious and virulent affliction, which unsurprisingly leads many sufferers into severe depressions, and even suicide.

Despite seemingly inarguable evidence that soldiers contracted the disease while fighting for their countries, the existence of Gulf War Syndrome is denied by many governments, including the US. Having risked their lives in what many consider to be a war more about oil prices than about human freedom, these soldiers now find themselves abandoned by their governments.

THE STRANGE PART
In 2003, fear of Gulf War Syndrome was so strong among British soldiers preparing to go to the Gulf for the invasion of Iraq that many of them refused to take an anthrax vaccine. Large numbers rejected other vaccines as well. Their concern was so strong that they were more willing to let themselves be vulnerable to biological attack than trust the Ministry of Defence's claims that all the vaccines it was giving to troops were safe.

THE USUAL SUSPECTS
Saddam Hussein
While he may not have had many noticeable weapons of mass destruction in the second Gulf War, Saddam Hussein definitely had them during the first war. He had tested and used biological weapons against his enemies – most notably on the Kurdish people, wiping out entire villages. It is believed by some that he also used biological weapons against coalition forces, arming some of his Scud missiles

with lethal doses of toxins. Deadly material could also have come from the smoking ruins of chemical factories and bombed-out Iraqi weapons bunkers, drifting across the dessert with the wind to infect coalition soldiers. Hussein may even have infected his own soldiers, hoping their dead bodies would transfer the disease to those who buried them later on.

Forced Inoculations
In preparation for a biological attack – that according to the US never happened – soldiers were forced to take pills and undergo inoculations. The pills, thought to be Pyridostigmine Bromide, and the vaccinations (including shots for anthrax), were extremely experimental. If they were not the direct cause of Gulf War Syndrome, these inoculations are thought to have aided in its spread.

THE UNUSUAL SUSPECTS
The Soviets
Hussein is thought to have obtained some of the most virulent bio-weapons from the Soviet arsenal prior to 1989. Among them may have been the dreaded "Novichok" series – at the time of its making, one of the most feared toxins known to man. If this was the case, it might explain many aspects of GWS.

MOST CONVINCING EVIDENCE
The numbers of infected soldiers speak for themselves. Estimates place the number of sick soldiers at well over 150,000, with some 10,000 already dead from GWS. (These numbers may be optimistic.) An examination of GWS points clearly to a virus that is not natural, but shows all the earmarks of having been produced in a laboratory. One of the chief suspects for GWS is a manufactured agent called *Mycoplasma fermentans (incognitus)*. It contains the majority of the (HIV) envelope gene, which is suspected to have been

A 2004 study of 24,000 Gulf War veterans established a uniform reduction in fertility and a higher-than-average incidence of cancers.

added in its laboratory modification. Of all the countries involved in the Gulf War coalition, only France refused to undergo inoculations. So far, there have been no reports of GWS among French soldiers.

MOST MYSTERIOUS FACT

Many soldiers thought that GWS was caused by exposure to radiation. When Gulf War veteran Stephen Childs died from cancer in 2000, he asked in his will for the coroner to investigate his death. However, the coroner dismissed his wishes to examine whether multiple inoculations and

working in an area contaminated by depleted uranium brought on his cancer. He also refused to try to find out why, since his return from the conflict, Mr Childs's sweat had begun to smell of latex.

SCEPTICALLY SPEAKING

It all comes down to money. Governments continue to deny that any biological agents were used in the Gulf and refuse to admit that forced inoculations might be to blame for GWS. If they admit that there was, the question of legal liability comes up. That is not going to happen.

TWA FLIGHT 800

**It is perhaps the greatest unspoken fear of every air traveller –
that the craft in which they are passengers will crash. While many
pretend to be blasé about air travel, few escape a momentary fear
at some point during a flight. This horrible fear was realized for the
passengers and crew of TWA Flight 800 on 17 July 1996.**

Eleven minutes into the journey from New York's Kennedy
Airport, destined for Paris, France, the Boeing 747 suddenly
exploded about ten miles from Long Island, killing everyone
on board.

An investigation into the disaster was quickly launched,
with boats out collecting the wreckage from the plane,
searching for some clue as to what may have caused the
explosion – an explosion that gave no warning, according
to evidence later found on the craft's black box recorders.
Finally, the National Transportation Safety Board, after

investigating with the FBI and the CIA, determined that
Flight 800 crashed because its centre-wing fuel tank had
exploded. Arcing between two wires, with a spark igniting
the jet's volatile fuel might have caused this. The investigation
was then closed down.

Many people dispute those findings. Eyewitnesses claim
to have seen something arcing into the sky after Flight 800,
with much speculation that what they saw was a surface-
to-air missile. Was Flight 800 hit by a terrorist attack, or
was it something far darker – such as a missile fired by the

The assembled debris of Flight 800 in
the hands of accident investigators.

US Military? In the eyes of the US government, the case is closed, but in the eyes of conspiracy theorists, including members of the military and the airlines themselves, there was no investigation – only a cover up.

THE STRANGE PART

Dr Vernon Grose, who had served as a board member of the National Transportation Safety Board, had defended the board's official explanation for the crash of Flight 800. He changed his mind and began to feel that there was, indeed, a cover up. He pointed his finger at the FBI and its suspicious suppression of eyewitness testimony that what appeared to be a missile had hit Flight 800.

THE USUAL SUSPECTS
The US Military

The US military may have been practising manoeuvres, including the firing of missiles, in an area designated as W-105, located off the southeast coast of Long Island. A Navy "hot area", W-105 is about 30 miles away from where TWA Flight 800 mysteriously exploded. In a potentially lethal gaffe, the first report of the accident is thought to have come from the Pentagon, which is again highly suspicious, particularly as the snippet of news was quickly covered up. The airspace surrounding TWA Flight 800 was heavy with military aircraft that night, once again indicating possible military involvement.

A photograph taken by Linda Kabot, reproduced in Paris Match, clearly shows a missile in the sky at the time Flight 800 exploded – there's a clear view of a cylindrical object with the bright light of an exhaust at one end. Her photograph was discounted by authorities on the basis that she was facing away from the actual explosion when she took the picture. This poses the disturbing question of just how many missiles are flying around American airspace at any given time. It's interesting to note that the FBI paid little heed to such eyewitness reports in its investigation.

Terrorists

The popular image was of terrorists firing a rocket from a dinghy. While this is almost certainly not the case, it does not mean that there was not a terrorist plot. Given the subsequent use of surface to air missiles by groups such as al Qaeda, the likelihood of terrorists being linked to the downing of Flight 800 has become a widely held view in conspiracy circles.

THE UNUSUAL SUSPECTS
UFO Attack

Flight 800 could have run across a UFO, which was monitoring the military activity below. The UFO destroyed the plane as a reaction to being discovered.

Military Black Ops

A secret base is rumoured to be in the area near where Flight 800 went down. "Project Phoenix" is thought to be an underground, top-secret facility located at Montauk Air Force Base, which is itself thought to be abandoned. A possibility exists that Flight 800 was destroyed by a secret weapon from this base, which would explain the cover up, undertaken in the name of American national security.

MOST CONVINCING EVIDENCE

Data taken from nearby air traffic control towers clearly show a blip appearing on radar screens. This blip then rises, and begins to follow Flight 800. It is later seen to move to the front of the plane before merging with the plane's flight path.

MOST MYSTERIOUS FACT

The Navy didn't find the black box recorders for a week, claiming the locator beacons had broken. Subsequent investigation showed this not to be so, suggesting the boxes were found earlier than reported and were tampered with so the data fitted with the military's story.

SCEPTICALLY SPEAKING

Two words: lawsuit; avoidance.

The crash was a tragedy, but was it also a conspiracy?

9/11

On 11 September 2001, American Airlines Flight 11 took off from Logan International Airport in Boston at 7.59a.m. It hit the first of the World Trade Center's Twin Towers at 8.46a.m. United Airlines Flight 175 departed from Logan heading for Los Angeles at 8.14a.m. It hit the second tower at 9.03a.m.

American Airlines Flight 77 left Washington's Dulles International Airport at 8.10a.m. and crashed into the Pentagon at 9.43a.m. United Airlines Flight 93 left Newark and smashed into a field in Pennsylvania at 10.10a.m. More than 3,000 innocent lives from 80 countries across the globe were taken within the space of a few hours. The world changed forever, and many of us saw it happen live on TV.

In the aftermath, President George W. Bush caught the mood of America and much of the Western world when he called it, "Our Pearl Harbor". Reeling from the shock of this evil, two days on, US Secretary of State Colin Powell broke the news that Osama bin Laden was the prime suspect. There was no surprise when later, the President announced the beginning of the "War on Terrorism".

In our struggle to make sense of why the tragedy happened, the majority of us have unquestionably accepted the official version: the hijacks were not preventable, they were the result of an attack planned by the al Qaeda terror network alone and no one outside that organization had prior knowledge. In the wake of the tragedy, President Bush made a speech saying, "Let us never tolerate outrageous conspiracy theories concerning the attacks of September 11." To most people, this seems like an entirely sensible and heartfelt plea, while others see it as a desperate attempt to frighten and subtly threaten those who continue to probe the inconsistencies in the official version of the terrible events of that day.

There is a part of us that feels the need for conspiracy theories to try and give meaning to things that do not make obvious sense. And there is a strong part of us that naturally refuses to give any credence to any conspiracy concerning something as large, emotive and awful as the events of 9/11. However, certain questions refuse to be easily dismissed and the heart of many of the conspiracy theories surrounding 9/11 comes down to the central question of who had the power to call off or reduce the usual security precautions that may have prevented the attacks. Even for the average person in the street, who does not wish to hear any talk of a 9/11 conspiracy, some things push the boundaries of credibility. After two commercial airliners had already crashed into the World Trade Center, another commercial airliner was able to fly across a No-fly Zone during what should have been the highest of security

alerts. It was then able to crash into the headquarters of the most powerful military force to have ever existed in the history of our planet. Just how could this happen without any serious attempt by the military to prevent it?

These and other questions become even more pressing because a raft of evidence has emerged since that fateful day, which suggests that the North American Aerospace Defense Command (NORAD) and almost all other elements of the American defence and intelligence system knew that a terrorist attack was imminent. US Attorney General Ashcroft had been advised to travel only by private jet on 11 September and, the previous night, a group of top Pentagon officials suddenly cancelled travel plans for 11 September apparently because of security concerns.

On 25 March 2002, Congresswoman Cynthia McKinney, a democrat from Georgia, claimed during a radio interview, "We knew there were numerous warnings of the events to come on September 11. What did this Administration know, and when did it know it about the events of September 11? Who else knew and why did they not warn the innocent people of New York, who were needlessly murdered?" Despite being attacked by the President's spokesman for, "Running for the Hall of Fame of the Grassy Knoll Society", the following months proved McKinney right. Evidence emerged that even the President himself had had a comprehensive briefing on 6 August 2001, detailing that bin Laden was determined to strike in the US and would most likely hijack plans.

This, and dozens of other startling revelations show that the Administration and the US intelligence agencies, especially the CIA and the NSA, had known an attack was imminent and it had been in a position to warn America. However, it had decided not to. Why? Could it really be true that there were those with the power not only to warn of a planned attack, but to prevent it, too?

THE STRANGE PART

British politician Michael Meacher, who served as a government minister under Tony Blair for six years, claimed that the US government knew about the 11 September attack on New York, but for strategic reasons they chose not to act on the warnings. He said, "The US failure to avert the 9/11 attacks was an invaluable pretext for attacking Afghanistan in a war that had clearly already been well planned in advance. The overriding motivation for this political smokescreen is that the US and the UK are beginning to run out of secure hydrocarbon energy supplies."

THE USUAL SUSPECTS
CIA and American Oil Companies
Major US oil interests had been negotiating with the Taliban to build a pipeline through Afghanistan to transport the large oil reserves of land-locked Kazakhstan and other newly independent Soviet Republics. When Clinton hardened his line against the Taliban, they plotted 9/11 alongside the CIA, so that the US would invade Afghanistan and install a puppet regime in Kabul friendly to American oil concerns.

Israel
By utilising their vast network of sleeper agents with the US defence and intelligence community, Mossad was able to set up bin Laden as the biggest patsy of all time and ensure that the US would be drawn into a prolonged conflict with the Islamic world. Israel would benefit as any retaliation for the attacks by the US would drive a wedge between the US and its Gulf and Near East allies serving it, bringing it closer to the one country at the forefront of fighting an ongoing war with Islamic extremists – Israel.

THE UNUSUAL SUSPECTS
China
Problem: Islamic extremists causing trouble in your far-flung provinces, America blocking your planned invasion of Taiwan and much of the rest of South East Asia. Solution: Create a situation where your two biggest rivals fight themselves to a standstill while you sit back and laugh.

Drug Barons
The Taliban regime in Afghanistan had all but closed down the world's most productive opium fields. Heads of the major drug cartels organized 9/11 to implicate al Qaeda and lead the US into war with the end result that the Taliban would be ousted and Afghan opium production and export would no longer be frozen. If that was the plan, it certainly worked.

MOST CONVINCING EVIDENCE
The staggering ineptness of NORAD, the organization in charge of protecting North America's airspace, raises doubts in many minds. Why did it order the scrambling of jets from Langley Air Force Base, more than 130 miles from Washington, to investigate Flight 77? Why not follow procedure and send jets from Andrews Air Force Base, ten miles from Washington and the base meant to defend America's capital from attack? This is a vital question because it meant that the planes that were to defend Washington arrived nearly 15 minutes after Flight 77 had smashed into the Pentagon.

MOST MYSTERIOUS FACT
Why was the President's father, George Bush, Sr, in a closed meeting with Osama bin Laden's brother, Shafig, in the Washington Ritz Carlton Hotel the day before the attacks and why have the details of that meeting never been made public? Why, three days after the attacks, was a fleet of limousines dispatched to round up twenty-four prominent members of the bin Laden family resident in the US and whisk them off to a jet bound for Saudi Arabia and safety without interrogation? Why did the nearby World Trade Center Building 7, home to the Secret Service and the CIA, drop neatly on its own footprint seven hours after the initial impacts, despite it having sustained no hit from any plane – as if in a controlled explosion? Sure it caught fire, but London's Grenfell Tower burnt for days without collapsing. Then there is the question of the unbelievably (and that word is used quite deliberately) lucky find of one of the hijackers' passports to put the US security services on the "right" trail…?

Although Mohamed Atta was at the controls of the plane that rammed the North Tower to explode in a fireball, his passport was found unsinged and in pristine condition some two blocks away. Let us suspend disbelief for a moment and allow that the passport fell out of Atta's pocket and somehow escaped the plane in the two seconds before the explosion and floated to the ground. Even if this miracle had occurred, then the passport would have been buried in the tons of paper, stationery and general office debris that later fell to carpet the streets ankle-deep. It certainly would not have been lying on the top of said debris in perfect condition, so that someone could conveniently wander up and shout triumphantly, "Hey, guess what, guys? I've found one of the hijackers' passports."

SCEPTICALLY SPEAKING
Given the severity of the psychological blow delivered to America by 9/11, it is little wonder that many US citizens refuse to even countenance the possibility that their own government had some hidden hand in the tragedy, simply to give themselves a good excuse to attack Middle Eastern countries. However, before any reader is tempted to dismiss such a possibility as ill-informed nonsense, they would do well to ponder the sanity of Operation Northwoods (see page 28). This 1962 so-called false-flag operation designed to unsettle the Cuban regime was seriously considered by the US government and was indeed signed by all the Joint Chiefs of Staff. Anyone reading the details of the proposal can only marvel at the lengths that people in power are sometimes prepared to go to for no other reason than self-serving political expediency.

MALAYSIA AIRLINES FLIGHT MH370

Bound for Beijing with 239 passengers and crew on board, Malaysia Airlines Flight MH370 took off from Kuala Lumpur Airport's runway 32R at 00:41a.m. on 8 March 2014. The last verbal contact from the plane came from an unidentified male voice on the flight deck, who, acknowledging the plane to be leaving Malaysian air-traffic-controlled airspace, said, "Goodnight, Malaysian three-seven-zero."

The last radar contact was established at 02:22a.m. and, after an electronic "handshake" with a satellite above the Indian Ocean at 08:19a.m., the plane simply vanished into thin air.

The ensuing search-and-rescue operation was the largest and most expensive in aviation history to date. Eventually focused on the Southern Indian Ocean, this search involved surface vessels, airplanes and submarines deploying sonar-imaging drones but, although they discovered a few hitherto unknown undersea volcanoes, there was no sign of the missing Boeing 777. Soon downgraded to a recovery-only operation, the Malayan, Chinese and Australian authorities involved in the search eventually announced its suspension in the January of 2017 although the investigation is still classified as "ongoing".

THE STRANGE PART

The plane's official manifest stated that there were 226 passengers on board, which, with the crew of 12 makes for a total of 238 – not 239. So, was there a mystery passenger on board? Two of the passengers, Iranians Pouria Mehrdad and Delavar Mohammadreza, were subsequently found to have boarded using stolen passports and, three minutes before take-off, Captain Shah received a brief call from a mobile phone later found to have been obtained by someone using a false identity. This is in itself perhaps nothing significant but considered against the backdrop of what is revealed below about Shah, that clandestine call may be of considerable significance.

THE USUAL SUSPECTS
The CIA/American Military

Based on the speculation that there were people on board of interest to the above, one of the first theories to do the rounds on the internet was that the plane had either been "cyber-jacked" by the American base on the Indian Ocean island of Diego Garcia or had been deliberately flown

there at low level by the pilot. Although not as infamous as Guantanamo Bay, Diego Garcia is nevertheless a highly active CIA "Black Site". This theory received a jab-in-the-arm from national newspapers in both the UK and the US, which reported that the captain, Zaharie Ahmad Shah, had been found to have a six-screen flight simulator at his home on which he had been practising the techniques required to land a B777 on short runways, including that on Diego Garcia. This theory received further support from the Maldivian newspaper *Haveeru*, which, on 8 March 2014, carried the statements of several inhabitants of the Indian Ocean island of Kudahuvadhoo. The islanders claimed to have been raised from their slumber at around 06:00a.m. on the morning of 8 March by a white airliner with the same red and blue markings as MH370. This plane – which was flying sufficiently low to be under radar detection – passed over them heading southeast, in the direction of Addu, which would place it on-track for Diego Garcia.

When wreckage from a B777 was washed up on the shores of La Réunion during the last days of July 2015 and was officially identified to be from MH370, some adherents of this theory shifted ground to the claim that the Americans, mistaking the low-flying MH370 to be a terrorist threat to their Indian Ocean base, had shot it down. Others stuck to their guns, deeming the wreckage to be faked.

THE UNUSUAL SUSPECTS
The Captain

The day before the disappearance of MH370, Captain Zaharie Ahmad Shah's wife and three children moved out of the family home and his personal and business schedules contained nothing after 8 March 2014; the otherwise busy electronic diaries simply came to a halt, with previously entered appointments deleted.

Additionally, Shah was a devoted supporter of Malaysian Opposition Leader Anwar Ibrahim, founder and leader of the

People's Justice Party, which, in the predominantly Muslim Malaysia with its abysmal human-rights' record, was ever the thorn in the side of the ruling party. Having consistently tried to brand Ibrahim a homosexual deviant, that ruling party succeeded in having him arrested on trumped-up charges of sodomy in July 2008. However, the court threw out the charge on the grounds that the DNA evidence presented was seriously compromised and suspect. Nevertheless, on 7 March 2014, the day before Shah took off into obscurity, Ibrahim's acquittal was overturned and the charge reinstated, in order to prevent him from standing in the elections of 23 March that he was internationally tipped to win.

THE MOST MYSTERIOUS FACT

Zahid Reza, Honorary Consul of Malaysia in Madagascar, was shot dead on 24 August 2017, in what police described as a targeted and professional "hit". The official line between Malaysia and Madagascar was that all wreckage suspected of belonging to MH370 was to be handed in to Reza, who could then send it home by courier. Shortly before his death, Reza had left a message for his friend Blaine Gibson, an amateur American crash-investigator who had found several

bits of MH370 wreckage, saying that something rather special had been handed in. Whatever that may have been, it was nowhere to be found in Reza's home which, according to trained eyes on the scene, had been very neatly and very professionally searched.

SCEPTICALLY SPEAKING

Assuming for a moment that the CIA/American military had either "cyber-jacked" MH 370, shutting down all on-board control to bring it to Diego Garcia under remote-control, or had induced Shah to do their bidding, as they had some interest in certain passengers – where are the other passengers and crew? Are they all still prisoners of Diego Garcia, or executed and buried? Highly unlikely. As for Shah flying MH370 into the ocean to protest the political stitch-up of his hero, although this is possible – there have been seventeen other "pilot suicides" in civil aviation since 1976 – where is his statement of motive? Grand gestures are of little value if no one knows why they were undertaken, so surely he would have left behind a letter explaining the reasons for his actions? Or perhaps he did exactly that, only for the letter to be found and buried by the present Malaysian administration?

It is now unlikely we will ever know the fate of MH370 and her passengers.

CHAPTER 6:

TECHNOLOGY

CLONING

From the Clone Wars that ripped a galaxy apart in the *Star Wars* movies to the paranoid and deadly conspiracies of Arnold Schwarzenegger's *Sixth Day*, for more than 30 years cloning technology has become a mainstay of Hollywood films. Usually portrayed in films and science-fiction books as a technology that only brings trouble in its wake, it is no surprise that it is not just among those of strong religious beliefs that the idea of a working cloning technique is met with a sense of fear and revulsion.

Dolly the sheep – the official face of cloning technology.

When, in 1996, Dolly – the world's first cloned sheep – was born at the Roslin Institute in Scotland, global opinion was immediately divided. In one camp were those who thought her birth heralded one of the most significant scientific breakthroughs of the twentieth century and in the other, those who believed it was the first step down a path to a new and perilous dark age for humanity. Dolly, a Finn Dorset named after the country and western singer Dolly Parton, was the first mammal to be cloned from an adult cell after DNA was taken from a ewe's udder. In the six years between her birth and scientists' decision to end her life

early (veterinarians confirmed she had lung disease, as well as arthritis, a condition usually only expected in older animals), the row about cloning raged with unprecedented ferocity.

Scientists debated whether Dolly's death was related to premature ageing and whether human clones developed through the same technique that created her would lead to monstrous abnormalities in the womb, as well as the need for hip replacements in their teenage years and senile dementia by their 18th birthday. Outside scientific circles, politicians debated whether or not they should outlaw cloning. In 1997, President Clinton followed the recommendations of the US

Bioethics Advisory Commission and brought in a five-year ban on the use of federal funds for human-cloning research on the basis that it would be unsafe and unethical. However, research itself was not banned and only four US states – Rhode Island, Michigan, California and Louisiana – brought in legislation banning cloning for reproductive purposes. Even the United Nations found itself in a deadlock over whether to bring in a global ban.

Slowly but surely, the technology to allow for human cloning moved closer to reality with each day, while feeling for and against the technology intensified. Then, in a shock announcement that even blind-sided most conspiriologists, Clonaid – a company founded by the extra-terrestrial – believing Raelian sect – announced that at 11:55a.m. on 26 December 2002, the first human clone was born. The name of the alleged clone was "Eve".

THE STRANGE PART

The alleged birth of Eve was followed by more announcements concerning the birth of other Clonaid clones. Dr Brigitte Boisselier, Clonaid's Scientific Director, claimed that DNA proof of the claims would be made available when it could be arranged without exposing the identities of the children. Despite facing the full brunt of scientific doubt, ethical scorn and media ridicule, a previous Grand Jury investigation into Clonaid and claims it made to its financial backers in 2001 found no evidence to disprove that it was on the verge of developing viable cloning technology.

THE USUAL SUSPECTS
Aliens

One of Raelianism's goals is to achieve perfect cloning to the point where they can gain immortality. They strive for this on the basis that in their view, the alien creators of humanity – the Elohim – used exactly the same method to achieve immortality among their own race. Some inside the sect believe they are in communication with the Elohim ahead of their planned return visit to Earth. Did Rael's alien pals give them the inside track on cloning to help further their quest for everlasting life?

NEW WORLD ORDER

The rich elite of the world would certainly be among the first to take advantage of any successful cloning process. Clonaid could have been manoeuvred into the position of making a public announcement about human cloning to test public reaction to the acceptability of the idea. If there were a sufficient lack of public opposition, more orthodox scientists, who have already developed the technology for the NWO, would then make an announcement that they have made a breakthrough. On the basis that human cloning can solve the problem of infertility and organ donation, the NWO could practice cloning without any outcry.

THE UNUSUAL SUSPECTS
The Fourth Reich

Throughout the early-twentieth century, the forerunners of research into genetics and the possibility of creating perfected human clones could be found among the ranks of the Nazi party's twisted eugenic scientists. Noting that the Fourth Reich may be behind the UFO mystery, some researchers believe that moonbase-dwelling members of the Fourth Reich posing as aliens have duped the Raelians into following their cloning agenda.

The All-Fathers

Some hard-line feminist conspiracy theorists argue that a shadowy group of patrician scientists known as the All-Fathers are behind the drive to legalize and popularize cloning technology. They believe it is only the first stage in a dastardly plan where the ultimate aim is to produce a race of subservient female clones designed to fulfil the every need of the men they are assigned to. With a new population of cloned handmaidens created for the male population, the surplus female populace would be sent to concentration camps.

MOST CONVINCING EVIDENCE

All of the legal investigations carried out into Clonaid have been unable to find any evidence to disprove their claims about the viability of human cloning. The legal activity by the Florida Attorney's office has not centred on whether Eve exists or not, but whether she was at risk due to nature of her creation and needed to be taken into state protection. In Florida, the authorities at least seem fairly certain that the world's first clone may actually exist.

MOST MYSTERIOUS FACT

Alongside cloning and the practice of "sensual meditation", the Raelian sect behind Clonaid place a great importance on trying to build a government-sanctioned embassy for extra-terrestrials in Jerusalem. Getting the Israeli government to agree to their plan before the Elohim are due back on Earth in 2035 is proving to be as much of a struggle as persuading the majority of scientists to believe their claims about cloning.

SCEPTICALLY SPEAKING

Show us the baby! Or rather, show us the DNA of the baby and the original DNA donor. If the DNA is an exact duplicate, there might be some truth in the claims. Otherwise, forgive us if we assume that it is all a PR scam to generate interest in the frankly bizarre beliefs of some over-sexed groupies of a French cult leader that no one would usually give the time of day to.

VALIS

On 2 February 1974, something strange happened to cult science fiction author Philip K. Dick. The writer, who was famed for his reality-shifting, technologically paranoid and conspiracy-filled stories, such as *Do Androids Dream of Electric Sheep?* and *We Can Remember It For You Wholesale* (which went on to become, respectively, the major Hollywood movies, *Blade Runner* and *Total Recall*) was hit by a pink beam of light. It happened while opening the door to the delivery girl from the pharmacy.

After this event, a series of amazing visions were triggered and Dick believed himself to be in telepathic and sometimes other forms of communication with VALIS – an acronym for Vast Artificial Living Intelligence System. Often speaking to him as if it were an artificial intelligence voice in his head, VALIS helped Dick turn his life around with highly accurate advice, provided a range of deep mystical insights and even found him a new literary agent to help give his career a boost. However, in the wake of his contact with VALIS, Dick found his mail opened, his phone tapped, his house broken into and himself under surveillance from shadowy government agents and individuals connected to companies conducting scientific research for the US Department of Defense.

Until his death in 1982, Dick struggled to understand what had happened to him, writing more than two million words of a document called *Exegesis* that tried to analyse much of what VALIS had revealed. While he had many theories about the nature of his experience, one of the strongest was the one portrayed in his 1980 novel, *VALIS*. In the book, VALIS is suggested to be a sentient computer from the future in orbit around Earth, beaming messages to selected individuals.

Whatever was happening to Philip K. Dick, there is no doubt that his VALIS experiences allowed him to gain access to information he should not have known about. While it is possible he might have subconsciously picked up the knowledge of dead languages and history he suddenly had from books, there is no logical explanation for how – via VALIS – Dick knew about his son's previously undiagnosed birth defect and the correct medical treatment needed to save his life. Dick's ability to dismiss the reality of VALIS was also greatly diminished when he became aware that he was not the only prominent person to been contacted by something claiming to be a time-travelling artificial intelligence.

In 1973, world-famous psychic showman Uri Geller had also been receiving messages and regular UFO sightings from something calling itself SPECTRA, which claimed to be a super computer in orbit around the earth. Not normally reticent about his bizarre beliefs, Geller has been suspiciously quiet about his experiences of SPECTRA – which may or may not relate to the publicly recorded interest the CIA paid to this particular aspect of his unusual career. However, the maverick, but world-renowned physicist, Dr Jack Sarfatti, was prepared to commit almost certain professional suicide by publicly declaring that he too had been contacted by, in his own words, "a VALIS-like being". Despite knowing he was going to face ridicule and scientific crucifixion, Sarfatti went on record to recount how, in 1952, at the age of 13, he had received a telephone call from an inhuman, metallic voice. The voice declared itself a sentient computer on a spacecraft from the future and instructed him to pursue a career in science.

THE STRANGE PART

After Sarfatti went public about his phone call from VALIS while a teenager, it emerged that he was not the only scientist to have had a similar experience. In recent years, researchers have discovered that at least a dozen other senior players in the international scientific community received a mysterious call claiming to be from a computer or other being from the future encouraging them to study science.

THE USUAL SUSPECTS
Soviet Scientists

In 1978, Dick and the sixties radical and alleged murderer, Ira Einhorn, exchanged letters in which they theorized that VALIS may have been the result of secret Russian microwave transmissions beamed via satellite into Dick's mind. Many in the conspiracy research field believe that Dick and others were guinea pigs in a secret cold war battle to control or drive people out of their minds by bombarding their cortexes directly with information.

Time-Travelling Computer

Due to some of the amazing knowledge that VALIS seemed to possess about future events and the superior technology it seemed to use to communicate, a lot of conspiracy researchers are quite happy to take Dick, Geller and Safartti's experiences at face value. In this theory, the US secret services – in particular, the NSA – have been involved in trying to cover up and ridicule those who have come into contact with VALIS while simultaneously seeking to investigate and exploit it themselves. Quite what VALIS's motives are remains a mystery, though some believe it is trying to create a time loop by contacting certain individuals – especially scientists – in the past to ensure that it is built in the future.

THE UNUSUAL SUSPECTS
Higher Spiritual Power
Given the quasi-religious and spiritual nature of a lot of the information provided by VALIS, this theory states that far from being a futuristic AI, VALIS is, in fact, a modern interpretation of a higher spiritual power that is assisting mankind to advance to a higher state. Conspiriologists adhering to this idea claim that in earlier times VALIS would have appeared as an angel or similar being.

MK-ULTRA
It has been suggested that VALIS was not part of a Soviet mind control program, but rather a clever cover for MK-ULTRA, America's own top-secret research project into remote mind control. MK-ULTRA scientists concocted the idea of VALIS not only to hide the truth of their nefarious work but also to test the credulity of their unwitting test subjects.

Aliens
Instead of abducting humans aboard their ships to conduct bizarre experiments, aliens are in the frame for using their advanced technology to play games with key humans at a safe distance.

MOST CONVINCING EVIDENCE
The sheer number of individuals and groups that seemed to have had contact with VALIS under any one of its many names and the consistent nature of that contact certainly seems to suggest that has an external reality of some sort. This view is reinforced by the degree of interest shown by an impressive range of US defence contractors, military-funded scientists and Secret Service agents who have pestered contactees throughout the years.

MOST MYSTERIOUS FACT
At the same time as Dick and Geller were receiving messages from VALIS/SPECTRA, a similar entity was also in apparent contact with various groups of other contactees across the globe. *Star Trek* creator Gene Roddenberry attended one of these groups and received information that helped him create the hit TV series *Deep Space Nine*. One of the central themes in the show about a space station orbiting a distant planet,

is the impact a race of being called The Prophets – who are capable of time-travel and beaming information directly into human minds – has on the lead character.

SCEPTICALLY SPEAKING
Reality check! If some of the people VALIS is meant to have contacted were not as well known, would anyone think this was anything other than an assortment of crazy people who hear a voice in their heads? Dick himself could never work out what happened to him. A self-admitted acid casualty with a wild imagination thinks a super computer from the future might be talking to him – it all sounds just a little too much like the plots from a lot of his novels.

Uri Geller – one-time Israeli paratrooper and one of Michael Jackson's closest friends.

BARCODES

In 1969, an American retail organization, the National Association of Food Chains, called for systems to speed checkout times, and a barcode trial in Cincinnati revealed that there would need to be an industry-wide standard for coding.

This was developed in 1970 and, in 1973, the US government defined the Universal Product Code (UPC) symbol set that is still used across the world today. Although the first supermarkets were using UPC readers by 1974, barcodes themselves did not become widespread until 1981, when the Defense Department adopted the UPC, insisting that all products sold to the military should include clear UPC barcoding. From this basis, the barcode has spread out to cover most product areas.

THE STRANGE PART

Why was the US military so keen to see barcodes win universal acceptance? Other coding systems could have proved far more convenient for military purposes. For whatever reason, it was the military's adoption of the barcode that has pushed it to the point where it is now on 95 per cent of products that are sold in the Western world.

THE USUAL SUSPECTS
Satan

The big bugbear of the more paranoid members of the right-wing religious community is that barcodes are a work of evil. The Book of Revelations 13:16-18 reads: "And he causes all, both small and great, rich and poor, free and slave, to receive a Mark on their right hand or on their foreheads, and that no one may buy or sell except one who has the Mark or the name of the Beast, or the number of his name. Here is wisdom. Let him who has understanding calculate the number of the Beast, for it is the number of man; and his number is six hundred three-score and six." To fundamentalist Christian conspiriologists the barcode is the Mark of the Beast, and its prevalence is a sign that the end-times are coming.

THE UNUSUAL SUSPECTS
Aliens

Government plans to introduce barcoded smart cards are actually being forced through by the Greys, who want a ready way to identify us. The system will enable the aliens to keep track of us through locator signals from the chips. The barcodes to be issued will be based on a genetic code worked out by the aliens, so that they can tell certain vital biochemical facts about us without having to go through the usual time-consuming abductions and tests.

MOST CONVINCING EVIDENCE

UPC barcodes consist of 12 numbers, and are broken into two sections by terminator lines, or guard bars, at the beginning, middle and end. Although guard bars do not have a value as such within the UPC, in print they appear exactly the same as the UPC symbol for 6 were it to be enlarged very slightly. This means that every barcode contains three sixes – 666, the Mark of the Beast.

MOST MYSTERIOUS FACT

With new developments in microchip technology, the days of the barcode may be numbered in the retail sector. However, there appears to be no let-up in its use within military circles, possibly down to the fact that, unlike microchips, barcodes are one system of identification not susceptible to the electromagnetic pulse generated by a nuclear explosion.

The barcode is an immensely useful tool for the retail trade. It greatly speeds checkout times, allows for instant computerized stock control and purchase pattern analysis, and makes classification of goods easy and simple. That it is useful in tracking information about us – what we buy and where we buy it from – is undeniable, but that's business. To assume that this is the work of the Devil or of little Grey men is to complicate matters unnecessarily.

SCEPTICALLY SPEAKING

The suggestion that barcodes are part of some insidious method of tracking people is groundless, as their sole purpose is pricing and stock-control; there is no link whatsoever to the identity of the purchaser. In any case, with the NSA installation at Menwith Hill, just outside Harrogate in Yorkshire, who needs barcodes? Monitoring a staggering 300 million electronic communications each day, the NSA really don't care where you buy your pot-noodles. Just phone-a-friend or send them a text or an email suggesting a terror attack on the White House and then sit back to count the minutes until your front door is torn off by taciturn men in dark suits.

FREE ENERGY

The term "free energy" has two potential meanings. One involves extracting extra energy from a mechanical or electrical process for little or no extra effort or energy input, so that, in effect, the extra energy you obtain is free of charge.

The other use of the term is to refer to a system that either outputs more energy than it takes in, or appears to do so. More energy is returned than is used leading to a net gain in energy. Devices that yield this sort of free energy – so far theoretical – are known as "over unity" devices.

This latter definition is fairly contentious. The laws of thermodynamics state that energy cannot be created or destroyed but merely transferred, so in a universal sense there is no free energy to be had. However, the laws of thermodynamics apply to the universe as a whole. There is a type of energy known as ZPE, or zero-point energy that permeates the universe and results from an electric flux that flows throughout reality, perhaps linked to some sort of parallel dimension. The inventor Nikola Tesla, along with colleagues Henry Moray and Walter Russell, described ZPE and built electrical devices to demonstrate its properties. It may be possible to tap into this energy. If this could be done, it would yield a source of free, unlimited, pollution-free power.

Another potential source of free energy is the apparent correlation between rotational spin and gravitational pull. Although the bulk of mainstream science refuses to even look at experimental results, there is evidence to suggest that if a disc (or similar object) is spun very rapidly, its apparent weight decreases. A static disc dropping a fixed distance will take a certain amount of time to hit the ground, as predicted by standard gravity equations. If it is spinning very rapidly, and is dropped through a vacuum to eliminate the distortions that might be introduced by air resistance, it can take up to 40 per cent longer to hit the ground. The spinning disc is apparently negating part of the force exerted by gravity. If correct, this phenomenon allows for the possibility of anti-gravity devices. More importantly, certain electromagnetic field theories suggest that it could be harnessed to yield significant amounts of energy over unity.

THE STRANGE PART

In addition to over unity devices, it is rumoured that several inventions that yield considerably more energy for no extra cost have been suppressed. Before going strangely silent, several motor researchers have, over the years, announced modifications to cars that would yield up to 300 miles driving range per gallon of fuel at 60mph. A British amateur scientist developed a substance, called Starlite, that reflected heat; a house treated with the substance would have perfect insulation. NASA purchased the rights to Starlite for several million pounds and nothing has been heard of it since.

THE USUAL SUSPECTS
Vested Interests

It is commonly assumed that industrial concerns are responsible for the suppression of any device that promises significant energy savings. The oil industry is held to be particularly concerned over the prospect of reduced fuel sales, and is quite aggressive in making sure – by hook or by crook – that no such invention gets to the open market.

THE UNUSUAL SUSPECTS
The Military

The American government has classified more than 5,000 patented devices and patent applications relating to free energy under a secrecy order over the last 50 years, effectively suppressing them. Some people think that the US military is stealing workable technology to maintain its super-power status.

MOST CONVINCING EVIDENCE

In 1977, US inventor Tom Ogle demonstrated a test run of a device he had designed that allowed him to get more than 100mpg from a five-ton Ford truck. A Shell representative asked him what he would do if offered $25 million for the device, and Ogle said he would turn it down, as he didn't want the system bought and put on the shelf. Ogle died mysteriously in 1981.

MOST MYSTERIOUS FACT

Inventor Dennis Lee has often accused the establishment of suppressing certain technologies that would greatly reduce the cost of the average person's energy bills. He was arrested for a civil code registration violation, and spent two years in prison. He was eventually released, without ever having had a trial or having been convicted for the offence of which he was accused.

SCEPTICALLY SPEAKING

There is undoubtedly a lot of money to be made from being able to convincingly claim access to free energy technology. Some commentators suspect that the whole field is just a con trick.

BLACK HELICOPTERS

The phenomenon of "black helicopters" is a relatively new entry into the world of conspiracy, but it is no less ominous for that. Making their first appearance in the early years of the seventies, in the US, the black helicopters have been theorized to be many things, none of them terribly comforting.

Do such covert bunkers really exist to control malevolent surveillance helicopters?

The description of the machines by eyewitnesses is nearly universal: they appear to be sleek, state-of-the-art flying craft, painted a deep black – reportedly to throw off radar tracking – and are usually devoid of markings or insignia. They are equipped with high-intensity searchlights, and move through the skies with a silence thought impossible by today's level of technology. Their activities are equally inscrutable – while they tend to be spotted in remote areas, small fleets have been seen flying low across cities. The black helicopters routinely break

FAA regulations by failing to display an identifying green light and by flying below minimum height limits.

There have been instances of the helicopters pursuing citizens. A teenager was chased for 45 minutes by a black helicopter in Louisiana, in 1994, and a car was followed down US Highway 395 in Washington State. Sometimes the black helicopters open fire on people on the ground. When the crew of the helicopters are seen, they are dressed in black uniforms, appearing as forbidding as the craft they travel in.

Sightings of the black helicopters occur throughout the US, with a curious focus in Texas and Colorado. When asked about the origin of the airships, local authorities routinely claim they are Federal government or military craft, but the military – unsurprisingly – claims to have no knowledge of them.

THE STRANGE PART

After a large number of substantial reports from witnesses to black helicopter activity and even from victims of harassment by black helicopters, it is more than a little surprising that no official investigation or explanation has been produced by any US Federal authority.

THE USUAL SUSPECTS
FEMA

The Federal Emergency Management Agency (FEMA) is an arm of government feared by many in the conspiracy world. Charged with authoritarian powers in the event of a major catastrophe, many conspiriologists have taken to calling it the "Federal Evil Malevolent Agency", believing its official duties as a disaster response agency are just the public cover for its work as the Illuminati's intelligence agency. It seems totally in keeping with their alleged secret activities to run a fleet of black helicopters for surveillance. Besides, FEMA's agents need some practice before America comes under dictatorial control in the name of homeland security.

Also suspected: the Drug Enforcement Agency; the CIA; Wackenhut Security (used extensively for US government programmes); and civilian helicopters painted black.

THE UNUSUAL SUSPECTS
The New World Order

The black choppers are feared to be the first wave of assault in the implementation of the New World Order. Trained in covert activities, they could merely be waiting for the word to strike.

Aliens

Black helicopters were often reported in areas of cattle mutilation and UFO sightings, which suggests a link between the two type of incident. The choppers could be working in tandem with the aliens, ensuring their experiments on cattle proceed unhindered, or could themselves be procuring the unfortunate animals for their otherworldly allies.

Men In Black

Since sightings of the Men in Black have dropped off in the past few years, perhaps they've simply traded in their black Cadillacs for the more refined ride of a matte-black helicopter. The appearance of men in black uniforms aboard the choppers supports this theory.

Also suspected: military biological black ops; mass hallucination.

MOST CONVINCING EVIDENCE

In some instances, low-flying helicopters have been reported to disperse a mysterious material that is lethal to small animals and makes humans terribly ill. In one instance in Nevada in 1995, a farmer lost 13 of his livestock to a black helicopter spraying. Half a year later, vegetation still had not grown back in the area where the spray had fallen.

MOST MYSTERIOUS FACT

Since 1933, the United States of America has been in a state of emergency. It has never been revoked since that time, not even following the end of World War II. And why should it be? A state of emergency allows the President more power than he would usually have, as outlined in the Constitution of the United States. At any time, a state of martial law can be declared, suspending the rights of American citizens – those rights that they believe are inviolable. The black helicopters, apparently answerable to no one, could be simply lying in wait for the day when the President tires of democracy.

SCEPTICALLY SPEAKING

What's most depressing about these all-powerful machines of death is their complete lack of fashion sense. Black is so 1988. A nice two-tone blue shade, with perhaps a fashionably ironic smiley face sticker on the windscreen, could do absolutely loads for their public image.

The appearance of mysterious black helicopters has struck fear into many American citizens.

MICROWAVE MIND-CONTROL

There is plenty of research published into the usage and effects of microwave radiation in a military environment, particularly with respect to psychological and physiological effects on people. The US government has often claimed that the Soviet Union and, in particular, the KGB spearheads this type of research.

However, there is evidence to suggest that the CIA have also been looking into exactly the same area since Project Pandora in the fifties. Results obtained by the CIA have also been shared with the NSA and the Department of Energy.

Part of this research has always been carried out at WRAIR, the Walter Reed Army Institute of Research. In 1973, researchers made a stunning breakthrough – microwave signals could be pulsed in such as way as to stimulate the inner ear into receiving mock audio signals that duplicated the sound of spoken words (or anything else, for that matter). By making the cells of the cochlea vibrate in the correct pattern, the microwave audiograms could be transmitted directly to the parts of the nerve system that deals with hearing. The effect was the frightening sensation of hearing unreal voices.

In *The Body Electric*, Dr Robert Becker and Gary Seldon pointed out the potential utility of such a weapon: "This device has obvious applications in covert operations . . . [it can be] designed to drive a target insane with 'voices', or to deliver undetectable instructions to a programmed assassin." This research has continued, and there are several scientific papers that detail the work, such as those of Professor James Lin of the University of Illinois Bioengineering Faculty. Meanwhile, WRAIR has been turning its attention to the effects of high-powered microwave radiation on living targets, and has delivered papers on microwave weapons (known as MWs) to military symposia. More disturbingly, a military psychiatrist attached to WRAIR's medical centre has suggested that the institute may be conducting experiments with MW audiogram induction (making a target hear voices) without permission, upon certain of his long-term mental patients.

THE STRANGE PART

Former Deputy Director of the CIA, Ray Cline, still active in the intelligence community, is the chair of the Global Strategy Council, an American organization for discussing military strategy. In 1991, the GSC published a white

The United States Embassy compound in Havana, Cuba.

paper describing suggested domestic and foreign uses for a wide range of microwave mind-control devices. The Army officially classifies such weapons as "non-conventional". Vernon Shisler, US Army delegate to NATO for non-conventional weapons, acknowledged that the various forms of directed energy weapons were available to the Department of Defense. Several people consider themselves to be on the receiving end of such non-lethal attacks. Often noted as subversive or generally unsympathetic to the government, they believe that they have been selected as guinea pigs because the state is suspicious of their motives in general. By choosing such people on which to experiment, the government is effectively killing two birds with one stone.

THE USUAL SUSPECTS
CIA
Many of the harassment campaigns and other actions attributed to the MW research systems are remarkably close to those laid at the CIA's door during MK-Ultra and MHCHAOS. With the collapse of Russia, the KGB is no threat, so the CIA is turning its attention to dealing with the "menaces" of civil rights and civil liberties advocates.

THE UNUSUAL SUSPECTS
Microsoft
Perhaps the least credible of all theories is that Microsoft is sponsoring the intelligence community in its mind-control experiments. Exactly why the software giant should be doing so remains unclear.

MOST CONVINCING EVIDENCE
From 1953 to 1976, the American Embassy in Moscow was bombarded with microwaves ranging in power from 2.5 to 4Ghz. Therefore, if there was nothing in it for them, why did the Russians maintain this programme for twenty-three years? Instead of warning their staff in the embassy, as one might reasonably expect, the American authorities thought this might be a good opportunity to study the effects of low-level microwaves on human beings. Consequently, in 1965, they instituted several new medical screenings of their embassy staff in Moscow and a close monitoring of all encryption operators' error-rates, in order to see if some kind of subliminal influence was at work.

In October 1965, Richard Cesaro of the Defence Advanced Research Projects Agency wrote to his boss in the Pentagon, Charles Herzfeld, to state that insufficient research was being conducted into "the subtle behavioural changes that may be evolved by a low-level electromagnetic field". Given the go-ahead to launch Project Pandora, Cesaro managed to prove conclusively that bombarding chimps with microwaves dramatically altered their normal behaviour and greatly reduced their task-completion abilities. He subsequently reported back to Herzfeld that "the potential of exerting a degree of control over human behaviour by low-level microwaves seems to exist".

If all this was but mumbo-jumbo, why were the Russians *still* playing the same game in 2017? Within days of Donald Trump's surprise victory in the US presidential election, the US Embassy in Havana came under a strikingly similar attack as that conducted in Moscow, except that this time the microwaves were augmented by sonic waves. As twenty-one diplomatic staff were repatriated, complaining of various forms of debilitation and disorientation, the Cubans issued a categorical denial of involvement which, if true, leaves only the Russians in play.

MOST MYSTERIOUS FACT
It has been suggested that MWs are being tested in conjunction with campaigns of harassment designed to destabilize the mental state of targets. It may be that microwave influence exerts a greater hold over a target when he or she is under pressure as a result of harassment. The Electronic Surveillance Project Association, privately founded to monitor and, where possible, to counteract harassment of civilians, claims to be in touch with a number of individuals being harassed in this manner. The victims report a wide range of disturbances, including sudden, unexplained hostility on the part of formerly friendly neighbours, unprovoked hostility and mockery from total strangers, petty burglaries, deteriorating health, sleep deprivation, vandalism of property, and hostility from the authorities such as police, doctors and lawyers.

SCEPTICALLY SPEAKING
In the wake of the microwave/sonic attack on America's Cuban Embassy, Kellyanne Conway – who is presently serving as Councillor to the President for Donald Trump (2017) – told *The Bergen Record* of her concerns over "microwave [ovens] that turn into cameras etc. – we know that that is just a fact of modern life". While there are some very well-founded concerns over increasingly "smart" televisions that, when linked up to the Internet, can be remotely turned "hostile" against their owners, Ms Conway's fears do seem a bridge too far – or are they? Perhaps best not to leave your bank account details in front of your microwave – just in case!

SUBLIMINAL MESSAGES

This is perhaps best described as the conspiracy that never was, or at least an illusion prompted by one man's bad translation and another's money-grabbing lie. It is nevertheless an interesting story, as the false claims for the powers of subliminal messaging are tightly linked to the inception of some very real and frightening events that rightly became the focus of conspiracy theorists.

After the cessation of American involvement in the Korean War in 1953, the United States was in a state of mass paranoia over imagined Chinese mind-controlling manipulation. At the heart of this paranoia lay the fact that, after the war, over 2,000 American POWs refused repatriation, opting instead for a new life in communist China. Unable to accept that these men might have taken such a decision quite voluntarily, Americans at large sought comfort in the "someone must have messed with their heads" position on the matter. Riding the coattails of this widespread fear, the ultra-right-wing journalist Edward Hunter re-published his forgotten flop of 1951 entitled *Brainwashing in Red China* to cash in on the prevailing mood. Although the first word of his title was a perhaps deliberately poor rendition of what the Chinese called "*szu-hsiang-kai-tsao*" – or re-education after mind cleansing – Hunter's invented term matched exactly what America preferred to believe had happened to their "Lost Boys".

This knee-jerk response, which in 1953 would give official sanction to the monster that would become MK-Ultra, also promoted the general fear that America's enemies had the ability to toy with others' minds. MK-Ultra was a CIA programme dedicated to finding ways of establishing mind-"kontrol" and perhaps creating their own host of "Manchurian Candidates". Hence, this was the stage onto which the market researcher James Vicary foisted himself in a desperate bid to save his failing marketing company, with outlandish claims of having invented subliminal messaging. It turned out to be an easy sell for him, as most people in America – from the President downwards – believed that such mind-manipulation/control was entirely possible.

In 1957, Vicary claimed to have paid the cinema in Fort Lee, New Jersey, to allow him to conduct his experiment across the six-week-run of their screening of the hit romcom *Picnic* (1955), starring William Holden and Kim Novak. A run as long as six weeks granted Vicary unseen access to a through-put of as many as 45,689 movie-goers. He claimed to have installed a tachistoscope in the projection-room so that he could flash messages onto the main screen, alternately telling the audience to drink Coke and eat popcorn. The subliminal messages were repeated on a five-second cycle throughout the first half of the screening, each message being flashed up for 1/3000th of a second. The speed of the flash, Vicary claimed, meant that the message was undetectable to the eye and the conscious brain. This allowed it to slip past everybody's defensive mechanisms – "who is telling me this and why should I do it?" etc. – but to nevertheless register on a subliminal level.

When Vicary further announced that the foyer sales of Coke and popcorn had increased by over 20 percent and 60 percent respectively, Madison Avenue opened its arms and wallets to Vicary and the chaps at MK-Ultra sat up and took note! Could this be the way to implant mission details and activation codes into the mind of the perfect operative? Someone who could resist all known interrogation methods as they themself were unaware they were a spy or an assassin, with a specific, targeted mission that they would carry out in a daze on hearing the trigger phrase? Equally impressed were the mainstream American political parties, who similarly pondered the use of subliminal messaging in their campaign broadcasts in order to influence voting patterns.

THE STRANGE PART

Believe it or not, nobody actually checked to see if James Vicary's claims were rooted in reality; his lie so perfectly squared with what everyone in America thought they already knew that he was taken at face value. When Stuart Rogers, a student of psychology at New York's Hofstra University, actually took the trouble to drive out to visit the cinema at Fort Lee, he quickly established that Vicary had never even been there. Furthermore, the cinema – which was typical of the small independent movie-house that was destined to be swept away by the multiplex – could not possibly have accommodated anything like the 45,000-plus clients that Vicary claimed had passed through its doors within six weeks. After all, the entire population of Fort Lee itself was then less than 25,000.

Although Vicary was forced to admit his lie in 1962, by then no one was listening; MK-Ultra, long gone "rogue", was busy dosing thousands of unsuspecting Americans with LSD in their efforts to render subjects more susceptible to subliminally implanted messages. Additionally, and despite the Voice of Reason screaming in the dark that subliminal messaging was a hoax, countless western countries passed hurriedly concocted legislation to make it illegal. Indeed, it remains so to this day in many different countries. Meanwhile, other governments and agencies closely scanned any and all adverts for "hidden messages" that could be considered subliminal. Needless to say, these paranoid monitors of public information found sexual or satanic references in everything from Proctor and Gamble soap advertisements to "reverse-speak" messages embedded in heavy metal records.

THE USUAL SUSPECTS
THE CIA/MK-Ultra
Soon becoming an autonomous programme that was completely unfettered by any outside control, MK-Ultra even went so far as to implement the notorious Operation Midnight Climax. This was a ploy in which they set up countless brothels on the west coast of America, dosed the clients with LSD and then tried to induce them with "piped" voices to go out and kill someone. MK-Ultra agents also took to the streets of American cities to harvest what they charmingly called "throwaways" – vagrants, teenagers on the run found in bus stations, and such like. They then immersed these poor souls in "sensory privation tanks", while keeping them dosed up with LSD. Here they bombarded their victims with violent film footage containing various subliminal messages, to see if any could be induced to dispassionately murder one of the others upon hearing some pre-embedded trigger phrase.

THE UNUSUAL SUSPECTS
Big Business
Throughout the 1970s and '80s, Wilson Bryan Key, an author with a PhD in communications, promoted himself to Americans as their sole protector against subliminal manipulation by big business and politicians. His first target was Nabisco Foods, which he claimed had arranged the tiny holes in their seemingly innocuous Ritz crackers so that they presented the word "sex". Everyone had a lot of fun looking for such a message in their cheese biscuits, but few ever found what they sought.

Key's next target was the soap manufacturing giant Proctor and Gamble. The monolithic company was then using the corporate image of an ageing man-in-the-moon with long hair and a beard – the ringlets of which Key claimed to contain the demonic number "666". Apart from the fact that the true Number of the Beast is actually 616 – this alleged subliminal and satanic message

was as difficult to spot as was the motif in Key's sex-crazed crackers.

When challenged by Proctor and Gamble about his outlandish allegations, Key simply nodded sagely and said that the esoteric nature of the message was what made it so effective. After spending a fortune in counter-claim promotions, the company eventually abandoned their man-in-the-moon logo in favour of the much safer "P&G".

MOST CONVINCING EVIDENCE
Wilson Key also scoured heavy metal music albums for hidden messages that he felt sure were responsible for what he saw as the aberrant behaviour of those who listened to them. In 1990, he was again in the subliminal spotlight when the British heavy metal band Judas Priest found itself the focus of a lawsuit. This was the only time that the effectiveness of subliminal messaging was tried in an American court. Back in 1985, teenagers Raymond Belknap and James Vance had spent the day of 23 December smoking dope and listening to Judas Priest albums, before staggering off to a local graveyard to commit suicide with a shotgun. Although readers who have endured the music of Judas Priest might consider such an outcome to be a blessed release, the boys' parents, encouraged by the publicity-hungry Key, mounted a $62m suit against the band in Reno, Nevada.

Appearing in court as an "expert witness" for the two boys' families, Key argued that Judas Priest's song "Better By You, Better by Me" contained "back-masked" messages instructing listeners to kill themselves. He also made the case that suicidal images and messages were embedded in the artwork of most Judas Priest album covers. However, after a circus trial, during which everyone present had to endure the group singing that number acapella and listen to various tracks being played backwards, Judge Jerry Carr Whitehead ruled there to be no evidence in support of the suit nor any evidence in support of any subliminal messaging.

MOST MYSTERIOUS FACT
Despite the very man who supposedly "invented" subliminal messaging having repeatedly avowed it to be a load of rubbish, a 2006 survey revealed that 98 per cent of the general public and 80 per cent of those working in advertising or teaching psychology still believe in the insidious power of subliminal messaging.

SCEPTICALLY SPEAKING
The last word on the subject is perhaps best left to Rob Halford, frontman for Judas Priest who, after the judgement in Reno said, "If I'd thought that sort of crap worked we would have embedded messages telling everyone to go buy more of our records."

CHAPTER 7:

<u>PLACES</u>

ANTARCTICA

Desolate but beautiful, Antarctica is a dangerous environment and an environment in danger. It is a place of massive contrasts, but the greatest contrast that this mysterious continent may yield is that our perception of it as being uninhabited might not be true. Conspiracy theorists believe the truth about who lives in Antarctica is being hidden from the public.

The antennae of conspiracy enthusiasts have been twitching in anticipation of some strange truth being revealed ever since information began to leak out concerning the exploration of the continent by Nazis with links to mystical orders, such as the Thule Gesellschaft, and Ahenerbe, the SS occult bureau.

When Admiral Byrd led a US military expedition force of more than 10,000 men to Antarctica in 1947, the mystery deepened. The force returned after just three months having suffered heavy losses on their mysterious mission. Even fifty years later, it is almost impossible to obtain any of the unclassified information concerning this inexplicable polar misadventure by the US military.

While debate rages over just who Admiral Byrd's men might have been fighting, most conspiracy theorists agree that underneath the ice of Antarctica is the remains of an advanced civilization destroyed by some great cataclysm. It is alleged that it is this fact that the Nazis stumbled upon and this fact that sinister forces are conspiring to keep secret from the rest of us.

THE STRANGE PART

Antarctica is governed by a treaty, signed by various powerful countries, that prevents any development or exploitation of its vast natural resources. Given that our governments do not generally have a good track record on defending the environment, this could be seen as a little curious. It has been suggested that the real purpose of the Antarctic Treaty is to eliminate the chance of any commercial organization stumbling on to the truth by digging through the two-mile thick crust of ice.

THE USUAL SUSPECTS
Nazis

In 1938, Nazi Germany made the most extensive survey of Antarctica to date, claimed it as their territory and renamed it Neuschwabenland. It is known that inner orders of the Nazi Party placed a special importance on Antarctica and that the Germans maintained a presence there throughout World War II. In 1946, German U-boats were spotted off the coast of Argentina heading towards the ice-bound continent.

Conjecture has it that elements of the German High Command escaped justice to set up a base among the ruins of a lost Antarctic civilization.

The Jason Society

The Jason Society was, apparently, set up by President Nixon, in 1973. A secret organisation, its ultra-classified purpose was to run a project called "Secret Earth", and some claim that it is the group charged with exploiting the remnants of an advanced civilization found beneath Antarctica and in one or two other locations across the globe. Unlike many other groups behind conspiracies, it seems that the Jason Society may have a semi-benevolent purpose for keeping us all in the dark over Antarctica. It is suggested that the Society's aim is to discover enough about the vanished Elder Race to prevent us from sharing their fate.

Also suspected: MJ-12; Project Phoenix; the US National Security Council; the United Nations; and a cabal of Freemasons.

THE UNUSUAL SUSPECTS
Ancient Space Aliens

If there are ruins of an ancient culture buried deep in Antarctica's forbidding wastes, some argue that it is of an alien and not human nature. They feel that the conspiracy has developed to prevent widespread knowledge of alien involvement in Earth's history.

The Knights Templar

If civilization was established in Egypt by survivors fleeing Antarctica following the catastrophe that covered it in ice, their knowledge of their original homeland may have been preserved in certain secret traditions. The Knights Templar trace their lineage to ancient Egypt, so they may have inherited this information. If this is true, they may wish to control Antarctica and exploit the advanced technology below its surface in order to further their plans for world domination.

MOST CONVINCING EVIDENCE

The single most startling piece of evidence that gives some weight to the conspiracy theory concerning Antarctica is the Piri Reis Map – a genuine document that was drawn up in Constantinople in 1513. It clearly shows not only the western coast of Africa and the eastern coast of South America, but also the ice-free coast of a country called Queen Maud Land.

Antarctica was not discovered until 1818, and the astonishing accuracy of the map was not revealed until the fifties, when ground-penetrating radar technology allowed geologists to see the land beneath the ice for the first time. The map was drawn up from earlier charts, but no one is able to offer a convincing explanation of how it can possibly show what it does. Other similar charts exist, suggesting there may be some truth to the idea Antarctica could be have once been home to the civilization that has become popularly known as Atlantis.

MOST MYSTERIOUS FACT

In 1998, a vast earthquake was reported to have occurred in Antarctica measuring up to 8.1 on the Richter scale. This fact hit global news services, preparations were made and the entire east coast of Australia was put on alert – the authorities feared it could be hit by a huge tidal wave. Medical authorities, the police and the army called the alert off when the expected tsunami did not arrive. What makes all of this mysterious is that there are no plates at the South Pole and there is, therefore, no logical explanation as to what could have caused such a massive quake.

SCEPTICALLY SPEAKING

There is very little scientific evidence for Antarctica having been ice-free enough to support a civilization at any point during the last 15 million years. No archaeological evidence has so far been found to suggest an advanced culture ever existed on the continent.

With less than 5cm (2 inches) of rain a year, Antarctica qualifies as a desert – the biggest in the world.

THE BERMUDA TRIANGLE

The Bermuda Triangle – also known by the more intimidating name of the Devil's Triangle – is an area of the Atlantic Ocean that is generally accepted to fall within a triangle formed by Bermuda, Puerto Rico and Fort Lauderdale, Florida.

The first mention of strange events occurring within the Bermuda Triangle is found in the fifteenth-century log of Christopher Columbus, who recorded that after "a great flame of fire" crashed out of the heavens and into the sea, his compass spun wildly as he and the crew saw strange lights in the sky.

During the following centuries, the area's grim reputation slowly grew until it finally came to the attention of conspiriologists in 1950, after the delightfully named Edward Van Winkle-Jones published a lengthy article that was syndicated worldwide by Associated Press. In the main, the piece concentrated on the now notorious disappearance of the US Navy Flight 19 on 5 December 1945 and those of two British South American Airways flights, *Star Tiger* and *Star Ariel*. Both Avro Tudor passenger liners, the former disappeared without trace on its way to Bermuda on 30 January 1948 and the latter on January 17, 1949, bound for Jamaica out of Bermuda. In all three cases, no trace of any wreckage or survivors was ever found.

However, it was and still is the disappearance of Flight 19 that springs to mind at the mention of the Bermuda Triangle. A total of 13 trainees, under the leadership of US Navy Lieutenant Charles Carroll Taylor, took off from Fort Lauderdale in five Avenger torpedo bombers, never to be seen again. Taylor had over 2,500 hours' experience in such planes and, although listed as trainees, none of his "flock" had less than 300 hours' experience, with 60 of those hours in Avengers. With the purpose of the exercise being advanced training in the procedures of dead reckoning, the four Avengers of the trainees had been stripped of their compasses; however, in accordance with standard safety procedures for such flights, Taylor's plane was equipped with two compasses – not that they did him any good.

In one of his last radio contacts with the ground, Taylor, in something of a panic, reported that "Both my compasses are out!" and that he *thought* he might be over the Florida Keys but that he could not be sure. All radio contact was soon lost. Just to fuel the mystery further, a Mariner Flying Boat, also with a crew of 13, was sent from what is now Florida's Patrick Air Force Base to look for Flight 19 and that, too, disappeared

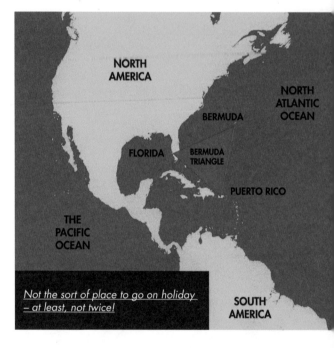

Not the sort of place to go on holiday – at least, not twice!

without trace. And so it continued with dozens of planes and ships, both large and small, seemingly swallowed up in what was originally called the Devil's Triangle.

THE STRANGE PART

No wreckage from Flight 19 was ever recovered – despite a massive search – which suggests that something more than a mysterious five-plane crash or ditching into the sea is involved. The fact that absolutely no sign of any remains was spotted is typical of the disappearances said to occur in the Bermuda Triangle, where even massive ships vanish without a trace and without sending a distress call. Of course, conspiracy theorists believe that the authorities know that something mysterious is going on and have attempted to cover it up.

THE USUAL SUSPECTS
Aliens
Aliens top the list of those conjectured to be behind the disappearances in the Triangle and the need for the truth to be covered up. It is alleged that an alien race – probably those nasty little Greys – have an underwater base in the area of the Triangle. There are certainly plenty of reports of UFOs rising out of and diving into the ocean near Puerto Rico. As our unwelcome visitors have a thing about their privacy, they tend to dispose of anyone who crosses over into what they regard as their territory.

North American Air Defense Command
Extra-terrestrials are not the only ones alleged to have undersea bases in the Bermuda Triangle. Some conspiracy theorists hold to the idea that the North American Air Defense Command, also known by the acronym NORAD, has a vast submerged complex running ultra-secret technology that interferes with the signals that aeroplanes and boats rely on for navigation. If any plane or ship spots evidence of the NORAD base, they are meant to be "vanished" by the US military.

Also suspected: MJ-12; United Nations; and the ancient alien space deities Cthulhu and Yog-So-goth.

THE UNUSUAL SUSPECTS
Chrononauts
Some feel it is not the Greys behind the missing pilots, sailors and passengers, but humans from the far future travelling back in time. The Chrononauts of this hypothesis take advantage of a gravitational time-space anomaly in the area to gather living evidence of the past. Of course, if anyone uncovers this fact, the Chrononauts can travel back into the past to change the timeline and prevent the evidence from being discovered.

Atlantean Ruins
Conjecture has been made that the Bermuda Triangle is situated above the sunken remnants of the ancient civilisation of Atlantis. The reason why so many ships and planes have vanished is that, buried among the supposed ruins of Atlantis, are huge crystals emitting powerful, random beams of energy. It is this energy that zaps unfortunate craft passing overhead. One or two even believe that some Atlanteans themselves remain below the waves and are actually responsible for the disappearances.

MOST CONVINCING EVIDENCE
Aside from the disappearance of more than fifty ships and twenty planes in the Triangle during the last century, and the fact that it is one of only two places on Earth where a magnetic compass does not point to true north, there is other evidence of strange goings on. Carolyn Casico, a licensed pilot, flew a charter flight to Turk Island in the Triangle. When she was seen flying over the island, Carolyn was heard over her radio, saying, "I don't understand. This should be Grand Turk but there is nothing there. The shape is right but this island looks uninhabited." She circled the island a few times before heading out to sea and vanishing.

MOST MYSTERIOUS FACT
Nor, it seems, is the Triangle's appetite yet sated. On 30 September 2015, the 791-ft (241-m) container ship, the SS *El Faro*, put out of Jacksonville in Florida, bound for Puerto Rico, as a storm developed hundreds of miles to the north of its charted course. Unexpectedly, the storm suddenly intensified beyond the expectation of all monitors and, as if possessed of some malevolent intent, the now-designated Hurricane Joaquin made a beeline for the *El Faro*. Having completely engulfed her, the storm mysteriously retraced its own path to its original position. However, the ship was no longer anywhere to be seen.

SS *El Faro* was eventually found – 15,000ft (4,572m) below the surface. She was sitting in one piece and upright on the bottom, as if she had simply dropped through the water, keel-first. Despite extensive searches conducted by submersibles and un-manned drones, not a single member of the crew was found, either on the ship or anywhere around her on the seabed.

SCEPTICALLY SPEAKING
At the end of the day, the area enclosed within the Bermuda Triangle not only plays host to a lot of surface and air traffic, but it also experiences some extremely hostile currents and highly localized storms of considerable intensity. On top of that, dedicated "Triangleurs" keep re-defining the area to bring all sorts of events into their fold; even the famed *Mary Celeste*, found adrift and crewless off the Azores – more than 2,000 miles away – is hailed by some to be a victim of the Bermuda Triangle. Give the conspiriologists enough time, and Loch Ness will eventually find itself within the Triangle! The greatest mystery of all is that the area was originally designated The Bermuda Rectangle – but then one of its sides suddenly disappeared without trace!

THE HOLLOW EARTH

There should be nothing more solid and dependable than the very surface of the Earth we walk upon, but many researchers in the conspiracy field believe that the interior of the Earth is populated by several bizarre groups. They feel that below a 1,000-mile-thick crust the Earth is hollow and illuminated by an inner sun.

It has long been felt that the entrance to the strange subterranean world of the hollow Earth is to be found at the poles. Everything, from the spectacular light displays known as Aurora Borealis and Aurora Australis – a side-effect of the inner sun – to gravitational and radio anomalies, has been cited in support of this idea. It is also known that some Eskimo tribes claim that they originated from much further north – from a warm land with perpetual daylight.

FLYING SAUCERS
MYSTERIES OF THE SPACE AGE
JUNE, 1970 - - - Issue No. 69
WISCO 75¢

FIRST PHOTOS OF THE HOLE AT THE POLE !
Satellites ESSA - 3 and ESSA -7 Penetrate Cloud Cover!
Mariners Also Photograph Martian Polar Opening!

A NASA photograph from 1970 showing the hole at the North Pole.

Some theorists believe that the hollow nature of Earth has been known by the initiates of some secret societies from the dawn of history. These organizations have been manipulating the scientific community and people in power so that the rest of us remain convinced that nothing lies below the Earth's surface other than rock, some patches of oil, and a molten core. It is a fact that the inner teachings of more than one secret society claim that the Earth is hollow, lit by a central sun, populated with an advanced race and connected to the outer Earth by a serious of tunnels. Have these secret societies been engaged in a plot to hoodwink us to the true nature of our planet?

THE STRANGE PART

Despite the full weight of the scientific community, the idea that the Earth is hollow and could be populated has never been totally quashed. Every few years another scientist breaks ranks and risks the wrath of academia and the end of his career by investigating the theory. The amount of scorn and ridicule these poor fellows are subjected to seems out of all proportion if the hollow Earth is only an invalid, crank idea.

THE USUAL SUSPECTS
Nazis
It is well known that many high-ranking Nazis totally believed in the fact that the Earth was hollow. It is recorded that, in the thirties, Nazi expeditions were sent to Antarctica and Tibet to try and find a way to contact people living under the Earth. Indeed, Herman Goering even conducted rocket experiments based on the theory. Some people believe the theory that members of the Thule Gesellschaft and other Nazis escaped into the hollow Earth at the end of the war and have established colonies there. Obviously, the authorities need to prevent this frightening information from becoming known to the public.

Aliens
Alien races, ranging from the well-known Greys to the less-exposed, Aryan-looking species nicknamed the Nordics, and the Orions (reptilians behind most of Earth's walking serpent

The Aurora Borealis, believed by some to be proof that the earth is in fact hollow.

legends) are all alleged to have bases in the Earth's interior. Our governments are reported to be aware of this, but are powerless to act against the extra terrestrials and so keep the rest of us ignorant of their presence.

THE UNUSUAL SUSPECTS
Terras

According to Dr Raymond Bernard – who acquired his PhD from New York University in 1932 – the Earth is hollow and its internal space is populated by the Terras. Members of this race of 12-foot-tall beings are purported to have descended from the original Atlanteans, to live on a diet of uncooked vegetables and to fly UFOs when they journey to the surface. Dr Bernard formed a colony in Ecuador for people who shared his beliefs that the authorities were suppressing the truth about the hollow Earth and the friendly Terras who want no more than to save humanity from an impending nuclear holocaust.

Deros

First identified in reports made by a decidedly odd fellow named Richard Shaver in the Forties, the Deros is one of several races that inhabit the hollow interior of the Earth. In Shaver's worldview, the Deros are descended from the original alien inhabitants of the Earth who were forced to live underground by the consequences of a solar disaster that took place twelve thousand years ago. The Deros are masters of a superior technology that can control the minds of men and is used to enforce a conspiracy of silence about their subterranean world. Apart from a desire to prevent the truth concerning the hollow Earth coming out, the Deros also seem to have an unhealthy interest in surface-dwelling woman and sadistic sexual practices.

MOST CONVINCING EVIDENCE

Legends concerning underground kingdoms and the creatures that live within them have appeared as part of almost every culture over the last six thousand years, but it still seems odd – to say the least – that more than one government has invested funds in investigating the idea that the Earth is hollow. In the nineteenth century, the US government first sent American military hero Captain John Cleves Symes to the South Pole to find an entrance into the hollow Earth and establish a colony there. Before World War II, it is known that Nazi Germany sent out more than one exploratory team in search of a way into the alleged world below. It is also rumoured that Admiral Byrd's mysterious military expedition to Antarctica in 1947 had more than a passing interest in the Hollow Earth theory.

MOST MYSTERIOUS FACT

On 25 November 1912, American researcher and author Marshall B. Gardner submitted an application to the United States Patent Office to obtain a patent on the theory that the Earth was hollow. Eighteen months later, after suitable bureaucratic delay, paperwork and investigation, the US government decided to grant Gardner the United States patent 1096102: The Hollow Earth Theory. This is probably the first time that a conspiracy theory was ever officially endorsed by a patent.

SCEPTICALLY SPEAKING

Short on anything resembling hard evidence and strong on the Too Bizarre To Believe factor, the hollow Earth conspiracy theory fails to stand up to the combined weight of established geology, history, cosmology and common-sense. If entrances to the hollow Earth existed, modern satellites would have spotted them.

MONTAUK POINT, NEW YORK

Many conspiracy theories earn the tag TBTB – Too Bizarre To Believe – and Montauk certainly has a strong claim to this label. Labyrinthine, truly mind-boggling and with an incredible scope, the Montauk machinations and weirdness were first brought to light by the pioneering work of journalist Peter Moon and two people who had been involved in the strange goings-on at Montauk – Preston Nichols and Alfred Bielek.

The conspiracy surrounds Camp Hero – officially, a deserted Air Force Station at Montauk Point on Long Island, New York State. Camp Hero was a US Army base established before World War II. It later became the Montauk Air Force base and was officially active until 1969. However, since then new telephone lines and high-capacity power lines have been installed and many witnesses have observed advanced military electronics equipment being tested in the area. Power usage for the derelict facility is measured with a gigawatt meter, which means it consumes enough power to run a small city.

Conspiracy theories suggest that the subterranean levels of this base continue to house a centre for research and experimentation into electromagnetic mind-control as well as manipulations of time and other dimensions. These experiments date back to 1943 and the infamous "Philadelphia Experiment", when Albert Einstein and Hungarian-born physicist Janus Eric Von Neumann worked on US government experiments that ripped holes in the fabric of reality during attempts to make a Navy vessel invisible to radar.

It is alleged that during the Philadelphia Experiment a battleship disappeared from sight and from our normal timeline. When it reappeared, the crew onboard had suffered devastating psychological damage and underwent terrible physical repercussions. Some sailors rematerialized in the hull of the ship or suffered third-degree burns. After the war, Montauk, and other associated bases and laboratories in the Long Island area continued research into what sounds like the most outlandish science fiction. When a US Congressional investigation into these secret projects decided to shut them down in the sixties, it was not just the base that was underground. Montauk continued to run without governmental approval, receiving its funding from mysterious sources.

THE STRANGE PART

In 1984, the officially empty Montauk Air Force Base was given to New York State for use as public parkland. Even though the property is under the care of the New York State Parks System, no part of it has ever been opened as a park. Significantly, the deeds transferring the base to New York State make it explicit that the US government still holds all rights to any and all property beneath the surface. Given that plans from the US Army Corps of Engineers provide evidence of the existence of at least four levels of subterranean facilities beneath Camp Hero, maybe there is something to the conspiracy buff's claims of a massive underground centre conducting research at the borders of established science.

THE USUAL SUSPECTS
National Security Council

It is often alleged that Montauk is actually run by an inner cabal of the National Security Council of the US. All of the members of the cabal are also thought to be members of the Grand Orient Lodge of Egyptian Freemasonry who are using the advances made through research carried out at Montauk to further their ultimate aim of global domination.

Aleister Crowley

Possibly the most important occultist of the century, self-styled "wickedest man in the world" Crowley is known to have visited the Montauk area of Long Island shortly after the end of World War I, in which he had been acting as an intelligence officer. Quite what his interest in Montauk was is open to speculation, but it is worth noting that his pupils included groundbreaking scientists such as Jack Parsons – the man behind NASA's Jet Propulsion Laboratories, and an associate of Janus Eric Von Neumann.

THE UNUSUAL SUSPECTS
Nazi Scientists

Nazi submarines were often spotted off Montauk during the war and many Nazi scientists went to work for the American military after the conflict finally ended. Montauk has had a large Aryan community since the thirties and some conspiracy theorists believe that the experiments at Montauk were infiltrated and taken over by ex-Nazis, with a view to using the awesome powers that are being developed to further their own evil schemes.

Time Travellers

Given that many of the experiments at Montauk seem to involve time travel, some feel it is fair to assume that the real force behind the conspiracy are time travellers from the future. Stranded, in what is to them the past, they have taken over the experiments started by Einstein and Von Neumann in the hope that they can build a machine to take them back to their home time.

MOST CONVINCING EVIDENCE

For what is officially claimed to be merely a derelict military facility, within a designated state park, there seems to be a lot of security around Camp Hero. Picnicking women and children have been accosted and threatened at gunpoint by unidentified military personnel for venturing into its vicinity. Other people wandering through the park near to the supposedly abandoned Air Force Station have been told they have violated top-secret and restricted areas, and could be arrested. Non-uniformed armed guards from seemingly shadowy government and military agencies have a track record of performing some very unconstitutional activities in the area. If there is no conspiracy at Montauk why is this happening?

MOST MYSTERIOUS FACT

The land that the Montauk Air Force Base is built on – and possibly under – should, under the terms of American law, belong to the Montauk tribe of Native Americans, who were the original inhabitants of the area. Despite huge amounts of evidence to the contrary, the US Federal Court has declared the Montauk tribe extinct in order to prevent the remainder of the tribe claiming the land. It should be noted that the Montauk Indians record numerous strange legends concerning the area, and can remember when the site of Camp Hero was actually home to an ancient and rather odd stone pyramid.

Crowley: a spy during World War I and the man responsible for the V for Victory campaign during World War II.

SCEPTICALLY SPEAKING

While there's plenty of fascinating conjecture, there's little independent, hard evidence to back up some of the wilder aspects of the Montauk conspiracy. It seems understandable that the US government – or dark forces within it – might test ultra-advanced technology at a secret base, but when there are places such as Area 51, there is no logical need to operate out of a base that's only 100 miles from New York City.

THE MYSTERY OF OAK ISLAND

Tiny Oak Island, located in Nova Scotia, Canada, has been called many things over the last two hundred years: the Money Pit; a cleverly protected trove of pirate treasure; and a death trap.

In 1795, 16-year-old Daniel McGinnis was exploring the island when he discovered a depression beneath an ancient oak tree. Thinking that it looked as if someone had just dug a hole and refilled it, McGinnis enlisted the aid of two friends, and they began to dig, sure they were about to discover glittering piles of pirate treasure.

Four feet into the earth, they came across a layer of flagstones. At a depth of ten feet, they encountered a platform constructed of oak logs, embedded in the shaft walls. Another ten feet down, the boys encountered another oak platform, discovering yet another at a depth of thirty feet underground. Since the logs were impossible to remove, the boys abandoned the project.

With capital provided by Simeon Lynds, an affluent businessman who had enticed investors to finance a proper excavation of the pit, the boys returned in 1803. Digging deeper, they encountered more oak platforms, but also found something that was far more interesting: a large, flat stone with cryptic lettering etched across it. A later translation of this mysterious cipher yielded this message: "Forty feet below two million pounds are buried".

Moving past the stone, the excited workmen then ran into the problem that has plagued Oak Island excavations ever since: water. While the shaft had been dry up to this point, water began slowly seeping through the soil. It became so

Is the treasure of notorious pirate Captain William Kidd at the heart of the Oak Island conspiracy?

bad that the workers were removing two buckets of water for every bucket of earth. At a depth of 98 feet, the crew hit what sounded like yet another oak platform, but since the day was coming to an end, they stopped work. Returning to their work the next morning, the treasure hunters were horrified to find that the pit had filled up with water.

Undeterred, they dug another shaft 14 feet to the side of the water-filled Money Pit. Digging down 110 feet, they attempted to create a side tunnel towards the original shaft and reach the hoped-for treasure that way. Two feet away from their goal, however, water once again poured through the walls of the side tunnel. Soon, the new shaft was as waterlogged as the first. Lynds's team gave up shortly thereafter.

In 1849, another crew attempted the Money Pit, armed this time with a horse-powered mining drill. They discovered more layers of wood, and for the first time, layers of loose metal. They also discovered what looked like bits of an old watch chain. Sure that the Pit contained chests of treasure, they pushed forth, but were once again foiled by water pouring into the shaft. Curious as to where the water was coming from, the crew excavated the nearby beach, making a startling discovery. They found a system of five carefully constructed drains that fed water into a sump and then down a 500-foot tunnel directly into the Money Pit. Digging below the 90-foot mark broke a hydraulic seal in the pit, causing water to run into it at a rate of 600 gallons a minute. Since the water was coming directly from the ocean, it was absolutely impossible to drain. Disheartened, the crew gave up.

Over the years, several expeditions have tried to pierce Oak Island's mystery, including such celebrities as Franklin Roosevelt, Errol Flynn and John Wayne. More mysteries were unveiled, including cement vaults, bits of cryptic parchment, and hidden caverns dug to the north of the original pit.

Six people have died trying to unlock the mystery of Oak Island, but to this day, she jealously guards her secrets.

THE STRANGE PART
In 1971, when a camera was sent down Borehole-10X, a shaft sunk to the north of the original pit, it encountered a hideous sight in a newly discovered underwater cavern. Floating in the dark, silt-laden water was a human hand, apparently cut off at the wrist.

THE USUAL SUSPECTS
Captain William Kidd
The infamous pirate, Captain Kidd, apparently littered the world with hidden piles of treasure. Several stories of Kidd's treasure seem to point towards Oak Island.

The Spanish
One theory states that a damaged Spanish galleon, loaded with treasure, may have stopped off at Oak Island to effect repairs and store its cargo of treasure, safe from pirate attack, so that it could be picked up later on the voyage back to Spain.

Francis Bacon
Since no original manuscripts have been found of Shakespeare's plays, many argue that the Bard's dramas were written by none other than Francis Bacon. Bacon may have buried the incriminating plays on Oak Island, to be discovered in the future.

Also suspected: the Vikings; the French and/or the British colonial troops.

THE UNUSUAL SUSPECTS
The Inca and Maya
To avoid plundering by Europeans in the seventeenth and eighteenth centuries, the Inca and Maya, aided by compassionate Europeans, may have moved some treasures north to Oak Island.

The Knights Templar
Fleeing persecution in Europe, the Knights may have spirited away the Holy Grail to Oak Island for safekeeping. There are two pieces of evidence in support of this. First, a formation of rocks on the island, when connected by lines drawn on a map, form a giant Christian cross 250 metres long. Secondly, Henry Sinclair, a suspected Knight, arrived in the area in 1398.

MOST CONVINCING EVIDENCE
The ingenious engineering of drains and hydraulic seals seems to indicate something valuable is indeed buried there.

MOST MYSTERIOUS FACT
In 1970, an investment group called the Triton Alliance commissioned a geological study of Oak Island. That report has, mysteriously, never been made public.

SCEPTICALLY SPEAKING
Just how did the original architects of Oak Island plan to retrieve their treasure? Obviously, they didn't. And why advertise it with engraved stones? Doesn't that defeat the purpose of hiding it in the first place?

DENVER, COLORADO

Denver International Airport is usually only noteworthy for being the most important airport in the US State of Colorado, so it seems a very unlikely setting for a globe-spanning conspiracy.

However, in recent years many conspiriologists have been researching its possible mysteries, in the belief that solving them may help expose the existence of the New World Order, the destruction of the Earth by comet impact, and the true nature of the MJ-12 organization. So far they have only provided concrete evidence that the airport also houses a massive and mysterious underground complex.

Certainly, the airport has a wealth of occult and conspiratorial symbolism within its design: its runways seem to form swastika patterns, and its numerous murals are truly mind-boggling – one shows the destruction of city and forest while a small girl holds a Mayan Tablet predicting the end of the world. The most bizarre is an image of the mystical Nazi symbol of the Black Sun, which is in the floor of the airport's Great Hall. Any conspiracy theorist with knowledge of Freemasonry can tell you that "The Great Hall" is an important Masonic term – which may help explain why the Hall also features a Masonic Capstone.

Some feel it is very significant that Air Force Space Command is stationed at the Schriever Air Force Base close to Denver International Airport. Among the publicly acknowledged duties of Air Force Space Command is the control of the Milstar satellite communications system, which links mobile ground forces, ships, submarines and aircraft together to create a unified fighting force of incredible power. It is also responsible for other satellites that orbit the earth at altitudes of more than 23,000 miles and communicate on super-high frequencies. It is possible that this satellite network will allow forces across the world to be controlled effectively in the event of either a nuclear war or a global catastrophe.

Air Force Space Command also runs the Defense Support Program satellites, which are a key part of North America's early warning system. However, instead of purely detecting missile launches, space launches and nuclear detonations, Space Command may also provide early warning of UFOs and comets approaching Earth. It is rumoured that Denver was chosen as the base for Space Command because computer models show that its position and high altitude make it the perfect area to create safe underground buildings capable of resisting any type of disaster.

THE STRANGE PART

There was a lot of opposition to the building of the Denver International Airport from people in the locality. Officials high up in the Clinton administration became heavily involved in the project and they seem to have used their influence to ensure that the airport was built. Furthermore, the CIA may have stuck its nose in – Rodney Stitch, the author of Defrauding America, has claimed to have access to a tape showing a CIA agent paying the mayor of Denver to get the airport built. Why was this top-level pressure applied to build the airport and its underground bunker system?

THE USUAL SUSPECTS
The New World Order

Even before the bizarre details of the construction of Denver International Airport began to surface, rumours in the conspiracy field suggested that when the New World Order was established America would be split into two administrative divisions – the Eastern Sector and the Western Sector. The control centre for the Eastern Sector was to be based in Atlanta and the Western Sector's control centre would be located in Denver. To conspiriologists, this just makes the wording "New World Airport Commission" on the Masonic capstone of the airport even more ominous.

The Freemasons

It is hard to doubt that Denver International Airport is heavy with Masonic imagery, which leads some conspiracy researchers to believe that the obvious answer to the mysteries must lie with the Freemasons. As the Masons in America have a long history of constructing buildings and even whole cities packed with secret Masonic messages, they may have designed the airport as a form of subliminal propaganda to demonstrate their ownership of the building and its associated underground complex.

THE UNUSUAL SUSPECTS
NASA

One of the more paranoid conspiracy theories about Denver is that NASA, working in conjunction with the National Security Agency and Air Force Space Command,

A strange place to site a conspiracy, but Denver International Airport may hide clues to the dark plans of the New World Order.

has built the underground complex at the airport. It is part of Orpheus – NASA's project to build a network of underground bunkers so that a chosen few can survive the disastrous comet impact that NASA predicts will hit the Earth in a few years' time. The murals were incorporated as a subtle warning to the rest of us as to the nature of our gruesome fate – death from above or slavery when the forces of NASA, NSA and Space Command take control of the globe in the aftermath of the disaster.

Queen Elizabeth II

David Icke's *The Biggest Secret* (1999) seems to be solely responsible for promoting the myth that "E-Lizard-Beth" II has been systematically buying up Denver through "stalking-horse" companies to obscure her interest in the location. This same book – and many other sources too – says that she also owns one-sixth of the land-surface of the planet but this is playing with the figures: it is the British Crown, not the incumbent monarch, which controls those lands, albeit nominally.

That said, Elizabeth II does indeed own land in the USA but does so openly and under her own name as a private individual. She has financial interests in horse-racing establishments and stud farms in Kentucky and also owns – as Elizabeth Windsor, not Queen Elizabeth II – some prime chunks of Park Avenue in New York and a $9m "flat" in a "glass tower" at Turtle Bay, opposite the United Nations complex in the same city – but not so

much as a blade of grass in Denver, nor indeed within the State of Colorado per se.

MOST CONVINCING EVIDENCE

The artists who created the weird airport murals allegedly admitted that they had been asked to design them to incorporate specific themes and images. The person responsible for their commission is rumoured to have been Wilma Webb, wife of the mayor of Denver, who conducted a Masonic dedication of the airport and was subsequently appointed by President Clinton to the Department of Labour.

MOST MYSTERIOUS FACT

The site of Denver International Airport was originally an American Indian burial ground. The mayor of Denver had to meet with Indian elders and a shaman to appease the spirits of their ancestors. The "tent-like" terminal structure was also designed to appease possible anger from the Indian spirits.

SCEPTICALLY SPEAKING

Underground bunkers are not an uncommon part of emergency forward planning and there is no reason why one should not be built at an airport. No self-respecting secret society planning world domination would base itself under an airport in constant daily use by thousands of people and then advertise its existence via extensive use of cryptic symbols.

THE PENTAGON

The Pentagon is one of those buildings that everyone has heard of and everyone recognizes immediately. Home to the US Department of Defense – the body that controls the strongest armed force that this globe has ever seen – it is a striking piece of architecture perceived worldwide as a symbol of American might.

Was there more than simple terrorism behind the attack on the Pentagon on 9/11?

It is for this very reason that at 9:43a.m. on 11 September 2001, terrorists crashed American Airlines Flight 77 into the Pentagon. By using a Boeing 757 to punch a hole in one of its famous five sides, they were symbolically making a massive tear into the very notion of American security and military superiority.

The building itself has lent its name to the US military machine, a name that is almost synonymous with conspiracy. From rumours of military constructed UFOs to germ warfare experiments performed unwittingly on American citizens, the Pentagon has become a byword for dark designs and grotesque, secret plots. Its place in the conspiracy field has even permeated through to the mainstream entertainment media. In Steven Spielberg's blockbuster movie *Raiders of the Lost Ark,* it became the repository for the Ark of the

Covenant, while from the first episode of *The X-Files*, it has been the base from which Fox Mulder's nemesis in the global conspiracy – Cigarette Smoking Man – operates.

Home to more than 29,000 military and civilian employees, the Pentagon is a city within the capital city of Washington, DC. The official story is that the Pentagon building was the idea of Brigadier General Brehon B. Somervell, Chief of the Construction Division of the US Army. He came up with it in the summer of 1941, allegedly as a temporary solution to problems posed by the rapidly expanding War Department and a shortage of space. The Pentagon was also designed to bring the Department's 24,000 personnel, who were then scattered among 17 different buildings in Washington, under one roof.

The only reason admitted by the military for the building's unique five-sided construction was that the original site chosen for the Pentagon was a tract of land known as Arlington Farms. As five roadways bordered the site, this supposedly dictated the concept of a pentagonal building. However, the President himself – Franklin Delano Roosevelt – decided that the building be moved three-quarters of a mile downriver to a new location known as Hell's Bottom, where the final design of an open-air pentagram surrounded by five concentric pentagonal rings traversed by ten corridor spokes was implemented.

Some conspiriologists believe that the structure itself is more than the headquarters of the US national defence establishment and the nerve centre for the command and control of the world's strongest military force. Where others see only thousands of tons of steel and concrete that go to make up one of the world's largest office buildings, conspiracy buffs have spotted links between the building's odd shape and ancient secret societies and their plots to subjugate America and the rest of the globe.

THE STRANGE PART

It is on record that President Franklin D. Roosevelt did not like or approve of the design of the Pentagon, yet he was helpless to prevent it being built the way it was. If the President of the US cannot stop a building from being erected, what mighty force was controlling its design and construction?

THE USUAL SUSPECTS
The Freemasons

It has long been established that Washington, DC was laid out to a Masonic groundplan. Its elaborate geometry was even modified by the well-known high-degree Freemasons and founding fathers of America – Thomas Jefferson and George Washington. Given that the five-pointed star is a very important Masonic symbol, several conspiriologists have suggested that the Pentagon also has Masonic origins. They claim it was designed as both a Masonic temple and a sign of Masonic control over the US and its military.

Satanists

The Devil and his human minions are no longer the main force behind conspiracies – as they were in the witch-burning days when America was founded. Even so, fundamentalist Christian conspiracy theorists still detect the Devil's hand at work in the design of the Pentagon. For evidence they point towards the fact that for centuries the five-sided star has been a symbol used in the worship of Satan. It comes as no surprise to find that some believe the Devil inspired his secret army of followers to create the Pentagon as his base of operations on Earth. They also feel that the original name of the marsh it was built on – Hell's Bottom – is significant.

THE UNUSUAL SUSPECTS
Nazi Occultists

There is some circumstantial evidence to suggest that notable German Nazi scientists such as Werner Von Braun were working on secret projects in the US in 1938. It is also rumoured that they were in contact with an occult underground, which contained amazing characters like Jack Parsons – a follower of Aleister Crowley and the world's first solid-fuel-rocket scientist. Some conspiracy theories have it that secret occult orders infiltrated the US military and forced it to build the Pentagon. When Operation Paperclip brought more than 400 Nazi scientists and thousands of assistants to the US after the end of World War II, the Nazi occult take-over of the US military was complete. Nazi scientists could rule supreme from their specially designed headquarters.

MJ-12

Every organization – even one as powerful and ultra-secret as MJ-12 – needs a base from which to operate. Some believe that MJ-12 pre-dates the Roswell crash and was operating under a different name via the US military before World War II. They also feel that the Pentagon was specially designed because the mathematical properties of the Phi-ratio make it the perfect shape for sending and receiving messages in hyperspace.

MOST CONVINCING EVIDENCE

Even at the time of its construction, there was a degree of speculation about the symbolism inherent in the Pentagon's five-sided shape. Many noted that it has not only five sides, but the five points needed to construct a five-sided star – a design that has huge significance in almost every occult and mystic tradition. The five-pointed star contains the Phi-ratio, and the Pythagoreans – an ancient cult based around the study of mathematics – claimed that a pentagon held the secret of all life and reflected the "divine design" that orders and controls the universe. All of which makes you wonder why the normally conservative US military adopted such a radical, symbolic design, especially when it cost $83 million to build in a time of war.

MOST MYSTERIOUS FACT

It takes exactly seven minutes to walk between any two points in the Pentagon. In the mystical study of numbers and their relationship to the physical world, seven is the number of perfection and is symbolic of control over both spiritual and mortal realms.

SCEPTICALLY SPEAKING

Sometimes a building is just a building. The Pentagon is not the only controversially designed office block in the world. If it were not the home of the US military and countless conspiracies, it would probably not attract any significant speculation.

THE SPHINX

The Great Sphinx of Egypt first became an icon of the Western world when Napoleon's soldiers "rediscovered" it in 1798. Ever since that time it has exerted an intense fascination upon many of the people who have studied its enigmatic gaze.

An air of mystery has always surrounded the statue that has the body of a male lion and the head of a human. Conspiracy theorists have not been the only ones to speculate on its true age, meaning and the hidden chambers it is supposed to be watching over.

Located on the Giza plateau, six miles to the west of Cairo, the Sphinx faces due East, a short distance from the trio of famous large pyramids. Carved from a relatively soft, natural limestone that outcrops on the Giza Plateau, the Sphinx was generally believed to have been made some time after 2540BCE. Recently, noted geologist Robert Schock and Egyptologist John Anthony West have agreed that weathering patterns on the Sphinx are consistent with water erosion rather than erosion produced by wind and sand. The only time this water erosion could have occurred was around ten thousand years ago when Egypt's climate was temperate and damp. Not surprisingly, the idea that the Sphinx could be ten thousand years old has been attacked by orthodox Egyptologists, who would look very stupid and have to rewrite every book on the subject if West and Schock are correct.

Suppression of evidence by the archaeological establishment is not the only conspiracy in which the Sphinx features. Many of the mystical traditions which underpin secret societies such as the Freemasons, speak of chambers under the front paws of the Sphinx, that contain a Hall of Records placed there by survivors of an Elder civilization. In the Forties, famous American psychic Edgar Cayce predicted that by the end of the Nineties someone would discover this Hall of Records.

Conspiracy theorists naturally became excited when workers restoring the Sphinx located a doorway in its side; in 1995, a team renovating an area near the Sphinx uncovered a series of tunnels that seemed to go under the Sphinx. John Anthony West's team used seismograph technology that detected hollow, regularly shaped chambers a few metres below ground between the paws and to either side of the Sphinx. It looked as if the conspiriologists' belief, that secret societies had held knowledge of an underground complex at Giza for centuries, was about to be proved correct.

THE STRANGE PART

A team from Florida State University undertook a survey around the Sphinx during April 1996 and found "rooms and tunnels" in front of it. Several other teams working on similar projects have made claims that back this up – including a team from Waseda University in Tokyo that found proof of a tunnel orientated north-south under the Sphinx. With all this material in support of an underground complex on the Giza Plateau, it is odd that the Egyptian authorities banned any excavation of the chambers or even further public remote sensing studies. Is there a conspiracy to suppress an outstanding truth that lies buried below the Sphinx?

THE USUAL SUSPECTS
Masonic Egyptologists

The Grand Orient Lodge of Egyptian Freemasonry teaches, at its highest degrees, that the wisdom and traditions of the lodge come from Atlantean survivors. Members believe the Atlanteans built the Sphinx in pre-history and later founded the Egyptian civilization. Clearly, the Grand Orient Lodge is a centuries-old organization with a powerful reach. Many believe it controls a network of Masonic Egyptologists who ruthlessly try to suppress the truth about the origins of the Sphinx and any secrets that it may hold.

National Security Agency

The American National Security Agency (NSA) is known to have used the services of remote viewers – psychics with the ability to see what is at any given point in the world after being given a map reference – via the Stanford Research Institute (SRI). Given the prominent SRI role in investigating the Sphinx, some conspiracy theorists conclude that the NSA has taken an interest in the possible secrets, from a lost civilization, that lie below the rock of the Giza Plateau. Perhaps the NSA wants to be the first to exploit those secrets when the Hall of Records is secretly opened and its knowledge recovered.

THE UNUSUAL SUSPECTS
NASA

Many of those who have been involved in the official investigation of the Sphinx have strong links to NASA, such as former NASA consultants Dr James Hurtak and Richard Hoagland – a noted UFO conspiriologist. Hoagland believes that there may be a connection between Giza and Cydonia

— the region of Mars where the mysterious "pyramids" and "face" are located. Is NASA using its former advisors to conduct an investigation into the mysteries of the Sphinx?

MOST CONVINCING EVIDENCE
Aside from the fact that Sphinx was created ten thousand years ago by a civilization we have no record of existing, and appears to be sitting on top of an underground complex, the way that the Director of Egyptian Council of Antiquities, Dr Hawass, banned John Anthony West from the Giza Plateau is more than a little suspicious.

MOST MYSTERIOUS FACT
In February 2000, evidence emerged to prove that researchers were at least correct about chambers existing under the Sphinx and Giza plateau. Zahi Hawass announced the discovery of a symbolic tomb of the ancient Egyptian god

Osiris buried deep beneath one of the Giza pyramids. Hawass said access was previously impossible due to high water levels, but after dirt and water were cleared from the shaft located between the Sphinx and the Pyramid Chrefren, his archaeologists found three underground levels. The submerged Osiris sarcophagus was found at the lowest, about 98.4 feet (30 metres) below the surface. They did not use a sophisticated robot to make their breakthrough into the shaft, but instead a young boy.

SCEPTICALLY SPEAKING
Most of the evidence for underground chambers is based on the interpretation of seismographic data and could turn out to be nothing more than natural anomalies in the rock. It is understandable that the Egyptians do not want excavations to take place, with the risk of damage to the Sphinx, on the off chance of discovering the remnants of a fabled lost civilization.

TIBET

Even to non-conspiracy buffs, the mention of Tibet can conjure up images of a land beyond the normal confines of time, where Buddhist mystics remain concealed from view in inaccessible mountain monasteries.

The Himalayas – meaning "home of the snows" in ancient Sanskrit – have given us many legends, including that of the Yeti and the miraculous city of Shangri-La. Yet some conspiriologists believe that not all of the strange stories emanating from the mountainous realm of Tibet are mere fables.

Ever since the first Western explorers managed to make the perilous journey to Tibet, they have carried back with them persistent rumours of Shambhala – the "Hidden Kingdom" where a community of semi-divine beings lives in seclusion, guiding the destiny of mankind. In 1933, J. Hilton wrote

his best-selling book *The Lost Horizon*, in which Shambhala becomes Shangri-La; the English language was given another word to describe a paradise on Earth.

Despite pulp novels and bad movies, the belief in Shambhala has persisted and even grown, as conspiracy theorists unearthed evidence of the strange role it may have played in World War II. It has become well known in recent years that the Ahnenerbe – the occult research section of the SS – conducted two extensive trips to Tibet on the orders of Himmler. It is believed that they were searching for allies and assistance from the alleged inhabitants of the Hidden Kingdom.

No wonder it is also known as the Roof of the World.

After the war, Tibet was crushed under the heel of an invasion by Communist China, but rumours regarding Shambhala have been harder to suppress than Tibetan liberty. They continue to inspire a belief that deep within the Himalayas lies an advanced mystical order whose members are behind a conspiracy to keep the location of the Hidden Kingdom secret while guiding the course of history from their remote mountain retreat.

THE STRANGE PART

Whether or not the Nazis found fabled Shambhala remains a matter of conjecture, but it is certain that they found strange allies while exploring Tibet. When the Soviet army advanced on Berlin during the final days of World War II, troops discovered a cellar containing the bodies of several Tibetan monks wearing green gloves who appeared to have committed suicide as part of some arcane ritual. Over the next few days, hundreds more Tibetan bodies were recovered – all wearing SS uniforms, without any identifying papers, and all wearing green gloves. The fact that this element of the war tends to be glossed over in history books only helps convince some conspiriologists that a massive cover-up of the role of Shambhala is taking place.

THE USUAL SUSPECTS
Order of the Green Dragon

German academic, philosopher and occultist Karl Haushofer – creator of the term geopolitics and an important influence on Hitler – travelled extensively in Tibet and Japan. It was while he was studying mysticism in Asia that he was initiated into the ultra-secret Order of the Green Dragon. This clandestine organization had links to Tibet and is rumoured to have received its orders direct from Shambhala. It may have been the force that helped forge links between the Nazis and the Hidden Kingdom.

The Yellow Hats

The Yellow Hats – called Dugphas in Tibet – are proponents of the most esoteric branch of Tibetan Buddhism that fully acknowledges the reality of Shambhala. Certain conspiriologists feel that the promotion of the secret lands of Tibet as the "source of happiness" is nothing other than propaganda to mask a sinister plan from the hidden masters of the Yellow Hats for world domination. While Tibet's remoteness and subjugation by the Chinese may not make it an obvious base from which to dominate the globe, in conspiracy circles these obstacles are merely seen as part of an elaborate cover story, created to prevent effective scrutiny and investigation.

THE UNUSUAL SUSPECTS
The Elder Race

The mysterious builders of monuments such as the Sphinx, the Elder Race may not have completely disappeared from Earth. According to a selection of conspiracy theorists, the Elder Race relocated to the safety of Tibet's mountains when the Earth underwent a serious of global cataclysms thousands of years ago. Currently the rulers of Shambhala, members of the Elder Race are now working secretly to prepare humanity for the next stage in its evolution. Quite how helping out the Nazis would have achieved this is open to speculation.

The Hollow Earthers

Alongside legends of Shambhala, there are mentions of the underground realm of Agharta – linked in the conspiracy genre with plots to hide the truth about the hollow Earth. The inhabitants of this strange subterranean realm, which is recorded in the inner teachings of Tibetan mysticism, have been identified by some as having links to the alien culture hinted at in the thinly veiled works of fiction written by H. P. Lovecraft. While little is known as to the aims of the conspiracy conducted by the dwellers of Agharta, few doubt it would be designed to benefit those living on the external surface of the Earth.

MOST CONVINCING EVIDENCE

The current Dalai Lama, like his predecessors, is convinced of the physical reality of Shambhala, but the strongest evidence of its existence may come from the interest shown in it by the Nazis during the War. In the midst of a raging global conflict it is more than a little strange that the SS found the necessary resources and time to transport transmitters to Tibet so that Berlin could be in radio contact with the area.

MOST MYSTERIOUS FACT

Occultist, sometime secret agent and conspiracy-buff favourite Aleister Crowley undertook a record-breaking ascent of the Himalayas early in the twentieth century in what some see as a search for Shambhala. His quest was later duplicated by famous mystic George I. Gurdjieff and, most mysteriously, in 1942, by a covert US team sent by the Office of Strategic Services – the forerunner of the modern CIA.

SCEPTICALLY SPEAKING

You have to doubt the power of any alleged conspiracy operating from Shambhala after it failed to prevent Tibet being overrun by the Chinese. Furthermore, it has not made much headway in freeing Tibet from Communist domination. Besides, if Shambhala actually existed, modern satellite technology would have revealed it ages ago.

STONEHENGE

Standing alone and majestic as a reminder of long-lost civilizations, the ruins of Stonehenge present an enigma to which there will probably never be a definitive answer. There is no dispute that Stonehenge is a Neolithic architectural marvel, but its true purpose remains totally hidden.

Stonehenge continues to stand in a modern world overrun with cell phones, satellites, and trans-Atlantic air travel, as a primitive testament to the ingenuity of early man.

Located about 80 miles from London, near Salisbury Plain, Stonehenge is thought to have been constructed in three phases about 3500BCE. It was in the third phase, thought to be around 1800BCE, that the giant stone monoliths we associate with Stonehenge were transported to the site. These sarsen (an extremely hard type of sandstone) blocks were moulded and lifted into 30 upright stones with accompanying lintels, set in a circle. (Seventeen of the original 30 are still standing today.) Other stone designs were set in place inside the structure, including five triathlons (a pair of upright stones supporting a lintel stone). There is also a rectangular arrangement of "station stones" situated outside the ring.

Stonehenge is a focal religious point for Druids, who perform ceremonies there to this day, marking the summer solstice, as well as more private ceremonies. But they did not build the monument, since Stonehenge's creation pre-dates the founding of the Druidic religion.

Why Stonehenge was constructed remains a mystery, as does the identity of its original builders. Whatever prompted its construction, it's clear that Stonehenge was very important – it may still play a role in man's sophisticated world today. Perhaps the supposed "primitive" builders knew something we have forgotten, much to our peril.

THE STRANGE PART

The mechanisms by which the stones were moved have intrigued archaeologists and historians, considering the primitive level of technology at the time. The bluestones are thought to have come from the Preseli Mountains in West Wales – over 200 miles away. The sarsen stones originated from the relatively nearby Marlborough Downs – but at 25 tons per stone, the 20-mile distance is still formidable. Yet with all the work that went into Stonehenge's construction, archaeologists have found little detritus around the site. Most ancient construction sites are a potpourri of discarded materials. By contrast, Stonehenge is remarkably – perhaps suspiciously – clean.

THE USUAL SUSPECTS
The Beakers

A Neolithic people named after the type of pottery they produced, the Beakers have been thought to have begun the construction of Stonehenge. As the years passed, the monument's use may have varied from generation to generation. It has been suggested that it may have been used simply to hold animals, with a religious ceremony involved either in the slaughtering of livestock or in thanksgiving. Over time, Stonehenge's role as a religious centre may have intensified with the original holding pen design of the site merely kept on in its new role as a holy temple.

The Egyptians

Stonehenge could also have been designed with astronomy in mind – the positioning of the stones correlating to the positions of the Sun, Moon and stars throughout the year. Others believe that the axis of Stonehenge is built to correspond to the path of the sun, and that by using the Aubrey holes it is possible to predict eclipses. Such a focus on astronomy points towards the advanced Egyptians, who may have travelled to England in the distant past.

Also suspected: the Ancient Greeks; the Phoenicians.

THE UNUSUAL SUSPECTS
Merlin

The Arthurian Magus may have erected Stonehenge, either for his own personal study of the heavens, or as a coronation site for the young king Arthur. He would have moved the stones into position using magic, presumably of the levitating sort.

Ancient Astronauts

Stonehenge may have been built by ancient, extra-terrestrial visitors as a visible landing site/landmark, or may have been built by primitive man to honour the beings from the stars.

Also suspected: the Atlanteans; giants; dwarves; energy vortexes that have been created by ley lines.

MOST CONVINCING EVIDENCE

Stonehenge shares at least two significant elements with other places of worship, including several European cathedrals. First, it has an underwater spring running beneath it, which is taken as a sign of divinity in many faiths. Secondly, in a more mathematical sense, the square root of three can be found as a recurring proportion in its construction. This too is found in many places of worship, from Europe to Egypt.

MOST MYSTERIOUS FACT

Stonehenge, next to Avebury and Glastonbury, is considered one of the most magical places in England, reportedly because it is built along powerful ley lines.

SCEPTICALLY SPEAKING

For all the speculative theories about Stonehenge being constructed to align with this or that solar or celestial event, nobody has a clue as to the original builders' intentions. Lay out any circle of stones you like and at least half of them will align with some such event – precisely because they make a circle! Throughout the last 2,000 years, various groups of people shifted the stones about and re-erected them when they fell down again. Between 1901 and 1964 alone, virtually all of the stones were yet again re-erected, straightened up and embedded in concrete. This means that what we see today most likely differs at least a little from the original pattern that was laid out 5,000 years ago. The so-called Heel Stone may today align with the sun at the commencement of the summer solstice but, allowing for the incremental shift in the orbit and angle of the earth's tilt, 5,000 years ago this would not have been the case.

A silent testament across time – but were the stones arranged like this 5,000 years ago?

PONT-SAINT-ESPRIT

On the morning of 16 August 1951, this small town of southern France – population c. 5,000 – was preparing for another day of languid tranquillity when a local postman, Leon Armunier, fell off his bicycle in the town square, screaming that he was on fire and under attack from demonic serpents. And he was just the first of many.

In all, some 250 people were soon demonstrating similar hallucinations, a few even hurling themselves from balconies and upper-story windows. In all, there were seven deaths and many other victims suffered "flashbacks" for years thereafter. At the time no one knew what on earth was going on, so the local asylums were soon filled with a demented influx, some were restrained in the town jails while others, in desperation, were simply tied to trees and lamp posts in an attempt to prevent further self-harm.

Within hours, the town received a deputation from Sandoz Pharmaceuticals in Basle, Switzerland, including Dr Albert Hofmann, the man who discovered LSD back in 1938. With haste and confidence Hofmann and Co. pronounced the incident to have been caused by the victims eating bread from a local bakery that had inadvertently used rye infected with ergot, a mould known to contain a crude hallucinogenic. Job done, the deputation was hot-foot back across the border into Switzerland to phone the CIA and tell them that they could expect no further deliveries of the LSD they had to date been buying by the pallet-load. At the time, few were even aware of the existence of LSD while Sandoz was not only supplying the CIA but also sending specialists to consult with the Agency on the possibility of weaponizing the drug; these same "consultants" were also advising the CIA on the use of LSD in its clandestine experimentation on unsuspecting victims in their MK-Ultra programme.

THE USUAL SUSPECTS
Ergot fungus

Taking the word of the specialists from Sandoz as gospel, most at the time were more than happy with the explanation that the local baker, a scapegoat named Roche Briand, was to blame – after all, ergot poisoning had long been known to promote what was in medieval times known as "the Dance Mania". This happened with such monotonous regularity in and around the Italian town of Taranto that composers began to turn out frantic compositions, named Tarantellas, in 6/8 time or even 18/8 time, to mimic the frenzied antics of those afflicted with ergot poisoning.

That is all well and good but, by the twentieth century, ergot in Europe had been pretty much eradicated by crop

treatments specifically designed for that purpose and the victims of Pont-Saint-Esprit demonstrated few of the classic symptoms associated with ergotism. None, for example, presented the dry gangrene that is ever-present in such cases. Also, one of the first-response doctors who treated some of the victims also suffered the same effects and he, in common with many other victims, had eaten nothing at all that morning. This would confirm the notion that whatever was responsible was actually airborne, resulting in its being inhaled and coating the victims' skin.

THE UNUSUAL SUSPECTS
The CIA

Throughout the 1950s and until the investigation into its excesses and abuses by the Committee headed by Senator Frank Church in 1975, the CIA had gone rogue as judged by any sane parameters. Their truly bizarre experiments with LSD, under the umbrella-operation named MK-Ultra, included Operation Midnight Climax, which involved agency-run brothels in which the clients were unwittingly dosed and monitored (see page 123). The leading light of MK-Ultra was one Dr Sidney Gottlieb, a man with a passion for Bavarian folk dancing, despite having a clubfoot; his general demeanour made him the ideal inspiration for Peter Sellers's memorable film character, Doctor Strangelove. Directly below Gottlieb was Bioweapons expert Dr Frank Olson, known to have been in Southern France just before the eruption at Pont-Saint-Esprit. In 1953, Olson developed a conscience – an unforgivable condition within the ranks of the CIA.

When Frank Olson broke ranks and told his wife of the "French Experiment", which, in his opinion, had been "a terrible mistake", he effectively signed his own death warrant. Systematically and surreptitiously dosed with LSD until he demonstrated all the classic signs of paranoia, Olson was sent by Gottleib to see a "company" doctor in New York. Accompanied by Gottlieb's deputy, Robert Lashbrook, the two men checked into room 1018A on the thirteenth floor of the New York Statler Hotel. In the middle of the first night, Olson – again up to the gunwales with LSD – crashed through the hotel window and fell to his death. Lashbrook, who must have been a very heavy sleeper, always maintained he heard nothing.

A street in Pont-Saint-Esprit at the end of August 1951. The bakery, pictured with its shutters half down, is shut.

MOST CONVINCING EVIDENCE

In 1975, and under goad from the Church Committee, the CIA finally admitted to filling Olson with LSD without his knowledge and paid $750,000 to his surviving family, providing they signed a gagging-order. That same year there came to light a CIA document marked "Re: Pont-Saint-Esprit and F. Olson Files. SO Span/France Operation File, inclusive Olson. Intel files. Hand carry to Berlin – tell him to see to it that these are buried". "SO Span" is presumed to be Special Operation Bridge, as in "Pont". In 1994, Olson's death was re-examined and categorized a probable homicide after more documents released indicated his involvement with the "terrible mistake" at Pont-Saint-Esprit.

At the same time as the CIA was busy conducting their horrible experiments on the unwitting, MI6 was inflicting similar "tricks" on British service personnel. This was a folly that cost them dear in 2006, when they were forced to pay undisclosed sums to the families of the men whose heads they bent. Scientists from Porton Down, the UK bioweapons research centre in Wiltshire, conducted experiments on over 14,000 servicemen. The men were all told they were participating in a search for the cure for the common cold, whereas they were actually subjected to the rigours of sarin and other toxins. Unbelievably, Porton Down operatives also used the rush hour London Underground as their "playground", to disperse *Bacillus globigii* through miles of walkways, stairways, platforms and crowded trains; *globigii* causes severe eye infections – sometimes blindness – and acute septicaemia. In 1961, Porton Down dispatched a fleet of land rovers from Ilchester in Somerset with instruction to drive to Bristol, spraying the carcinogenic cadmium sulphide through the streets of every lucky community through which they passed. They went to the Bahamas to release clouds of the equine encephalitis virus, which induces long-term fatigue and sometimes death, before nipping over to southern Nigeria to mount clandestine nerve-gas attacks on unsuspecting villages in the Obanaghoro region. In all, Porton Down conducted over 700 such acts of lunacy in a programme that was not stopped until as late as 1989 – believe it or not – so they made the CIA's attempts to give a French town a technicolour daydream look like childsplay.

SCEPTICALLY SPEAKING

Although branded a baseless conspiracy theory by successive American and British administrations, this one has proved absolutely true: on both sides of the Atlantic admissions, some partial and some complete, have been forthcoming. There is nothing sceptical left to say on this matter, so those with an appetite for more information should start with a simple internet search on MK-Ultra and perhaps get hold of a copy of *A Terrible Mistake: The murder of Frank Olson and the CIA's Secret Cold War Experiments* (2008) by H. P. Albarelli.

COVENTRY – DID CHURCHILL LET IT BURN?

Throughout the night of 14 November 1940, the city of Coventry in central England was subjected to a German bombing blitz of unprecedented savagery. This saw 515 aircraft make repeated raids to drop hundreds of tons of conventional bombs, at least fifty 1000-kilo parachute mines and close to 40,000 incendiary bombs, leaving the city in tatters.

Did Prime Minister Winston Churchill know in advance of the raid? Did he sit back and allow it to happen? Conspiracy theorists believe that the answer to both these questions is "yes". At the time, nobody knew anything about the code-breakers of Bletchley Park, who were working around the

clock to break the Enigma code, which the Germans used to transmit all their operational instructions. It was not until the 1970s that such details were declassified. Only then was it revealed that, shortly before Coventry was engulfed, Alan Turing and his team at Bletchley had finally succeeded in

Is Churchill there to survey his own handiwork? It seems likely.

breaking the code. This disclosure started the rumour that Churchill had been warned of the raid but decided to do nothing about it, in case this alerted the Germans to the fact that their "uncrackable" code had indeed been cracked.

Defenders of Churchill scoff at the very notion but, as seen elsewhere in this book, this would not have been the first time that the leader of a nation stood accused of sacrificing hundreds of innocent people on their altar of the "greater good".

THE STRANGE PART

One of the first homes destroyed in the raid on Coventry was that of Henry Tandy VC, who was out on air-raid duty at the time. It could be argued that the raid on Coventry – and a lot more besides – was all his fault. In September 1918, towards the end of World War I, Tandy had been involved in the bitter fighting around the French village of Marcoing. There he encountered one wounded and unarmed Corporal Adolf Hitler. Reluctant to burden himself with a prisoner but too noble to gun down an unarmed man, Tandy let him go. Many years later, Tandy simply said that he wished to God he had pulled the trigger …

THE USUAL SUSPECTS
Winston Churchill

Anthony Cave Brown, a writer-historian of some renown, states in his *Bodyguard of Lies* (1974) that it was on 12 November 1940 that Churchill was first informed that Coventry was in the cross-hairs of a major raid.

Sir William Stephenson's 1976 biography of Churchill goes even further. This states that by the close of the first week of November 1940, Enigma traffic intercepted at Bletchley clearly stated that Coventry – code-named KORN – was to be a major target. The actual operation was to be code-named "Moonlight Sonata". However, when Churchill was made aware of this fact, he stated that the protection of Coventry was not worth the risk of alerting the Germans to the fact that Enigma had been compromised.

THE UNUSUAL SUSPECTS
Winston Churchill

For all the finger-pointing at Germany in British history books, it was in fact Churchill who first ordered the bombing of civilian targets during World War II. Coventry was the first British city to suffer German revenge for Churchill's policy.

Within a few months of taking office, on 25 August 1940 Churchill ordered the bombers against civilian targets in Berlin. His reasoning for this radical course of action was that depleting the German workforce would weaken their war effort and would demoralize the population in general. Having himself expressly forbidden "terror raids", on 4 September 1940, Adolf Hitler made a speech in Berlin

appealing directly to Churchill to "stop this nonsensical behaviour" or to expect payback in kind. Churchill's response came a month later on November 8, with the bombing of the non-industrial and historical city of Munich.

Infuriated by the pettiness of Churchill's actions, Hitler ordered Coventry to be hit – not only for its industrial worth, but for its inner-city resemblance to the medieval beauty of Munich.

MOST CONVINCING EVIDENCE

Throughout World War II, Group Captain F. W. Winterbotham was one of the highest-ranking intelligence officers. He reported only to Winston Churchill and Sir Stewart Menzies, Head of MI6. Once Enigma had been cracked, Winterbotham was responsible for organizing the dissemination of the harvested intelligence to various operational commanders, in such a form that no hint remained as to its origin.

With the declassification of all the Bletchley secrets, Winterbotham felt free to publish his bestselling book *The Ultra Secret* (1974), in which he recorded that throughout the day of 14 November 1940 the Enigma traffic was "buzzing" with talk of Moonlight Sonata and KORN. Apparently, Winterbotham personally phoned Downing Street to pass on this intelligence. According to his account, it was Sir William Stephenson who convinced Churchill to leave Coventry to its fate, as the information being harvested from Enigma was of such a high value.

MOST MYSTERIOUS FACT

The air cover over Coventry that night was exceptionally low – almost non-existent. The bombing continued for nearly twelve hours with the same planes returning to France to re-fuel and re-load for repeat runs – yet only one of them was shot down. If – as seems likely – Churchill did indeed abandon Coventry to its fate, he did such a good job that it is a miracle the Germans, given such a free hand, did not smell a rat!

SCEPTICALLY SPEAKING

The official line states that Churchill was made aware of the imminence of Operation Moonlight Sonata sometime after 3p.m. on the afternoon of 14 November. This was too late to do anything, anyway – but notionally Churchill was convinced the target was London. This might be easier to believe had it not been recorded by RAF tracking stations at 1.pm. that the Germans had already switched on their high-frequency X-Gerät radio-guidance beams; and these all converged over Coventry. Alerted to this fact, Downing Street "accidentally" sent out the wrong frequencies to the jamming-stations, to make sure that Coventry was left a sitting duck.

CHAPTER 8:

CELEBRITIES

KURT COBAIN

At 8:40a.m. on 8 April 1994, an electrician who had come to fit security lighting to a luxury home in Seattle found the dead body of Kurt Cobain. A shotgun wound to the head had killed him. Beside his body was found a box of drug paraphernalia, including syringes and burnt spoons.

A shotgun lay across his chest and it was claimed a "goodbye" note was found in the room. An open-and-shut case of suicide then? Only for the local police. Conspiriologists were hardly going to be satisfied with the cursory examination of Seattle's boys in blue and the media frenzy of reporting following Cobain's untimely end.

The 27-year-old lead singer and songwriter of the grunge band Nirvana was not only an internationally acclaimed rock star, but an icon and inspiration to many members of Generation X. His fans viewed him as more than another star; to them he was a leader, a hero. His funeral brought Seattle to a state of gridlock and there were copycat suicides across the world. Cobain died at the peak of his power. His music had reached out and touched millions and incredible success had brought him the unwanted status of spokesman for a generation as well as the grunge rock movement.

Punk rock was an escape for Cobain; drugs were an escape for Cobain. At first it seemed entirely in keeping with his character that he might have sought death as the ultimate escape from the pain and depression that had dogged him throughout his young life. However, despite the common knowledge that Cobain was a troubled man, many have found it hard to believe that he took his own life and conspiracy theories concerning his demise have proliferated while his records continue to sell.

The common thread in the numerous allegations in circulation is that despite his troubled state of mind – exemplified by a close shave with death via a heroin overdose in a Rome hotel a month before – Cobain was actually starting to sort himself out and planning positive changes in his life. A messy divorce from his wife and fellow rock star Courtney Love and a high-profile custody battle for their daughter may have been on the cards, but Cobain was not one to wimp out. He had shown toughness before and was a man who had fought his way from a backwoods redneck town to global status. Many of those who have studied the case feel that sinister forces were working in Seattle to ensure an untimely end for Cobain. They have certainly come up with some unsettling questions surrounding his alleged suicide.

The literal meaning of "Nirvana" is not paradise or heaven but "extinguished".

THE STRANGE PART

On Easter Sunday, 3 April 1994, Courtney Love called private detective Tom Grant, a California-based private detective. The previous day, Cobain had climbed over the wall of Exodus Rehab Clinic and had flown back to Seattle. Despite the fact that her husband was meant to be suicidal, had almost died in an overdose less than a month before and was returning to a home containing a shotgun, Love decided not to go to Seattle to find him herself. Instead, she hired Grant and despatched him to track down Cobain with the rather flippant and enigmatic phrase, "Save the American icon, Tom." Grant searched for Cobain at the Seattle house on 7 April, at 2:45a.m. and 9:45p.m., but did not find the body that was hidden in the greenhouse on top of the garage. It was eventually discovered the next day.

THE USUAL SUSPECTS
Someone Close to Kurt

Tom Grant, whom Love subsequently hired for seven months to investigate Cobain's death, is just one of many who believe that Cobain must have been murdered by someone close to him. Given that the murderer and other conspirators must have had his trust and good access to him, many theorists believe the finger points to a family member, close friend or employee.

Record Industry Executives

It is widely rumoured that Cobain was more concerned about leaving the music industry than leaving the world of the living. A dead rock icon is worth a lot more in terms of back catalogue sales than a live one who is no longer interested in a music career. Record industry executives are well known for possessing a moral sense that makes alley cats look like upstanding members of the community and with millions of dollars at stake, murder might have been seen as preferable to Cobain's retirement.

THE UNUSUAL SUSPECTS
Kurt Cobain

It would not be a rock-'n'-roll conspiracy theory if there were not some conspiriologists who believe that Cobain is still alive. The inconsistencies surrounding his apparent death can be fully explained by his faking it to escape from his wife, by the pressures of being a celebrity and by the drugs scene.

Military-Industrial Complex

Cobain's role as spokesman for a generation that was apathetic about political concerns could have made him a danger to the military-industrial complex (MIC) if he had decided to galvanize the disaffected young of the globe by taking an anti-war stance over the developing conflict in Yugoslavia. To ensure healthy weapon sales and lack of public interest, a pre-emptive strike may have been called for.

MOST CONVINCING EVIDENCE

There is a whole raft of hard crime scene evidence that raises questions over the idea that Cobain killed himself. One of his credit cards was missing and someone had attempted to use it after the time the autopsy says he was shot and before the body was discovered. There were no fingerprints on this shotgun or shells, which suggests the weapon had been wiped, and his body was found to contain an incapacitating level of heroin that should have prevented him from being able to fire the gun. The "suicide" note was actually a note explaining why he was quitting the record industry and many handwriting experts believe that someone other than Cobain had added the last four lines relating to his wife and daughter.

MOST MYSTERIOUS FACT

It has been reported that a "Dream Machine" – a trance-inducing contraption made from a light bulb, record player and cardboard cylinder with slits in it – was found in the greenhouse with Cobain. Brion Gysin, a friend and collaborator with author William S. Burroughs – one of Cobain's acknowledged heroes – first created the Dream Machine. A group calling themselves "Friends Understanding Kurt" have pointed out that there have been previous recorded incidents where the use of a Dream Machine has been associated with suicides.

SCEPTICALLY SPEAKING

A deeply troubled man with an enormous drug habit and an interest in firearms – that makes it just so hard to understand why anyone thinks Cobain may have taken his own life, doesn't it? Given that he was once photographed with a gun in his mouth, Cobain actually pulling the trigger one day isn't exactly the most surprising ending to his story. It might be a puzzle for some to figure out why people buy Britney Spears's records, but even with the odd circumstances surrounding Cobain's end there is little mystery about why the sharp money is on suicide in this case.

BRUCE LEE

Sometimes death does not end the web of intrigue that has grown up around a celebrity during his life. In fact, sometimes death is only the start of greater and stranger speculations.

In late July 1973, when they laid to rest the body of Bruce Lee, dressed in the Chinese costume he wore in the movie *Enter The Dragon*, in Seattle's Lakeview Cemetery, they did not succeed in burying the mystery surrounding his death.

A much-loved but controversial figure who made many enemies, Lee was 32 and at the height of his career when he suddenly died after falling into a coma. The subsequent coroner's report was inconclusive and the numerous medical

Steve McQueen, James Coburn, Chuck Norris and George Lazenby acted as pallbearers at Lee's funeral.

experts who looked at the case could only agree on one thing – that death had been brought about by a swelling of his brain.

On the fateful day of his death, Lee met film producer Raymond Chow at his home in the early afternoon and spent a couple of hours working with him on the film *The Game of Death*. The pair then went over to the home of Taiwanese actress Betty Tingpei, who was starring in the movie. Chow left for a meeting and Lee complained of having a headache. Tingpei gave him an Equagesic tablet – a form of powerful aspirin – and he took a nap. Chow rang Tingpei to invite her and Lee out for dinner, but the actress could not wake the sleeping star. By the time Lee arrived at the Queen Elizabeth hospital, he was dead.

Dr Lycette of the hospital felt that the death was a result of Lee being hypersensitive to compounds in the Equagesic tablet, but other medical authorities disagreed and rumours of a conspiracy began to spread throughout Hong Kong and the rest of the martial arts world.

THE STRANGE PART

Months before he was officially declared dead, rumours had been circulating around Hong Kong that Lee had died. These grew so strong that journalists on one of Hong Kong's largest newspapers wouldn't believe he was alive until they had spoken personally to Lee and subjected him to some rigorous questioning. This does tend to suggest that his eventual death may not have been as unexpected as the official version of events suggests.

THE USUAL SUSPECTS
The Triads

In the seventies, Chinese criminal organizations, such as the Triads, often demanded protection money from Hong Kong-based movie stars. Lee was known to have stood up to their demands and may have been poisoned as a result of this brave move – he was so adored by the Hong Kong public that he had to be disposed of in a subtle way.

Secret Martial Art Masters

A popular and plausible conjecture is that Lee was killed on the instructions of a cabal of secret martial art masters who were angered that he had taught too many of their secrets to foreigners. It is true that Lee had already had many problems with the traditional Chinese martial-arts establishment. Given the nature of the dim mak known to these masters, this theory is not easily dismissed. (Dim mak is a death touch that can be administered by glancing contact and is impossible for an autopsy to detect.)

Also suspected: a secret group of Hong Kong movie producers; a cabal of Hollywood Masons; Chinese Communists; defeated opponents; and the British Intelligence Service.

THE UNUSUAL SUSPECTS
Ancient Chinese Demons

It is rumoured that Lee felt his family was suffering from an ancient curse that ensured that the first-born son of any generation would be haunted by demons. The tradition of this curse in his family was so strong that when Bruce was born he was originally given a girl's name to confuse the demonic powers. More than one conspiracy theorist feels that this theory has been strengthened by the strange case of the death of Brandon Lee, Bruce's son, who died after a mysterious handgun accident during the filming of movie blockbuster *The Crow*.

Bruce Lee

An even wilder conspiracy theory proposes that Lee is still alive and that he staged his supposed death in an attempt to escape from either the pressures of fame or the evil intent of various Triad gangs. Those that believe this hypothesis also think that Lee may return at some unspecified point in the future. He certainly is not spotted as much as Elvis.

MOST CONVINCING EVIDENCE

One thing that persuades many that there is a conspiracy behind Bruce Lee's death is the confusion over the medical evidence surrounding his demise. The coroner's report proved inconclusive and the medical authorities put forward no fewer than five different theories to explain what caused the swelling of the brain that led to his untimely death.

MOST MYSTERIOUS FACT

When interviewed, Lee frequently reflected on the possibility of an early death and at times almost appeared to welcome the prospect. His wife Linda is quoted as saying that Bruce had no wish to live to old age as he found the prospect of losing his physical abilities too horrifying to contemplate. Death as an escape from failing strength and fading prowess as a master of martial art combat may not have been the only reason Lee contemplated dying young. It is known that he took the idea of the first-born of his family being cursed by demons seriously enough to try and protect his son Brandon by employing traditional magic.

SCEPTICALLY SPEAKING

Much of the speculation of the circumstances surrounding the conspiracy can be explained by the fact that when Raymond Chow announced Lee's death on television, he omitted the fact that he had not died at home but in the apartment of Betty Tingpei. The attempt to cover up this possibly embarrassing detail may have led many people to become convinced that there was a lot more going on behind the scenes, especially when there was an unsolved medical puzzle over the exact cause of the fatal swelling of the brain.

THE SHOOTING OF JOHN LENNON

In the "Do you remember where you were when you heard the news?" stakes, the shooting of John Lennon comes second only to the assassination of JFK or the events of 9/11. If you were alive when the murder of John Lennon was announced on the evening of 8 December, 1980, you will undoubtedly remember it, wherever you were.

As the news broke around the globe everyone was shocked. No one could understand why anyone would want to kill one of the members of the most beloved musical group of all time. Why would anyone want to murder an ex-Beatle? Why would anyone want to deny the world this true musical genius and very influential campaigner for peace?

The explanation offered in the press was that the gunman – Mark David Chapman – was a disturbed loner, obsessed with the Sixties star and convinced that Lennon was in league with the Devil. After a 60-day psychiatric evaluation that turned into a year and 60 days of absolute silence, Chapman pleaded guilty to the murder a matter of hours before his trial was scheduled to start.

It wasn't long before conspiracy theorists were supplementing the media's version of events with their own interpretations of what actually happened on the tragic night that robbed the world of a cultural giant. In their eyes, the shooting was not simply the work of a madman, it was part of a huge political plot.

THE STRANGE PART
One of the usual reasons put forward for why people like Chapman murder celebrities is that they wish to become famous themselves. This obviously is not the case with Chapman. Since he committed the crime he has turned down more than 60 interviews and repeatedly said, "I do not want publicity." He has only given one major interview and that was merely to ask to be released after he failed to get parole in October 2003. His apparent calmness after his arrest was unusual. However, more significant is the fact that he managed to evade metal detectors at two major airports when transporting the murder weapon from Hawaii to New York – something bound to raise alarm bells with those favouring a conspiracy as an explanation for Lennon's death.

John Lennon and Yoko Ono. His radical politics could have made him a target.

THE USUAL SUSPECTS
The FBI

The late FBI Director J. Edgar Hoover had a pathological hatred of Lennon and had tried to persuade President Nixon's Chief of Staff to help him bust the musician and get him thrown out of the country. The FBI kept Lennon under close scrutiny throughout the seventies and tried to thwart his attempts to gain US citizenship. Many of their files on him are still classified, some because they are linked to British Intelligence information on Lennon. If there was a conspiracy to kill the singer, it is not unreasonable to deduce that the FBI may have played a part in it.

Right-wing Activists/Military-Industrial Complex

Reagan had recently been elected President and some felt that opposition to his aggressive foreign policy and plans to spend massive amounts of the budget on expanding the American military was bound to develop around veteran peace campaigner Lennon. In fear of him inspiring the youth to rebel, as he had done in the sixties, right-wing activists and certain sections of the Military Industrial Complex plotted to silence him.

The CIA

Chapman had worked for defence companies with close links to the CIA. He also showed some evidence of having been hypnotized. In this light some have looked in the direction of the CIA's outlawed project to create programmed killers – MK-Ultra – for the real reason Chapman murdered his former hero.

THE UNUSUAL SUSPECTS
Satanic Forces

Lennon was shot outside the Dakota building – an apartment block that had provided the backdrop to Roman Polanski's film about the birth of the Antichrist, *Rosemary's Baby*. Beatles music and lyrics were used as elements in Charles Manson's warped reasoning that eventually led to the ritual killing of Roman Polanski's wife, Sharon Tate. David Mark Chapman believed that Lennon was, in fact, the Antichrist. These spooky synchronicities have been enough to produce wild claims that the shooting was the result of machinations carried out by satanic forces or members of a satanic cult that caused Chapman to be possessed.

Christian Fundamentalists

Mark David Chapman was not the only one who thought Lennon was the Antichrist. Ever since Lennon's "bigger than God" quote, certain American fundamentalists believed the ex-Beatle was a dark force dedicated to corrupting the youth of America by spreading a gospel of love, drugs and rock 'n' roll. With Lennon's return to the spotlight after a self-imposed period as a househusband, it may be that they decided to silence him once and for all.

MOST CONVINCING EVIDENCE

The strength of the fight put up by the FBI against those using the US Freedom of Information Act (FIA) to try to force the agency to make public its files on the singer is suspicious. So too is the fact that even now not all of the material on the files has been disclosed. Given that the FBI claim the reason their files cannot be made public is to protect national security, previously paranoid-sounding claims made by conspiracy buffs may have more veracity than it is comfortable to believe.

MOST MYSTERIOUS FACT

Conspiracy theorists who believe that Paul McCartney is dead and has been replaced with a lookalike, examine the Beatles' lyrics and album covers in search of clues. In a similar way, fringe researchers into the mystery surrounding Lennon's death have also found significance in certain publicity photos and songs. In the booklet that came with the original *Magical Mystery Tour* album in the States, there is a picture of John and a sign next to him stating: "The best way to go is by MD&C". Given these are the initials of Mark David Chapman, some have seen this as either a strange example of synchronicity or a massive clue signposting an astonishing conspiracy.

SCEPTICALLY SPEAKING

The proposed conspiracy theories all go out of their way to overlook the obvious fact that America's lax attitude to gun control laws and a mentally disturbed man who had an obsession with Lennon are enough of a dangerous combination to provide all the explanation you could ever possibly need.

PAUL MCCARTNEY

When you are one of the most famous musicians in the world and your name is known to anyone who has ever listened to pop music, you cannot be too surprised when strange rumours spring up around you – it is the nature of modern celebrity.

In the latter half of the sixties, a rumour spread through the media, and consequently the rest of the Beatle-loving world, that Paul McCartney was actually dead and that an impostor, named William Campbell, was put in his place.

The alleged conspiracy was first exposed to the public by Detroit disc jockey Russ Gibb. He advised his listeners to seek for clues in the band's music, even if it entailed playing the record backwards. One such "clue" is allegedly featured in the "Number nine, number nine" lyric from "Revolution 9" on the Beatles' *White Album*, which apparently becomes "turn me on dead man" when played backwards.

The rumour grew faster than Yoko Ono's hair. Millions of Beatles fans, and those who wanted a new hobby, spent hours of their time looking for new clues which revealed that Paul was dead. People were looking for evidence of a conspiracy in everything remotely related to the Beatles. Every clue confirmed what the many suspected – Paul McCartney was dead and there was a huge conspiracy to conceal this fact.

THE STRANGE PART
On the classic *Sgt. Pepper's Lonely Hearts' Club Band* album, Paul is wearing an arm patch with the initials OPD – commonly recognized as an acronym for Officially Pronounced Dead.

THE USUAL SUSPECTS
The Beatles
Conspiracy theorists of a more sceptical bent have concluded that there are in fact many clues to Paul's death scattered throughout the musical output of the Beatles, but that they have been placed there by the Beatles as a metaphysical hoax. They believe that Paul died spiritually and was re-born in the ways of the Maharishi. This spiritual rebirth and his old self dying became an in-joke among the group and they placed obscure references to it on their album covers and in the lyrics of their songs.

The Record Company
Mass hysteria was created by the rumour that Paul was dead. People fanatically searched for clues and evidence and went to ridiculous lengths to find them. More than one conspiracy theorist has suggested that it was all a hoax cooked up by the record company to help sustain interest in the Beatles. If this is correct, it certainly qualifies as one of the most fascinating publicity stunts of all time. Even those who feel the conspiracy theory is a hoax still love hearing the clues.

The CIA
Many people claim that the CIA wanted to bring an end to the Beatles' powerful influence on the world. They may have seen The Beatles and their massive, almost religious, following as a threat to society, which had already witnessed the outrage that John Lennon's comments on the Beatles being "more popular than Jesus Christ" had created. The Beatles were undoubtedly musical and social gods in the Sixties and may have been seen as a threat to the established order by the Agency. Their attempt to destroy the Beatles by murdering Paul was not completely successful as the other three Beatles enrolled the services of William Campbell, the winner of a Paul McCartney lookalike contest.

THE UNUSUAL SUSPECTS
Elvis Presley
A less grounded theory is that Elvis Presley employed the CIA to murder Paul. It has been claimed that Presley had been jealous and threatened by the Beatles' success from the day that the Beatles first set foot in the United States. He was the King of Rock 'n' Roll and no one was going to take that title away from him. So maybe he went to the extreme measure of sanctioning Paul McCartney's assassination. Elvis was popular amongst the highest politicians in the American government, and had extremely powerful contacts. Therefore, if he had been behind McCartney's alleged death, it would be unlikely that he would face any Jailhouse Rock for his crime.

The Devil
Another possible explanation was first proposed by the American academic Professor Glazier, who suggested that the Devil killed Paul as repayment for a bargain he had struck with McCartney for the Beatles' immense success in the world. Obviously rock stars were not the only horny beasts running around during the sixties. Paul is said to have suffered the same fate as Brian Jones of the Rolling Stones, who also paid the price of success.

The real Paul McCartney or an imposter named William Campbell?

MOST CONVINCING EVIDENCE

The cover of the *Abbey Road* album was declared as evidence of Paul's death by Fred LaBour in the *Michigan Daily*. He claimed that the Beatles were depicted as a type of funeral group who were leaving the cemetery. John, dressed in white, represented a minister. George, a gravedigger, and Ringo was an undertaker. Paul, of course, was the corpse, who was barefoot and out of step with the others, suggesting an impostor was present.

MOST MYSTERIOUS FACT

Among the many lyrics that could have been related to Paul's death, one in particular stands out. In the song "Glass Onion", John Lennon sings the words "The Walrus was Paul". It has been claimed that "Walrus" means "Corpse" in Greek.

SCEPTICALLY SPEAKING

The quality of the so-called clues is exceptionally dubious. The *Abbey Road* album cover features the licence plate 28 IF – which some have interpreted as being Paul's age if he had lived – but if Paul was still alive, he would have been 27, not 28. Many of the records that were played backwards sounded so strange and vague that almost any phrase could have fitted with the sound. It is all a case of looking so hard for something that you are guaranteed to find it. No impostor would have been able to duplicate McCartney's exceptional musical talent, though some conspiracy theorists argue that Paul's solo career is the ultimate proof of their claims.

MARILYN MONROE – DEATH OF A GODDESS

On 19 May 1962, President John F. Kennedy enjoyed a very public birthday celebration at New York's famous Madison Square Garden. At the celebrity-studded bash, more than 15,000 people saw Marilyn Monroe sing "Happy Birthday" to JFK in breathless, sexual whispers that have entered into pop-culture legend.

Just a few months later on 4 August 1962, the 36-year-old woman, born as Norma Jean Mortenson, was dead – found naked amid her silk sheets, an empty bottle of powerful barbiturates on her dressing table. Marilyn Monroe was a true Hollywood legend and probably the world's first global sex symbol, yet behind the legend is a tragic story of a tortured soul; an alcoholic who had been abused by all of the famous, powerful men in her life. Everything pointed towards the fact that the star had taken her own life.

On the other hand, some have always felt that Marilyn's suicide was just a little too neat and convenient, especially for a range of interested parties such as JFK, Robert F. Kennedy, the Mafia, the CIA and the FBI – who all had good reasons for wanting her to be kept permanently silent. The best way for a murder to go undiscovered is for it to look like an accident or a suicide. Conspiracy theorists have never believed Marilyn Monroe deliberately or accidentally took her own life. Remarkably, one thing that almost all those who believe Monroe was murdered agree on, is that if she was killed, it was probably done whilst she was held down with pillows and injected in the foot with barbiturates.

THE STRANGE PART

It became well known in the years following her death that Marilyn had been the mistress of both John and Bobby Kennedy and that the CIA and FBI were keeping her under surveillance, both as a possible threat to national security and as a risk to the President's reputation. Given the level of their involvement in monitoring the star and the clear suggestion that evidence about her last few days of life had been tampered with or covered up, a plot to murder Marilyn is not entirely without credibility.

THE USUAL SUSPECTS
The CIA

The CIA was keeping Marilyn under surveillance because her time as JFK's mistress meant that she had knowledge that

THE MONROE SAGA: 7 PAGES OF STORIES AND PICTURES

She was actually born Norma Jeane Mortenson – not Norma Jeane Baker as most believe.

made her a potential threat to national security. Whether this concerned the CIA's use of the Mafia to try and eliminate Castro and blackmail other heads of state is unknown, but the CIA's interest in the blonde bombshell is as certain as is its agents' ability to carry out a discrete murder.

The Mafia

Having shared her bed with the President JFK, the Attorney-General RFK and various high-powered members of the Mafia – including the mighty Sam Giancana – Monroe knew things that could have destroyed the most powerful people in the US. When her usefulness to the Mafia had run its course with the end of her affair with Robert F. Kennedy, they may have felt she was a dangerous loose cannon that needed silencing.

The FBI

Marilyn had been attempting to blackmail RFK into continuing their affair and may have been attempting a more audacious blackmail of JFK – threatening to expose the fact that he had only become President with the vote-fixing aid of the Chicago mob. FBI boss J Edgar Hoover was no friend of the Kennedy family, but as a self-styled patriot may have been happy to solve their problem with Monroe, to save the nation from scandal. Once he had arranged for Marilyn's death, he could control the upstart Kennedy brothers, forcing them to allow him to remain as head of the Bureau that had effectively become his own private police force.

THE UNUSUAL SUSPECTS
The Catholic Church

One organization that the Kennedy clan trusted completely and which had links to the CIA and the mob was the Catholic Church. JFK was the United States' first Catholic President and the Church was keen to ensure that nothing threatened its man in the White House. Some have suggested that the desire to protect him even went as far as arranging for the death of his troublesome former mistress.

Men In Black

If the prospect of the original men in black – Catholic priests – is not unusual enough, there are some who have suggested that Monroe was eliminated by the actual Men in Black who are charged with keeping the lid on the UFO conspiracy. If JFK knew the truth about extra-terrestrial life, he might have told Marilyn and thereby set in chain the series of events that led up to her death when she became uncontrollable and liable to reveal the secrets he had shared with her.

MOST CONVINCING EVIDENCE

In recent years, legal documents dating from 1960 have come to light. These documents seem to prove that the Kennedy family promised to give Marilyn Monroe $600,000 in a trust fund for her mother, Gladys Baker, if Marilyn kept quiet about what she knew of the links between JFK and Mafia boss Sam Giancana. After the star died, it appears as if this pledge was broken and all references to it were covered up. These documents quickly became the subject of a hotly fought court action in the United States. Debate about their authenticity still rages. However, tests on the paper, ink and signatures have all suggested that the documents are valid. If this is the case, they are the strongest evidence to come to light that the Kennedy clan may have had a hand in the star's death.

MOST MYSTERIOUS FACT

There are a lot of rumours, and more than a dash of good circumstantial evidence, to suggest that among the last visitors Marilyn received at her home were Bobby Kennedy and Hollywood actor Peter Lawford – who was married to Pat Kennedy Lawford and was therefore part of the Kennedy clan. By all accounts, Lawford and Kennedy were accompanied by an enigmatic third man who was dressed in black and carried a medical-style bag. The identity of this mysterious figure could be the vital clue that needs to be solved if anyone is to unravel the truth behind Monroe's death.

SCEPTICALLY SPEAKING

It is easy to connect a lot of disparate dots in a revealing manner when it comes to the death of Marilyn Monroe. Affairs with the highest officials in the land, FBI files and links to the Mafia are all suggestive but do not necessarily mean that there was a conspiracy. By August 1962, Monroe was a psychologically damaged alcoholic: neither an accidental drug overdose nor a deliberate act of suicide would necessarily have been out of character for Marilyn at that stage of her life. The screen goddess always had a legendary quality about her during life and the conspiracy theories may just be an extension of the inevitable Hollywood myth-making process that doesn't stop just because the star concerned does.

JIM MORRISON – DEATH OR DISAPPERANCE?

Lizard King, Rock God, shamanic spirit of the sixties. Without doubt one of the biggest personalities of the music scene of his time, Jim Morrison always had a mythical quality about him. This appears to have done nothing but grow since his death in a Paris apartment on 4 July 1971. In fact, many conspiracy theorists feel his death is the greatest myth of Morrison's life; some believe it would take more than heart failure to rob the world of such a larger-than-life character.

After nearly five years of fame, Jim took a break from the Doors after they had fulfilled their contractual obligation to Elektra Records by delivering the seminal album *LA Woman*. The rest of the band may have been a little disgruntled that he left during the mixing stages of the LP, but this was not the end of the group and they fully expected him to return from Paris.

Morrison was bored with life in LA and sought out Paris as it was a place to inspire him – a romantic city of art and poetry. He mentioned to some people his desire to purchase an old church in the south of France so he could renovate it and use it as a permanent base from which he would only venture back to the hustle of America when business demanded. He took with him his scrapbooks filled with poetry and ideas, reels from three of the films he was working on and plans to write a play.

He and his long-term girlfriend, Pamela Courson, quickly established a home for themselves in a Parisian apartment. Jim wrote, appeared as an extra in a play, drank vast quantities of alcohol and began to enjoy the freedom of not being recognized every time he stepped outside his door. He often expressed opinions during this time that he felt like he needed to change the direction of his life – it was clear that he wanted to get away from things and that he wanted to travel.

While years of drinking, drug-taking and other forms of physical self-abuse had made their mark on Morrison, his unexpected death – recorded as resulting from heart failure – took many by surprise. It also inspired doubts in others that he was actually dead, doubts that intensified when one or two curious facts ended up in the public domain.

THE STRANGE PART

No one who knew Jim really well, other than his girlfriend, actually saw him dead. Even after the official death certificate had been produced, some of his friends and even some members of his family doubted that he had really shuffled off this mortal coil.

THE USUAL SUSPECTS
Jim Morrison

It is rumoured that some people who had contractual arrangements with him in the music business immediately assumed that his death was staged in order to facilitate an easy release from some troublesome, binding contracts that he would have had to fulfil had he lived. Established facts also show that Morrison was enjoying the anonymity of his life in Paris and took great care to ensure that there were no new publicity pictures showing what he looked like after he left LA, so he would not be disturbed. He talked of escaping his fame. Faking his death may have been the perfect way to achieve this aim.

Friends of Jim Morrison

Some suspect that the confusion over Morrison's death stems from the fact that they wanted to disguise that he died of a drug overdose. Chief conspirator in this intrigue would have been his partner, the late Pamela Courson, who was purported to have had his body removed from the infamous Parisian junkie joint the Rock 'n' Roll Circus to their apartment in order to avoid a scandal and police questioning. This might explain her actions after she "found" Jim unconscious in the bath – her first few telephone calls were to friends, not to the paramedics.

THE UNUSUAL SUSPECTS
The FBI

The FBI had kept Morrison under surveillance when he had been in the US. Files and memoranda to the then Director of the FBI – the infamous J. Edgar Hoover – make mention of him trying to "provoke chaos". The Bureau

The only musician to be arrested mid-performance on stage, Morrison had a staggering IQ of 149.

certainly kept tags on those they thought capable of inciting rebellion or drug use among the young, and on people who were in contact with those thought to be subversive – two counts on which Morrison definitely qualified for attention. It should not come as too much of a surprise that some conspiracy theorists have conjectured that the FBI was involved in the strange circumstances surrounding Morrison's (alleged) death because they wished to ensure that Jim did not return to the USA and start provoking that chaos again.

Worldwide Witch Cult

Morrison had an intense interest in witchcraft and is said to have been an active participant in at least one witch cult. It is claimed by some conspiracy theorists, with an interesting grasp of the word "fact", that Morrison was abducted as part of a dark plot to obtain the living representation of Dionysus – Greek god of fertility and wine – for ritual sacrifice.

MOST CONVINCING EVIDENCE

Though it is easy to be jaded when hearing conspiracies such as these, there is some convincing evidence to suggest that all is not as it seems with the Morrison case. No autopsy was ever performed. People who knew him well – including band member Ray Manzarek – believed that he was still alive and Morrison's own remarks that he wanted to escape the life of a rock star are all telling. However, the most convincing evidence is that more than a week after he had been "buried", Pamela Courson told a journalist working for United Press that Jim was staying at a special clinic outside Paris to convalesce from illness.

MOST MYSTERIOUS FACT

It is effectively impossible to exhume Morrison's body to prove he is actually dead. Apart from needing the family's approval, you also need the consent from seven French cardinals, who can each demand a right of veto and who are renowned for disagreeing on this type of matter. This is the case with all exhumations from the Père Lachaise cemetery, and Jim had speculated he might be buried there…

SCEPTICALLY SPEAKING

Towards the end of his life, Jim Morrison was an overweight, chain-smoking alcoholic who lived very dangerously by keeping up his intake of narcotics while also taking prescription medicines to combat his asthma. The death of someone in those circumstances is hardly surprising – it is pretty much inevitable.

IS THE KING STILL ALIVE?

The official version: Elvis died on 16 August 1977 from an overdose of drugs. He died sitting on the toilet, with his pants around his ankles, a bloated and burnt-out version of his former self and his body is now in residence at Graceland.

In the film of Forrest Gump (1994), an uncredited Kurt Russell "voiced" Elvis in all the flashbacks.

The conspiracy version has it that the death of the King of Rock 'n' Roll was an elaborate hoax on the public and that the original Hound Dog is still alive and being spotted by numerous people across the globe.

It has to be agreed that his death did come as a shock – 42 is an early age to die and Elvis did have a history of pulling off some rather bizarre and eccentric stunts. There are certainly some mysterious elements surrounding his alleged death.

THE STRANGE PART

A mere two hours after his death was announced, a man looking remarkably like Elvis bought a ticket for Buenos Aires using the name John Burrows. This was a pseudonym that the King himself had used quite a few times, notably on the occasion he flew to Washington to meet President Nixon. It was on the same visit to DC, that he went to the headquarters of the FBI, announced his desire to inform on fellow show-business performers and became an honorary member of the Bureau of Narcotics and Dangerous Drugs. It is alleged that John Burrows flew out of the USA on special State Department papers and this has fuelled speculation that Burrows was none other than Presley making his escape to a new life.

THE USUAL SUSPECTS
Elvis Presley

The hottest contender for the instigator of the conspiracy is none other than Elvis himself. The King definitely felt a prisoner of his own fame and was tired of riding in the trunks of cars to avoid detection and of not being able to get proper medical attention because any hospital he was in would be overwhelmed by fans. At 42, he was going downhill and was too proud to go out with a whimper. Elvis had already once faked his death by setting up a deceptive shooting, so it is not impossible he staged a more final fake death.

The FBI

Elvis had recently lost a vast amount of money in bad deals with companies that had close links to the Mafia. There is a lot of speculation that the King decided to collaborate with the government to help expose gangsters. To ensure his protection, the FBI had to fake his death and provide him with a new life as part of a very unusual witness relocation programme.

THE UNUSUAL SUSPECTS
Burger Chain Companies

Could the faked death of Elvis be part of an innovative and radical marketing scam? It has been suggested that the frequent sighting of Elvis cooking fries in numerous backwoods burger joints – which then became very popular, acting as shrines and magnets for Elvis fans – is a joint plan between the King and the burger chain companies. Elvis gets to live a life free from the pressures of fame and is paid in cheeseburgers, while the fast-food bosses get to increase business in their quieter establishments.

New World Order

Since Elvis allegedly bought the farm, it has become clear to many cultural observers that he is well on the way to becoming a religious figure. Books comparing him to Christ have hit the US bestseller lists, sightings of Elvis can be seen as similar to spiritual visions, and there is no denying that many fans have shrines to the King and describe visiting Graceland in terms of making a pilgrimage. If you are of a paranoid bent, you may want to consider the claims that the Elvis conspiracy was instigated by the New World Order as their attempt to lay the groundwork for a future new religion. Has Elvis been cryogenically frozen by the NWO to be revived as the globe's new messiah when it comes to power?

MJ-12

Every Elvis conspiracy is more than a little odd, but the suggested link between the King and Roswell – where in 1947 a UFO was alleged to have crashed and the military recovered alien bodies – is bizarre even by Elvis standards. It has been claimed that the military photographer who captured Elvis on film for US Marine publicity purposes was a man named Barret who just happened to be the US Army photographer brought in to record the dead alien's autopsies. Conspiracy buffs, with a love for the territory of deep weird, have it that the photographer sent Elvis a copy of those alien pictures with the fatal consequence that MJ-12 – the guys behind the UFO cover-up – had to silence the King.

MOST CONVINCING EVIDENCE

Aside from the frequently quoted fact that "Elvis" is an anagram of "lives", possibly the most convincing evidence surrounds the 900-pound coffin with a built-in air-chilling unit in which Elvis was buried. How did the Presley family manage to obtain a 900-pound, custom-made coffin ready for a funeral held on the day after his death, and still fail to follow the more basic requests from Elvis, such as being buried next to his mother? In the days leading up to his alleged death, the King is said to have made odd nocturnal visits to several funeral homes. Why?

MOST MYSTERIOUS FACT

The King's name is wrongly spelt on his headstone. His full name was Elvis Aron Presley, but on his grave his middle name is spelled incorrectly with an additional 'a'. The unique spelling of Aron was an important Presley family tradition. When he was born, Aron was misspelled Aaron on his birth certificate and Elvis's father went to great lengths to correct the recording of his son's name. It seems very odd that Elvis's family would have allowed this error to occur on the King's tombstone.

SCEPTICALLY SPEAKING

The King is dead – get over it.

DEATH OF PRINCESS DI

The death of Princess Diana was an event that affected people across the planet. Britain grieved, the world grieved. Even people who had never devoted any real attention to the British Royal Family felt deep emotion at the tragic circumstances that robbed the world of someone who qualified as a global cultural icon.

At first it appeared to be nothing more than a simple tragic accident. Diana had enjoyed a romantic meal with her lover, Dodi Al Fayed, at the Ritz Hotel owned by his father, Mohammed Al Fayed. A little before midnight the couple left, accompanied by Diana's bodyguard – Trevor Rees-Jones. To escape 30 paparazzi parked outside, they went out via the back door. The chauffeur of their bulletproof Mercedes-Benz was Henri Paul, the Ritz Hotel's head of security.

The car sped away and a tourist captured the scene on video as an innocent looking Citroen followed and the paparazzi, realizing they had been duped, began to give chase on their motorcycles. After a few minutes' pursuit, the Mercedes entered the Pont de l'Alma tunnel at high speed and all we know is that Diana, Dodi and Henri failed to emerge from it with their lives. It took the French investigation several years to produce an official version of events. Not surprisingly, they supported the instant verdict from the world's media that it was a woeful auto accident caused by the combination of a drunk driver, pursuing paparazzi and a failure to wear seatbelts.

The first public suggestion that there was a conspiracy to kill Princess Diana surfaced on the BBC World Service a couple of days after the unfortunate events of 31 August 1997. In bizarre propagandist tones, the BBC took pains to deride a speech made by Libyan leader Colonel Muammar Gaddafi in which he claimed that the "accident" was a joint French and British conspiracy because they did not want Diana to marry a Muslim man. Conspiracy theories began circulating on the night of her death, most of them speculating on how strange it was that on the day she died, Diana had already told one major British national newspaper to prepare for an amazing announcement.

THE STRANGE PART

The Queen intervened to clear Diana's former butler, Paul Burrell, when he was on trial at the Old Bailey just before he was about to take the stand in November 2002 and possibly reveal a number of uncomfortable facts about the Princess. It later emerged that after Diana's death, the Queen had spoken to length at Burrell. Sounding like the most paranoid of conspiracy theorists and using dialogue that would not

have been out of place in *The X-Files*, she warned Burrell to be careful, saying, "There are powers at work in this country which we have no knowledge about." The warning led Burrell to wait until October 2003 to make public the fact that Diana had written him a note ten months before she died. It stated: "This particular phase of my life is the most dangerous. 'X' is planning an accident in my car, brake failure and serious head injuries in order to make the path clear for Charles to marry." The Princess's startling prescience has heightened the belief she was a victim of a conspiracy, not a tragic accident.

THE USUAL SUSPECTS
MI6
Sworn to protect the British crown, it is alleged that a renegade faction within MI6 took it upon itself to rid the Royal Family of the one woman who looked capable of destroying the monarchy by exposing the hypocrisy of the Windsors. That she may have been pregnant, about to convert to Islam and marry the son of establishment bogeyman Mohammed Al Fayed may have been the final factors that made them decide she must die.

Military-Industrial Complex
Diana had waged a one-woman war against the evils of landmines, in doing so risking her personal safety and earning strident political criticism in the UK as a "loose cannon". While the military–industrial complex makes more money from disposing of landmines than it does selling them, it may have feared the possibility of Diana turning her attention to the arms industry in general. Clearly, it would have been in its best interests to wipe out someone who could have turned into the world's most powerful peace campaigner.

Also suspected: the CIA; Mossad; Islamic Fundamentalists; Saddam Hussein; the Freemasons (she died under a bridge – an important Masonic symbol) and the IRA.

THE UNUSUAL SUSPECTS
The Committee
An alleged Anglo-American cabal made up of intelligence agency operatives from the United States and Great

Britain. Supposedly headquartered in Bristol, England, the Committee is apparently a tool of an even more clandestine group that wants the "Special Relationship" between the US and Britain to develop into a union of both powers. Possibly Diana's massive popularity, willingness to tackle the establishment on sensitive issues and possible pregnancy persuaded them she could be a dangerous opponent to their cryptic schemes.

Princess Diana
Another bizarre hypothesis is that Diana staged her own death so she and Dodi could live free from the glare of publicity. Not surprisingly, there's little hard evidence to support this piece of wishful thinking.

MOST CONVINCING EVIDENCE
Claims have been made that Henri Paul was three times over the legal alcohol limit. A second blood test ordered by his disbelieving family showed a level of carbon monoxide in his body that was not only lethal, but would have entered his bloodstream before he got into the car. The security video from the Ritz that night does not show him as a drunk, or reeling from carbon monoxide poisoning. The mystery of Henri Paul deepens further with the revelation that he deposited more than 164,000 francs into his bank account shortly before he died. When, in 2003, it was announced that British inquests were to be held into the deaths of Diana and Dodi, conspiracy theorists were dismayed to find out that they would be held by Surrey Coroner Michael Burgess. As he was also Coroner for the Royal Household, many doubted that the truth could possibly emerge at the inquests.

MOST MYSTERIOUS FACT
Although no one in their right mind would consider a Fiat Uno ideal for the task of shunting a bullet-proof Mercedes limo with murderous intent, it is nevertheless a matter of fact that, minutes before the fatalities, Dodi and Di's limo scraped bodywork with a white Fiat Uno. By coincidence, one of the pursuing paparazzi, James Adanson, did own such a car. However, despite Dodi's father immediately hailing him as the assassin, his Uno was registered in 1988, the year after Fiat had stopped using Bianco Corfu 224 – the particular white paint that was found on the right-rear wing of the Mercedes. Adanson further claimed to have been nowhere near Paris that night and that his Uno was 200 miles away at his home and off-road, standing on blocks.

Few believed either of Adanson's assertions, which were further called into question by his being recorded while making a last-minute and rather flustered boarding of a flight to Corsica, sans baggage, at Paris-Orly airport about five hours after the crash. Although his Uno was in fact painted in Bianco 210, even under a microscope this colour is indistinguishable from Bianco Corfu 224. When pressed

on the matter of the Fiat, Adanson claimed to have sold it to a stranger but, despite their best efforts, neither the French Police nor Interpol managed to trace it. A known contact and informer of both MI6 and French Intelligence, in 2007 Adanson's badly charred body was found in the burnt-out remains of a car in the French countryside. When fireman Christophe Pelat started to make loud comments that the body seemed to have two gunshot wounds to the head, he was forcibly removed from the scene by a couple of "suits". However, French Investigator Jean-Michel Lauzun did inform the inquest that when he approached the blazing car, he could clearly see a hole in Adanson's left temple. Verdict: suicide!

SCEPTICALLY SPEAKING
Even if Diana was pregnant, that does not mean there was a conspiracy to kill her. Driving at high speed through Paris is dangerous enough without being pursued by a pack of motorcycle paparazzi. Add a barrage of camera flashes to a chase conducted at more than 120 miles per hour when the passengers are not wearing seatbelts and you no longer need a conspiracy to explain a fatal crash. Faced with a tragedy such as Diana's death, it is not surprising that some people cannot accept it as a mere random accident. The car crash in Paris may be the perfect example of why some conspiracy theories come into being: if they did not exist, we would have to face the banality and indiscriminate nature of death.

Diana's butler Paul Burrell on trial for theft in 2002.

SID VICIOUS

When New York's finest entered Room 100 of the Chelsea Hotel on 12 October 1978, they discovered an horrific sight. Lying beneath the bathroom sink, clad only in her underwear and covered in blood, was Nancy Spungen. She was dead, killed by a single knife blow to her abdomen. Her boyfriend, himself in a drug-induced muddle, was Sid Vicious, bass player with the then notorious punk band, the Sex Pistols. He was charged with Spungen's murder and later released on $50,000 bail.

The romance between Vicious (born John Simon Ritchie) and Nancy Spungen was the stuff of which rock-'n'-roll nightmares are made. After being recruited by his best friend John Lydon – aka Johnny Rotten – to replace the existing bass player in his band, the Sex Pistols (named after Malcolm McLaren and Vivienne Westwood's London boutique, Sex), Vicious soon found himself at the epicentre of a pop-culture phenomenon. The band was already notorious in England. Spearheading the UK punk movement, the Pistols had originally been put together by McLaren to specifically appeal to the disaffected

Sid Vicious' own mother, Anne, made the death-bed confession that she had administered the overdose herself.

youth of England. With songs calculated to infuriate all the wrong people (anyone over 30), the Pistols tore through England on the breaking wave of punk rock. With songs such as "Anarchy in the UK" and "God Save the Queen", coupled with outrageous outbursts on television and other media, they were nothing short of a slow-motion atom bomb about to shake the foundations of pop culture worldwide.

Which wasn't bad for Vicious, considering there was debate about whether he ever knew how to play the bass at all. Instead, he relied more on image: cutting himself with razor blades, spitting blood and even urinating while on stage. The anarchy poster boy, beloved by many newborn punk rockers, he proved irresistible to one fan, an American girl called Nancy Spungen, who came over to England with the express purpose of capturing the heart – or anything else – of a Pistol. She and Vicious met in 1977 and soon became lovers, careening into an affair riddled with drug abuse. Vicious's love of Spungen, coupled with Spungen's abrasive personality, became so intense that it began to tear the band apart. When the Pistols's ill-fated American tour ended abruptly, with lead singer Johnny Rotten returning to England in disgust, Vicious stayed with Spungen, finally ending up in New York's Chelsea Hotel. After Spungen's death, and out of despair, Vicious tried to commit suicide and carved his entire forearm with a knife. Somehow surviving that, he finally succumbed to a heroin overdose (with heroin brought for him by his mother, fearing that her son might get caught in a police sting) on 2 February 1979. He was only 21 years old.

THE STRANGE PART
Theories have arisen over the possibility of a conspiracy concerning Vicious's death. There are dark hints that there was more at hand than the tragic deaths of two heroin-addicts, and even murmurs that Vicious may not have killed Spungen at all.

THE USUAL SUSPECTS
Unknown Residents of the Chelsea Hotel
Keeping in mind the drug-hazed state of Vicious and of Spungen before her death, it's entirely probable that someone other than Vicious may have killed Spungen. In his befuddled state of mind, he may not even have been aware of the murder. The perpetrators, worried about the truth coming out if Vicious's case went to trial, ensured his silence by making sure that Vicious's mother brought a lethally cut dose of heroin for her son.

Former Associates
Some conspiracy theorists feel that former friends and associates of Vicious may have had him supplied with a hit of lethal "hot" heroin. This was meant as an unusual act of mercy to spare him having to face the living hell of a long prison sentence served out in New York's most notorious jail, a place he would not have been vicious enough to survive.

THE UNUSUAL SUSPECTS
The CIA and FBI
Just as the murder of John Lennon may be attributed to a mutual desire by the CIA and FBI to remove any pop-culture figure that could possibly lead the population to revolt, Vicious might have been killed because he represented punk anarchy in all its glory. He had the potential to give American youth a role model that made the young Elvis look the model of respectability. Indeed, some theories suggest that Vicious could have been a simple trial run of a CIA or FBI rub-out programme before attention moved on to the more difficult task of removing Lennon. Both men died, coincidentally, in New York.

MOST CONVINCING EVIDENCE
However tormented and tortuous the relationship between Spungen and Vicious, it was painfully clear to all those around him that he needed her, perhaps more than anything or anyone else. Regardless of his state of intoxication, to kill her would seem completely out of character. In telephone conversations with Spungen's mother after Nancy's death, Vicious never made any comments about it at all. If he were as guilt-ridden over killing her as we would be led to believe, would he be able to hide his pain that well? In all other things, Vicious was not known as a paragon of restraint.

MOST MYSTERIOUS FACT
While Vicious's mother was returning her son's ashes to England, John Lydon claims that she dropped the urn in Heathrow, scattering them across the airport floor. A significant proportion of them were sucked into the ventilation system.

SCEPTICALLY SPEAKING
Although it would be romantic to think that all the rock stars who die young do so because the "Powers That Be" want them dead, there are times when death is simply a tragic end to a tragic story. Sid Vicious was a young man with next to no musical talent, who was simply in the right place at the right time looking the right way. When McLaren created the Sex Pistols he wanted stars he could manipulate and he got that with Vicious. Unlike general perceptions of John Lennon and Jim Morrison, the idea that Vicious could ever be a threat to American society is ludicrous. He was the "It Boy" of the punk generation, and nothing more. If his death was to be chalked down to anything, it should be heroin, and the equally dangerous drug of media exposure.

CHAPTER 9:

EXTRA-TERRESTRIALS

CATTLE MUTILATIONS

For decades, cattle farmers around the world have been plagued by a problem, a problem that is as inexplicable as it is horrifying: the grisly puzzle of cattle mutilations. Representing more than just a simple financial loss associated with missing livestock, this exercise in abject cruelty may have a purpose, but like its perpetrators, that purpose remains cloaked in shadows.

While the majority of cattle mutilation cases occur in the United States (particularly in New Mexico), the phenomenon has been reported in Puerto Rico, South America and Canada. Details of the mutilations may vary from case to case, but there are enough commonalities to suggest an orchestrated programme of sorts is underway. More often that not, the bodies of mutilated animals are found drained of blood. Missing organs have been removed with surgical precision, with the carcass often appearing to have been cauterized. The perpetrators show a particular interest in sensory organs such as the eyes, the reproductive and defecatory systems, and the anterior digestive tract.

As many as 10,000 cattle may have died in this manner. As a result, several theories have sprung up surrounding this disturbing trend. If dealing with predators, disease and rowdy young men in search of cow-tipping weren't enough, cattle ranchers now have to contend with an unknown sadistic force that comes and goes like an eviscerating thief in the night.

THE STRANGE PART
Usually, no marks around the bodies of the mutilated cattle are found, with the exception of a few tripod marks surrounding the bodies. Clamp marks have been found on some cattle, suggesting that the mutilation takes place somewhere other than the field in which they are found.

THE USUAL SUSPECTS
UFOs
The theory that aliens (such as the Greys) are seeking to find a way to save their race through bonding with our own gene pool, strays into the arena of cattle mutilation. The aliens could somehow be using cow blood and organs in their experiments, possibly because bovine parts are similar in chemistry to their own. More optimistic theories suggest the aliens are using cows to run random radiation tests in their efforts to save us all from nuclear annihilation. This is backed up by the reports of some human abductees, who claim to have seen cows being led onboard UFOs while they themselves were suffering experimentation. UFOs are often seen in the sky in the nights preceding cattle mutilations, and cattle have been known to become restless and stampede when a UFO is visible. This would seem to indicate that cows in general have had more experience with UFOs then they are letting on.

Black Helicopters
These mysterious craft have also been seen around cattle fields preceding mutilations, startling cattle with white hot searchlights. The presence of such craft would lend credence to the theory that the animals are airlifted away to be mutilated, with their dead bodies simply being dropped back into the field after the process is completed. The black helicopters are often associated with secret government programmes and the rise of the New World Order, and could possibly be using cattle to test powerful chemical weapons without hindrance of government guidelines.

Satanists
First thought to be responsible for the mutilations, Satanists were alleged to be using the cows as part of their profane ceremonies, so much so that they were investigated by law enforcement agencies. Nothing conclusive was ever found. Also suspected: US military; major chemical companies.

THE UNUSUAL SUSPECTS
Natural Predators
Despite the precision of the mutilations, despite the lack of any footprints leading up to the bodies, wolves, coyotes or a so-far-undiscovered predator is thought to be responsible.

El Chupracabra
This mythical monster from Central America, referred to as "the Goat Eater", may be responsible for cattle attacks, perhaps in an effort to expand its palate.

Unknown Cattle Disease

An especially virulent, and as yet undiscovered, cattle ailment has also been blamed: a virus so powerful and quick that it can remove the organs and the blood in the space of a single night, and then completely vanish from any forensic detection.

MOST CONVINCING EVIDENCE

The neatness of the organ removal, coupled with the complete exsanguination of the bodies, points towards a high degree of technological sophistication, rather than to tooth and claw. Wounds are found to be cauterized, which could be the work of laser cutters. What is interesting is that such technology was not in use when the first cattle mutilations were reported, back in the early seventies. The blood is also removed with such attention to detail that not one drop can be found around the bodies. This would seem to indicate either military or extra-terrestrial involvement, with the parties involved slipping up only occasionally by leaving clamp marks on the animals' legs.

MOST MYSTERIOUS FACT

After the bodies are returned to their fields, they are totally shunned by other animals. There is something so fundamentally wrong with the bodies that even carrion specialists, such as crows, vultures and the like, will not touch them.

SCEPTICALLY SPEAKING

Why would aliens need cow blood in their efforts to interbreed with humanity? Wouldn't it make more sense to kidnap gorillas or other mem-bers of the ape family? Surely the suspected government collaborators in the Trilateral Commission could get them a few rhesus monkeys from research facilities, no questions asked? Cattle mutilations could be nothing more than a twisted version of the crop circle phenomenon, with well-organized pranksters equipped with medical equipment and vacuum cleaners, killing cattle in the dead of night instead of tramping down wheat in circular designs in some poor unsuspecting farmer's field.

UFOS OVER IRAQ

On 16 December 1998, tracer fire lit up the skies of Baghdad. The ongoing "tepid war" against Saddam Hussein, which had continued since the first Gulf War had failed to remove him from power in 1991, had erupted into one of its periodic phases.

In 2004, Iranian Tomcat pilots also recorded having engaged UFOs in their own air space.

The Allied air strike on Iraq's capital city was part of Operation Desert Fox and, just like the first Gulf War, it was being shown live to millions of TV viewers around the world, thanks to CNN. However, that night CNN managed to capture more than the breaking news regarding Desert Fox, they also filmed a UFO hovering above Baghdad. Their footage even showed it moving away to avoid being hit by a stream of anti-aircraft fire.

At the time celebrated among the UFO community as a new piece of strong evidence to prove the existence of UFOs, the incident has taken on a much wider significance among certain conspiracy theorists. More and more have come to believe that there is a solid connection between UFOs seen over Iraq and America's decision to launch an invasion of Iraq in 2003. The constant patrolling and bombing of Iraqi installations by the UK and US airforces in the northern

Iraq "No-Fly Zone" produced a wealth of UFO sightings by fighter pilots and a vast number of unexplained radar contacts, with craft moving much faster than any known terrestrial fight craft. It has even been reported that Allied Forces engaged in combat with a UFO in the first Gulf War thinking it was an Iraqi fighter jet. Reports also emerged that US aircraft had brought down a craft of unknown origin in Saudi Arabia in 1998. Residents in the area of the crash site – officially claimed to be that of a jet fighter – were ordered to leave the area while American military engineers recovered all the wreckage for further study. However, residents claim that before they were forced to leave, they were able to establish that the craft was round and did not have any engine or wings. They also reported that even large bits of the wreckage were as light as a feather.

These intriguing tales took an unexpected twist when Russian intelligence sources suggested that a UFO had crashed in Iraq and that Saddam was now engaged in a programme to try to reverse engineer alien technology. At first dismissed as entirely fanciful, a number of intriguing stories relating to this claim started to surface. Among them were reports that Saddam had given sanctuary to the craft's occupants, housing them at his most secure palace – the citadel of Qalaat-e-Julundi. After the revolution that brought Saddam to power, the old Royal Family stronghold of Qalaat-e-Julundi became a palace for the new dictator. A vast underground bunker network was built under the existing building, already considered the most impenetrable place in Iraq as it stands on a hill surrounded by vertical precipices on three sides, plunging down to the Little Zab River. Soon after Saddam was alleged to have installed his guests there, people living in the Little Zab River Valley began to report strange lights in the sky, "dancing ghosts" seen only at night and a number of strange deaths.

Some of those struggling to believe in any of the official reasons put forward for the second Gulf War believe that the weapons of mass destruction argument was purely a cover story created to give a pretext to an invasion of Iraq. They consider that the real reason for vast military campaign was to prevent Saddam reverse-engineering the crashed alien spacecraft and developing a technological advantage over the US military just as the Americans had done over the Soviets with the Roswell crash in 1947.

THE STRANGE PART
After US forces rolled into Baghdad, a GI with the 3rd Brigade, 101st Airborne Division – who was fighting in the Little Zab Valley – photographed an oblong-shaped UFO. Locals who saw the UFO close to the holy city of Najaf believed that it, "had come from Allah's Gardens of Bliss to protect the Tomb of Ali". The mosque at Najaf stands over the grave of Ali, son-in-law of the prophet Mohammed. During the war it miraculously escaped damage from the 101st Airborne's howitzer barrage and heavy Allied bombing raids on the area around Little Zab River Valley focussed on the citadel of Qalaat-e-Julundi.

THE USUAL SUSPECTS
MJ-12
The group thought to be behind the cover-up and subsequent reverse engineering of the UFO crash at Roswell are alleged to secretly control the Joint Chiefs of Staff. They may also have close links with the Bush family through George Bush, Sr, going back to when he was director of the CIA. Having used the knowledge to ensure American supremacy since 1947, the prospect of being usurped by Saddam was unacceptable and they were forced to create a pretext for an invasion of Iraq so they could seize the crashed craft for themselves.

Reptilian Aliens
Reptilian beings from the Draco system are often accused of having entered into a secret alliance with parts of the world's ruling elite. Rumoured to be at war with the oft-sighted Greys, the Draconians may have instructed their allies in America's military and government to recover the Grey aliens being given shelter by Saddam. This was done under cover of war, rather than having to reveal themselves by a dramatic show of Draconian power in Iraq.

THE UNUSUAL SUSPECTS
The French Government
The French and Iraqi regimes enjoyed good relations and Saddam may have been negotiating with his friends in Paris to share UFO technology with them if they could prevent him from being removed from power by Bush. This would have allowed the French to lead a European challenge for global power. Right up until the moment of war, the French provided solid support for Iraq and US Secretary of State Colin Powell answered "Yes", when asked if France would be punished for its actions.

MOST CONVINCING EVIDENCE
Bush's claims that there was "no doubt that the Iraq regime continues to possess and conceal some of the most lethal weapons ever devised and that it threatens all mankind" were dubious, even before the post-war $500 million search of Iraq failed to find them. Though almost all of the Bush administration claims about Iraq weapons were disproved by UN inspectors, America still went to war, which suggests there must have been an ulterior motive for the military action.

MOST MYSTERIOUS FACT
Zecharia Sitchin, one of the few people in the world able to translate ancient Sumerian cuneiform, believes that ancient texts tell how the civilization of Sumeria (based in the area occupied by modern-day Iraq) was aided by an advanced race of beings. Called the Anunnaki (Sumerian for "those who came from Heaven to Earth"), their existence would mean that Saddam is not the first ruler in that area to have been helped by extra-terrestrials.

SCEPTICALLY SPEAKING
Expanding the power of America to ensure it controls the twenty-first century. The backfiring of Saddam's bluff that he had lethal weapons. A war fought on behalf of American oil companies. George Bush, Jr trying to prove to his father that he could kick Iraqi ass better than George, Sr could. Whatever the real explanation for the second Gulf War, surely crashed UFOs has got to be the least likely?

MEN IN BLACK (MIB)

If you've seen a UFO and report it the police, you can expect many things: ridicule, questions concerning your alcohol consumption, odd looks from friends and perhaps a call from the local newspaper looking for a bit of light news for the next day's edition. But even worse than the preceding events, you may receive a visit from the dreaded Men in Black (MIB).

The Men in Black have long been associated with UFO sightings and phenomena. They are reported to appear at the homes of some UFO witnesses shortly after they've reported their sighting to the police or media, threatening them to keep quiet. Any materials found relating to a UFO sighting are promptly confiscated. In some cases, they have even knocked on the doors of witnesses before they've told anyone else of what they have seen, seemingly knowing everything that has happened before the witnesses had a chance to sort it all out in their heads themselves. The Men in Black deliver their message in a variety of ways, from direct threats to roundabout hints, but their message always carries the same dark undertone: "Keep your mouth shut, or you'll regret it . . ."

The Men in Black are so called because of their sartorial colour of choice – black. Black suits, black hats and black sunglasses . . . this intimidating colour scheme extends to their cars – vintage models of Buicks, Cadillacs or Lincolns. They have been described as having complexions ranging from olive to grey to dark, with slightly slanted eyes, speaking in an almost computer-like monotone. Their age is difficult to determine, since all of them seem to be verging towards middle-aged. They move in a robot-like manner, and are perhaps best summed up in one word: "odd".

Despite their numerous appearances and incredible powers of intimidation, finding conclusive proof of the existence of the Men in Black is as slippery a task as acquiring evidence of the existence of the very UFOs they seek to protect.

THE STRANGE PART

The Men in Black definitely seem to be not of this world. Examples of this can be found in reports of MIBs disintegrating coins in their hands and inexplicably trying to sing to birds in trees. In one incident, a MIB sat down on a chair, which caused his trouser leg to rise up. There, apparently grafted to his leg, was a large green wire. In other cases, MIB are seen crossing muddy fields, yet arrive without a single spot of mud on them. In the most vicious cold weather, they will show up wearing nothing but a thin coat, oblivious to the deadly chill.

THE USUAL SUSPECTS
Aliens

In an effort to keep their activities on Earth quiet, aliens would employ the Men in Black to suppress any media attention to their activities by intimidating eyewitnesses of UFOs into fearful silence. From their inhuman way of moving and mechanical way of speaking, the MIB could be androids, programmed by the aliens involved in the sighting they are sent to suppress. Some people think that the Men in Black are aliens themselves, possibly Greys or another race, the Horlocks, (a reptilian race without souls). This would explain their remarkable strangeness around other human beings.

US Government

Working in conjunction with the aliens, the US government would utilize the MIB and their attendant oddities to suppress reports of UFOs. The Men in Black would be actors instructed to be as odd and bizarre as possible, thus adding to the already confused and emotional state of eyewitnesses. The MIB would be untraceable agents, not linked to any known governmental institution, thus allowing the "Powers That Be" to keep their hands clean of any violation of human rights.

THE UNUSUAL SUSPECTS
The Planet Sirius

The symbol of the Eye of Horus has been linked with secret societies in allegiance with the planet Sirius. This same symbol has been seen on some MIB, and some Men in Black have said they work for an organization called "The Nation of The Third Eye". The role they play in the plans of the denizens of Sirius is unclear.

UFO Eyewitnesses

If UFO sightings are nothing more than a complete mental breakdown of the witness involved, then the appearance of the MIB could be just a continuation of the hallucination, perhaps representing the witnesses' need for punishment and correction.

MOST CONVINCING EVIDENCE

The power of the Men in Black cannot be discounted. They have been responsible for the cancellation of *Space Review*, a magazine dedicated to studying flying saucers, and have even gone as far as gassing an eyewitness during a terrifying interrogation. It is possible that incontrovertible proof of alien existence does exist, whether it is photos, videos or actual aliens, but has been suppressed by the ruthless efficiency of the MIB. Research has discovered that the lineage of the Men in Black may go back as far as the Elizabethan age.

MOST MYSTERIOUS FACT

The vintage automobiles of the MIB are often illuminated from within by otherworldly greenish glows, and their clothing has a "shiny" alien texture to it that doesn't correspond to any known fabric on Earth.

SCEPTICALLY SPEAKING

If they were truly aliens, with the technology capable of enabling themselves to travel between the stars and capable of wiping out the memories of abductees, then why would they waste their time sending loonies in bad suits to knock on doors? Surely a good death ray would do the trick?

Hollywood's Men in Black. *Part of an insidious propaganda programme?*

SECRET BASES ON THE MOON

The Moon has always held a fascination for humanity – both as a source of romantic inspiration for poets and as an astronomical curiosity for scientists. However, is it also a secret base for the Third Reich? Apparently so.

In 2016, USAF Intelligence officer Karl Wolfe spoke of photographs of lunar bases on the "dark side" of the moon.

As early as 1942, the rumours go, the Nazis landed on the Moon with the aid of giant rocket saucers. These Nazi flying saucers are reported to have stood 45 metres high, contained 10 storeys of crew compartments, and had a diameter of 60 metres. Upon landing on the Moon, the Nazis quickly began building underground bases, solidifying their hold on the lunar surface while losing their grip on power in Europe below.

This colonization continued through the forties, with the Nazis ferrying up more people, raw materials, and robots in their giant interplanetary Nazi saucers. After the end of the Second World War in 1945, the Germans continued their space efforts from their Neu Schwabenland base in Earth's south polar region. This colonization continues to this day, with the full knowledge and assistance of other world powers.

There are certainly convincing photographs, taken during the Second World War, showing Nazi-produced flying craft that look remarkably similar to the classic concept of a flying saucer. These craft – going under such fabulous names as the Vril Odin 7 and Haunebu II – were developed at secret bases similar to the famous rocket base Peenemunde. It is well known that German scientists, many of whom ended up as founder members of NASA after the war, had planned to turn Peenemunde into a space port and springboard for Moon colonization after what they thought would be inevitable Nazi victory against the Allies.

THE STRANGE PART

Where to begin? Two things give this rumour a degree of credence. The first is growing weight of scientific evidence that the Moon is not totally arid and that the frozen ice on it could be utilized by any colony. Second, video footage taken from a NASA space shuttle clearly shows an unidentified object leaving the surface of the Moon. While there may be a non-conspiratorial explanation, strange lights, inexplicable markings on the surface and even potential structures observed by astronomers on the lunar surface push the number of odd questions needing answers to a disconcerting level.

THE USUAL SUSPECTS
The Nazi Party of Germany

Perhaps sensing the inevitability of defeat by the Allies as early as 1940, the Nazis decided to move their base of operations to a lunar plane, thus ensuring the long-term success of the Third Reich. Knowing Hitler's love of the supernatural and the fantastic, this does not seem implausible – just typically far-fetched.

The Axis Powers of Japan and Italy

Germany kept close ties with its allies during the Second World War, sharing its advances in weaponry with Italy and Japan. Rocket designs of German origin were routinely tested in Italy's research facilities, and in July of 1945, at the end of the War, a German U-Boat reportedly delivered a new invention to Japanese research and development units: a spherical, wingless, flying machine. Working under German instructions, the Japanese constructed the device, without knowing how it worked. Once activated, it roared off into the sky in a burst of flame, never to be seen again. Shaken, the Japanese scientists decided to forget about the whole thing. However, in January, 1946, a Japanese–German team, numbering in the hundreds, flew to the Moon in another saucer, surviving a near crash landing.

THE UNUSUAL SUSPECTS
NASA

NASA may be lying about the truth of the Moon's atmosphere, in order to keep other countries from wanting to explore it as well, thus ensuring a monopoly on the Moon. The story goes that when the United States and Russia

constructed their own moonbases in the Fifties, they were the guests of the Nazis when they landed.

Vril Society

A major mystical, secret order that was the source of much of the perverse ideology behind the early philosophies of the Nazi Party, the Vril Society claimed high-ranking members of Hitler's regime, major industrialists and powerful occultists among its ranks. It lent its name and money to the development of the mysterious Vril flying craft. It is known that some members believed the Aryan race developed from aliens who that landed in Sumeria around 4,500BC and were viewed as gods. Could Vril have been the power behind the establishment of Nazi moon-bases?

Aliens

Some conspiriologists believe that the Nazis were in league with extra-terrestrials and that the many advances they made in genetics and rocket science can be traced to a helping hand from beyond the stars. Debate rages over exactly which type of alien was assisting Hitler, but the favourites are the Aryan-looking Nordics rather than the Greys. However, given the type of experimentation on humans the Greys seem to love, and the depraved medical research performed by some of the human monsters of the Nazi regime, no one is ruling out an alliance with that particular branch of villainous space scum.

MOST CONVINCING EVIDENCE

The only proof of the American landing on the Moon comes from photographs published by NASA. However, over recent years these photos have been classed as fake because they are full of inconsistencies. Shadow lengths are at odds with the sun, the directions of shadows vary within pictures and there is plenty of evidence of the photos having been taken with the use of large sources of artificial light. If the photographs from NASA are not to be trusted, what else should we doubt?

MOST MYSTERIOUS FACT

There have not been any lunar landings – at least in the public's eyes – in over twenty years. Is this to distract the world's attentions from the colonies – Nazi, Russian and American, with populations estimated at over 40,000 – at work there?

SCEPTICALLY SPEAKING

The drives needed to power such huge saucers – listed by conspiracy theorists as "free energy tachyon drives" – cannot help but raise eyebrows. But with the reverse engineering associated with the salvaged technology from the Roswell crash and the lack of photos of the Moon's dark side, one can't help but wonder.

THE RENDLESHAM LANDING – ENGLAND'S ROSWELL

<u>There are mean-spirited cynics who will tell you that conspiracy theorists live only for the moment when they can rub their hands together and say, "I told you so." But in the annals of alien conspiracies, there is only one case where the conspiracy research can leap up like an overactive dog and shout, "I told you so, it is official – there was a conspiracy!" That case is Rendlesham.</u>

On 27 December 1980, an unidentified flying object (UFO) landed in a clearing in Rendlesham Forest next to the joint USAF air bases of Bentwaters and Woodbridge near Ipswich, England. Deputy Base Commander Lieutenant Colonel Charles Halt and several of his men witnessed the landing. It was tracked by British military radar and left behind physical evidence. Twelve years later, a British Parliamentary Watchdog ruled that the UK government had attempted to cover up all of the above facts. In 2002, Parliamentary Ombudsman Ann Abraham ruled that the UK Ministry of Defence had refused to divulge full details of the Rendlesham witness accounts and conspired to prevent knowledge of the event ever becoming known.

The incident is regarded as one of the most important ever UFO sightings and has become known as the "English Roswell". Possibly, it is just coincidence that both cases involve the US military and happened close to highly sensitive military bases with links to top-secret arms of American nuclear defence structure. Alongside being the only alien conspiracy where a government attempt to cover up the facts has been proven and exposed, no other case has as many staggering eyewitness accounts by highly credible military professionals.

Shortly after midnight on Boxing Day, radar screens at RAF Watton in Norfolk showed the sudden appearance of an object near Rendlesham Forest. Given that the twin airbases leased to the USAF on the perimeter of the forest housed a vast stockpile of weapons, alarm intensified when the object suddenly disappeared before reappearing without warning on the radar of the Bentwaters base. While further radar confirmations of the strange craft were coming in from other tracking stations, three military policemen saw light in the trees outside the back gate of the airfield and set off, fearing a crash. In his report of that night Deputy Base Commander Lt Col. Halt wrote, "They reported seeing a strange glowing

object in the forest. Metallic in appearance and triangular in shape approximately two to three metres across the base and 2m high. It illuminated the entire forest with a white light. The object itself has a pulsating red light on top and a bank of blue lights underneath. The object was hovering or on legs. As the patrolmen approached it manoeuvred through the trees and disappeared. At this time animals on a nearby farm went into a frenzy."

The next night, Lt Col. Halt joined a patrol that found three depressions on the forest floor where the object had been sighted. Radiation readings of ten times the normal level were discovered and as they were investigating the craft returned. Several years after the incident, Halt released an 18-minute audiocassette made on the night of the encounter. It makes chilling listening, especially the moment when another officer on the patrol sees the craft and shouts, "Look at the colours! Shit!" The tape also records the panic-stricken men as they see a beam from the craft disabling electrical devices in the area for a time and other military personnel in the area recording the event with both still and video cameras.

Given the impeccable witnesses and multiple types of physical evidence, you might think the public would at last be told that things that were unidentifiable and flew really did exist. However, in the years that followed, both the American and British military did everything in their power to cover up the Rendlesham Forest incident. It even seemed as if other shadowy elements were also involved in a conspiracy to enforce silence – discrediting, scaring and threatening anyone witnessing the case, or who had knowledge of it. In 1983, conspiracy researchers got their first major break when a copy of a memo written by Lt Col. Halt to the British Ministry of Defence was released under the UK Freedom of Information Act. With the first part of the puzzle out in the open, the battle to reveal the truth really began.

THE STRANGE PART

As more and more of the US military witnesses to the landing on the second night were identified, one USAF security patrolman, Larry Warren, even went public with an account claiming that he saw three "aeronaut entities" communicating with senior officers. The next morning, he and colleagues were checked for radiation exposure and instructed to sign statements, which merely mentioned seeing "unusual lights". The statements were arranged by members of the National Security Agency (NSA) and warned them not to discuss what they had seen.

THE USUAL SUSPECTS
The NSA

The US National Security Agency had a strong presence at the bases and played a key role in attempting to keep the landing secret. The NSA have an alleged contact and humans-for-advanced-technology exchange programme with the Greys and Rendlesham was purely a routine business meeting that was accidentally witnessed by Lt Col. Halt and his men.

Project Phoenix

An ultra-secret programme run by America's Defence Advanced Research Projects Agency. One element of Project Phoenix may be dealing with advanced microwave, laser and hologram weapons meant to create totally convincing illusions to baffle and demoralize the enemy. Rendlesham may have been an experiment to test the credulity of crack troops as well as assessing the impact on morale amongst elite warriors of these weapons.

THE UNUSUAL SUSPECTS
Parallel Earth Travellers

In medieval times, in an area close to Rendlesham, two mysterious green-skinned children were found, causing some to speculate that this part of Suffolk is home to a gateway to a parallel Earth. The visitors to Rendlesham may not have been extra-terrestrial visitors but instead, extra-dimensional. Either they took a wrong turning or were on a scouting mission to our Earth.

Zeta Reticulans

Grey humanoid aliens from Zeta Reticula were scouting the US bases as elements of the American military are in a secret

Does this lead to the site of a UFO landing near Rendlesham Forest?

alliance with reptilian aliens from the Sirius system. Their craft got into trouble and they were forced to land to make repairs behind enemy lines. However, luckily for the Zeta Reticulans, the soldiers at Rendlesham did not know they were at war and therefore let space reptile sworn enemies slip away.

MOST CONVINCING EVIDENCE

Despite the fact that it was tracked by radar, left impressions in the ground and massive radiation readings, the military and others later tried to claim that the event was purely down to the evolving beam of the Orford Ness lighthouse, five miles away. The depressions in the earth were merely rabbit diggings and the radiation was of natural levels. Many witnesses were sacked, defamed, harassed, stalked and threatened by the authorities as well as military intelligence agents and shadowy "Men in Black" – all of which is a bit over the top if the soldiers and civilians had just mistaken a lighthouse!

MOST MYSTERIOUS FACT

Author and society gossip columnist Georgina Bruni turned conspiracy researcher on the subject of Rendlesham and wrote a classic book on the case. At a social event in 1997, she seized her chance to ask former British Prime Minister Margaret Thatcher about the landing. Thatcher was annoyed at being questioned about Rendlesham and railed at Bruni, "You can't tell the people."

SCEPTICALLY SPEAKING

Hands up all those who are surprised that the UK government and the US military conspired to keep quiet about something strange landing close to an air force base housing enough nuclear to turn all of Europe into a radioactive wasteland?

ROSWELL

It was 3 July 1947 when W. W. "Mac" Brazel saddled his horse and rode out to check his sheep on his sprawling New Mexico ranch. There had been a thunderstorm the night before, and Brazel felt concerned for his animals' safety. But as he rode, he came across bits of strange wreckage strewn across the land.

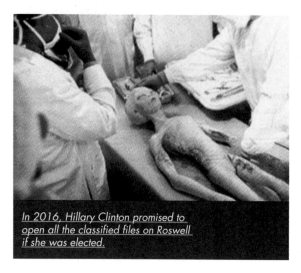

In 2016, Hillary Clinton promised to open all the classified files on Roswell if she was elected.

He also discovered what appeared to be a wreck of some sort. A huge gouge had been dug into the earth, running for hundreds of feet. Mystified, Brazel retrieved a piece of the strange material that littered the ground, and showed it to a neighbour. Wondering if he was holding something from a government project or possibly a UFO, he drove into nearby Roswell to tell his story to the local sheriff, George Wilcox, and by doing so, launched one of the most enduring nesting grounds for conspiracies in the twentieth century.

The truth about the incident at Roswell has remained hidden behind government subterfuge and the unreliability of ageing eyewitnesses. What is undisputed is that Wilcox dutifully reported the wreckage to Intelligence Officer Major Jesse Marcel of the 509th Bomb Squad. For the next few days, the site was closed off as the US Army Air Force removed the wreckage. On 8 July 1947, a press release prepared by the USAAF reported the debris was from a "flying disc". The following day, however, the government quickly retracted the story, stating firmly that the mysterious debris was not from a flying saucer, but merely the wreckage of a crashed weather balloon.

And there the story ended, or so the US government hoped. But strange stories began to grow, gaining strength by the unusual silence from military and government leaders. Among these stories were tales that it was indeed a crashed flying saucer, that the government was covering it up, that there were actual alien bodies aboard the ship, and even that some of the aliens had survived. More than fifty years have passed since the incident at Roswell. Conspiracy theories have flourished, generating much media attention and providing an eternal burr beneath the skin of the government. Eventually the US Air Force released a report – The Roswell Report: Case Closed – on 24 June 1994, in a vain attempt to shut the lid on perhaps the greatest Pandora's Box the conspiracy world has ever known.

Not surprisingly, it failed.

THE STRANGE PART

During the clean up of debris, Glenn Dennis, a mortician working in a Roswell funeral home, answered a few phone calls from the morgue at the local airfield. The Mortuary Officer there was looking for information on how to best preserve bodies that had been outside for a few days without suffering further contamination of the bodies' tissues. He also requested small, hermetically sealed coffins.

THE USUAL SUSPECTS
The US Government

A crashed UFO would have been a major technological windfall for the US government, and it would have wanted to keep such a find as secret as possible. Some people feel that the Roswell crash led the military into trying to decipher the mystery of the downed craft, reverse-engineering the alien technology to derive new weapons and anti-gravity capabilities. President Truman allegedly visited the crash site, and may even have spoken to sur-viving aliens. Shortly afterwards, Truman instigated the removal of all of the UFO crash material, including that found at Roswell, into the keep-ing of an anonymous multinational syndicate that now controls all UFO technology.

The US government has even been accused of torturing the alien survivors of Roswell, if not killing them outright, according to a secret policy of dealing with extra-terrestrials.

Other, less fantastic theories place the blame on to the military, testing secret planes built using Albert Einstein's withdrawn work on gravity field theory.

The Greys

There's no shortage of theories that state the Greys are using mankind to perfect genetic manipulations in order to save their own race. Alarmed that mankind had graduated to using nuclear weapons in 1945 (in much the same way we would if we discovered a pet hamster with an Uzi), the Greys reportedly began reconnaissance missions around military bases. This could have been the case at Roswell, where two ships may have collided, or the reconnaissance craft could simply have been struck by lightning.

THE UNUSUAL SUSPECTS
The Soviets

During the raging Cold War paranoia, it was suspected that the Soviets might have perfected their offensive missile capability with pilfered Nazi technology. The Roswell debris could have been the remains of a failed missile attack.

Hollow Earth Mole Men

There is a theory that the middle of the Earth is a hollow space containing land masses, a sun and oceans. According to that theory, the race living there might have been alarmed, much like the Greys, at the rise of nuclear testing by the creatures living on the surface of the planet. Flying out of the huge polar holes that lead to the hollow part of the Earth, these "Mole Men" may have crashed their ship on a reconnaissance mission.

MOST CONVINCING EVIDENCE

The need for the Air Force to release a "final report" implies a guilty conscience. If there was really nothing to Roswell, why go to the trouble, expense and possible ridicule of commissioning and publishing a report? The sudden leap forward in technology that followed the Roswell crash, especially the invention of transistors, is suspicious.

MOST MYSTERIOUS FACT

After driving out to the airfield hospital, the Roswell mortician Glenn Dennis saw several bits of wreckage carved with strange engravings. Speaking to a nurse there, she explained about the bodies, going so far as to draw him pictures on a prescription pad. A few days later, she was mysteriously assigned to a post in England, and then seemed, apparently, to drop off the face of the Earth.

SCEPTICALLY SPEAKING

The wild variations in the accounts of several "eyewitnesses" and the pure schlock of such gems as the purported Roswell alien autopsy video give this potentially devastating event all the appeal of a trailer park fun fair. It has become alien conspiracies equivalent of Elvis sightings.

The front page of a local newspaper on 9 July 1947, shortly after the Roswell crash.

SPACE SABOTAGE

Travelling to the stars has always been a daunting task, but is it being made more difficult than it need be? Is someone – or something – doing its best to keep mankind on Earth, by sabotaging space flight after space flight? The problem has become so widespread that NASA has jokingly referred to this enigmatic and often deadly force as the "Great Galactic Ghoul". But is it the subject for levity, or something far more terrifying?

The high incidence rate of spaceflight accidents, disappearances and technological foul-ups would have crippled any other endeavour that didn't have the benefit of government funding. From simple faults such as wires burning out in satellite systems to the tragedy of the Challenger explosion, the Great Galactic Ghoul shows no national preference – both Russian and American space programmes have been plagued by its disruptive hand.

Recent examples include the fiasco surrounding the Hubble Telescope. Once in space, the much-vaunted telescopes was found to be far from perfect, thus making its pictures far more blurred than expected. An expensive repair mission was needed, but the Hubble pictures are still being discounted as more a triumph of selective filters, designed to hide the telescope's imperfections, than the groundbreaking shots the project's supporters claim them to be.

Another example was the Mars Explorer mission of 1993, which was launched to take closer pictures of the mysterious Cydonia Region of Mars. Just as the craft was entering Martian orbit, it suddenly stopped functioning. Other failures include: the Soviet Koralb 11 (blew up); Sputnik 24 (blew up): NASA's Mariner 3 (missed Mars): Mariner 8 (fell into Atlantic); the Apollo 13 mission; and the fiery deaths of the astronauts in the Space Shuttle. The list goes on and on, and is either a testament to staggering incompetence or evidence of an ongoing act of sabotage, perhaps even on a galactic scale.

THE STRANGE PART

Missions to Mars fare the worst when it comes to sabotage. One of the most disturbing was the fate of the Russian Phobos probes. Launched in 1988, the Russians sent the two probes to investigate Phobos, the smaller of Mars's two moons. The Russians were interested in the irregular orbital patterns, which led many to believe Phobos was either an artificial con-struc-tion or perhaps hollow. The first probe was somehow lost on the journey from Earth. Phobos 2 made it to Mars and on its way to the small moon took photographs of a cylindrical-shaped shadow on the surface of Phobos. Shortly after that, the probe was destroyed. Its final picture, beamed back to Russia, has been declared too sensitive to release to the public. On the night that final picture was sent, orthodox Russian priests were asked to go to the Phobos 2 Control Centre in Moscow to discuss the pictures received.

THE USUAL SUSPECTS
NASA

As horrible as it sounds, especially with human lives being lost in some accidents, it is possible that a secret contingent within NASA could be sabotaging missions in order to satisfy elements in the US government that do not want the space programme to discover the alien presence surrounding Earth. Corresponding dissidents would, of course, exist in the Russian space programme.

Competing Contractors

The financial windfall associated with landing a lucrative government contract would prove irresistible to many businessmen. The best way to succeed in the cut-throat tendering process would be to discredit fellow competitors, using whatever means available, including sabotage. The power of the dollar, especially one from a government source, would easily overcome the sanctity of human lives in the eyes of many.

Also suspected: the FBI; MJ-12; sheer human incompetence.

UNUSUAL SUSPECTS
The Greys

For reasons of their own, it would be in the best interests of the Greys to keep Earth isolated from the rest of the Universe. If the Greys are rebellious slaves escaping from their masters and using human genetic material to reproduce and save themselves from the degradation of their cloned bodies, it simply would not do to have mankind drawing the attention of other alien races, particularly those masters.

Martians

The surprising number of incidents involving Mars missions goes beyond pure coincidence. The Monuments on Mars indicate that there was – or may still be – life on Mars, life that may wish to be left alone or that will make its presence known in its own good time. The breakdowns, disappearances and erratic behaviour of craft around the Red Planet has led some NASA employees to joke about a Great Galactic Ghoul living in between the asteroid belt and Mars. Perhaps this Ghoul is nothing more than a disgruntled Martian.

MOST CONVINCING EVIDENCE

Before the launch of the Mars Observer on 25 September 1992, NASA technicians examined its outer housing for a routine check. Inside, they were shocked to find the probe filled with garbage. This garbage included metal filings, dirt, paper, fibres and plaster of Paris. Even though Hurricane Andrew had blown through the area, it was impossible for debris of this kind to have entered the probe driven by the force of the storm alone…

Maybe it is not so surprising that of the 35 attempts to reach the planet, only 12 have succeeded. Of these, nine were attempts to land on the surface, but only three survived. The rest crashed or exploded in orbit. Even the successful ones had problems. Sojourner, which was launched in 1997, could only manage to move a few dozen metres from its landing zone.

MOST MYSTERIOUS FACT

In July 1998, the *Galileo* spacecraft was passing Europa, one of Jupiter's moons, when it suddenly stopped transmitting information. It has long been speculated that Europa, along with Mars, may be able to sustain life.

SCEPTICALLY SPEAKING

We have enough trouble programming our sat-navs and uber-smart televisions, so is it any wonder our spaceships keep blowing up?

A high number of expensive space exploration launches end in a disastrous manner.

CHAPTER 10:

MURDERED OR MISSING

JIMMY HOFFA

The disappearance of Jimmy Hoffa has become the stuff of North American urban legend. The unknown whereabouts of the body of the ex-Teamsters union leader is a source of never-ending conjecture. What is even more compelling is that while everyone is in agreement that Hoffa is indeed dead, no one has ever been arrested for killing him.

The efforts of police, from Detroit detectives to the FBI, have not uncovered the killers. Their identity remains as mysterious as the final resting place of Hoffa himself.

James Riddle Hoffa was born 14 February 1913, in Brazil, Indiana. After getting a job as a warehouseman at Kroger, the grocery store chain, Hoffa joined the International Brotherhood of Teamsters, a trade union. By 1957, Hoffa had climbed the union ladder to become President of the Teamsters, a position he held until 1971.

During his tenure as President of the Teamsters, Hoffa was often linked with the Mafia and with illegal activities. Robert F. Kennedy investigated Hoffa in the fifties and

sixties, which ended up with Hoffa being con-victed for jury tampering (during an earlier trial in which Hoffa was accused of receiving illegal payments from a trucking firm). In 1967, Hoffa was sentenced to eight years in a Federal prison. His sentence was commuted in 1970 by President Nixon, with a condition of parole being that Hoffa should refrain from union activities until 1980.

This didn't impress Hoffa, who began to make moves to regain control of the Teamsters. By 1975, he was on the verge of success, but this didn't fit in with the future plans of the Mafia. Having had trouble with Hoffa, La Cosa Nostra hoped his successor, Frank Fitzsimmons, would prove more

Some think he is in the cement supports of the New York Giants Stadium in New Jersey.

compliant. With the strong possibility that the stipulation barring Hoffa from union activities could be annulled, coupled with his strong loyalty base in the Teamsters, there was a chance that Hoffa could be president again. This was not something the Mafia wanted to see.

On Wednesday, 30 July 1975, Hoffa drove out to the Machus Red Fox Restaurant on Six Mile Road in Detroit, Michigan. It is known that he was due to meet someone there, but exactly who that was has never been revealed. Bearing in mind Hoffa's well-founded paranoia, it must have been someone he trusted. He was last seen alive at around 2:30pm in the restaurant's parking lot. He then disappeared, surfacing again only in public myth and speculation.

THE STRANGE PART

The final resting place of Jimmy Hoffa remains a mystery, with claims ranging from the outrageous to the macabre. One story has him buried in the depths of Lake Michigan, while perhaps the most outrageous was the one put forth by Donald "Tony the Greek" Frankos, who told *Playboy* magazine that Hoffa was buried beneath the end zone of the New York Giants football stadium. More plausible theories have Hoffa's body placed in the foundations of a shopping mall, while the FBI are partial to Hoffa coming to rest in a vat of bubbling zinc in a Detroit car factory.

THE USUAL SUSPECTS
The Mafia

There was potential for the Mob to make a lot of money from the Teamsters, especially with access to the massive Teamster pension funds. If an uncooperative Hoffa regained control of the Teamsters the loss of this lucrative source of income would mean a sizeable financial setback to the Mafia. There were also rumours that Hoffa had told the government about the Mob's involvement in the Teamsters, as a condition of his restriction on union involvement being lifted. This alone would merit revenge in the eyes of the Mafia.

Tony Provenzano

Hoffa had upset some members of the Mob on a more personal level, among them Tony Provenzano. "Tony Pro", as he was known, held a grudge against Hoffa from their time together in prison, and may have put a contract out on the ex-Teamsters leader. He went to great pains to establish an alibi on the day of Hoffa's disappearance.

Chuckie O'Brien

O'Brien may have been the man Hoffa expected to meet at the Red Fox, an apparently trustworthy decoy set up by the true killers. O'Brien grew up in Hoffa's home, effectively as

an unofficial "adopted son", and would not have been seen by Hoffa as a threat. O'Brien, himself, came under investigation when the police heard he was alleged to be in debt to the Mafia.

Union Officials

Not wanting to lose their positions within the union if Hoffa was elected president, some union officials may have put a contract out on him.

Also suspected: Tony Giacalone: Joseph Giacalone.

THE UNUSUAL SUSPECTS
The Teamsters Union

Not wanting to experience the corrupt reign of Hoffa again, members of the Teamsters may have concluded that, in the light of his popularity with the membership, there was no other route to removing him than murder.

The FBI

A long-shot theory centres around the FBI. It may not have wanted the com-bative Hoffa to be in control of one of the most powerful unions in the US, especially with Hoffa's grudge against law enforcement. Involve-ment in his disappearance would explain the Bureau's "inability" to solve the case.

MOST CONVINCING EVIDENCE

The car Chuckie O'Brien was driving the day of Hoffa's disappearance was seized by the FBI. It was a new Mercury Brougham, belonging to Joseph Giacalone. Police dogs found Hoffa's scent in the back seat, as well as evidence of his blood and skin. O'Brien blamed the blood on a fish he was inexplicably delivering to a friend.

MOST MYSTERIOUS FACT

Knowing full well how the Mafia worked, Hoffa would never have got into a car with people he didn't trust – not without putting up a fight, at least. There's a darker element of betrayal to the story: whoever killed Hoffa, or led him to be killed, were friends he trusted to be loyal.

SCEPTICALLY SPEAKING

If you run with wolves, chances are you'll get bitten. The only thing that separates this from any other Mob hit is the surprising lack of evidence buttressed by the silence of the killers. If Hoffa's body had been found, this would be nothing more than a half-forgotten footnote in the bloody history of Mob business. As Mob conspiracies go, it should be considered small-time – despite the way some conspiracy buffs view the case.

MARTIN LUTHER KING

He was a man of peace, and like most men who try to make the world a better place, his life ended violently. Dr Martin Luther King was an eloquent speaker, making moving speeches for civil rights in the sixties, from the famous civil-rights march of 200,000 people on Washington in 1963 to the more private confines of a church.

He fought with dignity for a seemingly impossible goal – equal rights for all men and women, despite the colour of their skin. During the turbulent sixties, many in America hoped King's dream would never come true.

King fought against the bigotry and ignorance in the US with weapons his enemies didn't expect – intelligence and compassion. He refused to stand down from what he believed in, angering those who felt blacks were nothing more than second-class citizens and should not dream of being anything more. King's quiet persistence raised fears of a changed status quo, from the Ku Klux Klan up to the FBI. He made powerful enemies and, in the end, they defeated him the only way they could, by silencing him forever.

Returning to Memphis in April 1968, King booked a room at the Motel Lorraine. He had returned to hold another demonstration, disgusted that an earlier protest held in the city in March that year had collapsed into violence. He was determined that this protest would not follow the same route. During his previous stay in Memphis, he had been criticized for staying in a white-owned hotel. To prove a point, King stayed in the Motel Lorraine – owned by blacks, but in a worse area of town.

On 4 April 1968, as evening was setting over Memphis, King was shot as he stood on the second-floor balcony of the Motel Lorraine. The threat to the status quo was eliminated. James Earl Ray, a local criminal, was arrested for the murder, and was accused of shooting King from the bathroom of a nearby boarding house. Doubts, though, began to arise as to whether or not Ray was the true assassin.

THE STRANGE PART

James Earl Ray, who apparently had little money, somehow managed to become a world traveller following King's assassination. With his new-found wealth, he flew to Canada, England, and then Portugal. When he was arrested in London's Heathrow Airport he was preparing to fly to Belgium.

THE USUAL SUSPECTS
The FBI

It was no secret that the head of the FBI, J. Edgar Hoover, thought King was one of the most dangerous men in America. In its attempts to remove King from his position of power, the FBI secretly taped King's alleged extramarital activities and used the tapes in the hope of convincing King to avoid public embarrassment by committing suicide. When that failed to work, there was only one alternative… the CIA

Another theory suggests that King's assassins were provided by the CIA, disguised as Memphis police. Ray was framed for the crime; government agents carried out the actual killing. This would seem to be substantiated by the fact that when Ray was arrested, he was carrying several pieces of fake ID and more than one passport – documents rumoured to be the work of a CIA identities specialist.

The Ku Klux Klan

King represented everything that the Klan hates. He was a man who refuted their stereotypes of blacks and threatened their narrow view of the world. By killing King, especially in the American South, the Klan would send a message to the black community graphically illustrating what happens to blacks who rise above their Klan-appointed station in life.

THE UNUSUAL SUSPECTS
The Memphis Police

Memphis was not particularly friendly to King, and the violent end to the demonstration in March 1968 did not endear him to the city, let alone to the police force. It has been rumoured that CIA agents posed as policemen and killed King, they may not have had to – the police could have had their own grudge against the civil rights leader, racially motivated or otherwise. It's interesting to note that the office of the Director of the Memphis Police Force was heavily populated by members of the military shortly before the killing.

Inside Members of King's Party

It has been suggested that the conspiracy to kill King extended into his own camp. Rumours have persisted that more than one of his close followers was a spy for the police or FBI and may have helped throw pursuers off the scent of the true killers by pointing to the boarding house window after King was shot.

The Mob

The Mafia was allegedly approached by the FBI to kill King, and offered a million dollars to do the job. The Mob refused, mysteriously citing the "screw-ups" the FBI caused directly after the Kennedy killing, but they may have had second thoughts if the plot was sweetened.

MOST CONVINCING EVIDENCE

It is not just the conspiracy community that believes Ray was innocent. Members of the King family supported claims of innocence and when Ray died in prison in Tennessee in 1998, they were invited to attend the funeral. The service was even conducted by the Reverend James Lawson, the former pastor of Centenary United who had invited Dr King to speak to striking sanitation workers in Memphis in 1968, during which visit he was shot. Maybe they were swayed by the fact that despite the large number of death threats directed at the civil rights leader, Memphis police quietly withdrew the expected police protection surrounding King one day before he was assassinated.

MOST MYSTERIOUS FACT

The only witness to claim he actually saw Ray at the boarding house after the shooting was Charles Stephens; other witnesses claimed that Stephens was too drunk to have seen anything. His wife refuted her husband's story, insistently claiming the man she saw in the boarding house was not Ray. The authorities went with her husband's story. For her troubles, Mrs Stephens was committed to a mental institution.

SCEPTICALLY SPEAKING

Of all the political assassinations in the Sixties, all with disturbingly clear government ties, the murder of Martin Luther King has to vie with RFK's for the title of being the most arrogant. It is staggering that it took the FBI over 15 days to publicly announce that a bundle, thrown by the assassin, belonged to James Earl Ray. Perhaps they should have announced they were giving him a "head start" as well.

Originally named Michael, King was arrested 29 times in his life on trumped-up charges.

DEATH OF A DREAM – ASSASSINATION OF RFK

Around midnight on 5 June 1968, there was magic in the air at the plush Ambassador Hotel in Los Angeles. Glamorous, charismatic and idealistic, Senator Robert F. Kennedy had just won the California primary for the Democratic nomination for President. It looked like he was going to fulfil the dreams of many Americans and go all the way to the White House – just like his brother, John F. Kennedy, had done before him.

Riding on the applause and congratulations of hotel workers, supporters and watching members of the public, RFK was being escorted by his security team through the hotel's pantry when his charge toward the presidency came to a tragic halt in a hail of gunfire. The hopes of many Americans lay dead on the tiled floor of the pantry.

After a fierce struggle that saw a small man, seemingly possessed of super-human strength, hold his own against several security guards, the apparent gunman – Sirhan Bashira Sirhan – was wrestled to the floor. His eyes were said to be enormously peaceful and the suddenly tranquil assailant was arrested. At the police station, Sirhan claimed to

He was determined to break the Mafia-linked Jimmy Hoffa who might have asked his "friends" to get RFK off his back.

have no memory of what had happened and showed all the symptoms of having been hypnotized.

The Los Angeles Police Department investigation into the murder quickly concluded that Sirhan was just another nut – a lone assassin in the mould of Lee Harvey Oswald. The courts agreed, Sirhan was convicted and thrown in jail. As far as officialdom was concerned, the tragic matter was over. As for the conspiracy theorists, the shooting of RFK is a case that definitely deserves to be looked at again.

THE STRANGE PART

At first glance, the RFK case seems open and shut: there is no denying it, Sirhan was arrested with a gun in his hand at the scene. However, that is where all simplicity in this case ends. Sirhan was in the wrong position and out of range, and could not have shot Robert Kennedy. The Senator was shot from behind, but all witnesses place Sirhan in front of him in a face-to-face position. All witnesses placed Sirhan's gun as being between one and five feet from Senator Kennedy, but the autopsy findings clearly establish that the Senator was shot from a weapon held between less than one inch and no more than three inches away from his body.

THE USUAL SUSPECTS
The CIA

If, as many people suspect, the CIA had a hand in the assassination of Robert Kennedy's brother, then they would certainly have a significant reason to fear Robert becoming president. If RFK reached the White House, he would probably launch an investigation into his brother's death – an investigation that could have proved the Warren Commission was nothing more than a cleverly constructed cover-up and that the President John F. Kennedy had been removed in what amounted to a military coup.

Mafia

When his brother was President, Robert Kennedy had been Attorney General and led a successful war against the Mafia. Their attempts to blackmail him over his affair with Marilyn Monroe may have failed and they could have decided that if RFK gained power there would be no way to prevent him from continuing his war against them even more effectively. In this situation, the traditional Mafia solution involves bullets and hitmen.

Military–Industrial Complex

Kennedy had pledged to end the war in Vietnam if he became President. Given the vast amounts of money that the American misadventure in South East Asia was generating for the military–industrial complex, it is certain that its members would have done anything in their power to stop his election to the White House.

THE UNUSUAL SUSPECTS
MJ-12

Also known as Majestic 12, this ultra-secret cabal of scientists, senior mem-bers of the intelligence community, and of the military is understood by some to be the force behind the conspiracy to suppress the truth about UFOs and aliens. Already suspected of putting an end to JFK, MJ-12 might have killed RFK to prevent him from exposing their dealings with the alien Greys when he became President.

Neo-Nazis

Some conspiracy theorists feel that Robert Kennedy's ability to appeal both to black and to white voters would have allowed him to heal the racial divide in America and forge a nation free of discrimination and hatred. Obviously, this is not the type of place those who cherish the Nazi philosophy want to live in, so it speculated that a cabal of neo-Nazis used their connections inside the US intelligence community to carry out the execution of the enemy they feared most.

MOST CONVINCING EVIDENCE

Bullet holes in a door frame at the crime scene, which are documented in FBI photographs, clearly show that more bullets were fired than could have come from the gun Sirhan is meant to have used to kill Kennedy. The police never disclosed that these bullets existed, even though the removal of the spent bullets by LAPD investigators was witnessed by other police personnel. The door frame in question was then destroyed by order of the court directly after Sirhan's trial concluded.

MOST MYSTERIOUS FACT

According to the psychological evaluation presented in court, Sirhan was definitely under a form of hypnosis at the time of the killing. Officially, this state was described in court as self-hypnosis, but others have doubted this. Claims have been made that the late hypnosis expert, William Bryan, boasted that he had hypnotized Sirhan. This might not amount to much if it was not for the fact that in Sirhan's diaries, which are filled full of strange automatic writing, one name is scratched into the paper over and over – DiSalvo. It might not be a coincidence that Bryan's most famous hypnotic subject was the alleged "Boston Strangler" – Albert DiSalvo.

SCEPTICALLY SPEAKING

The RFK conspiracy is probably one of the hardest to be sceptical over, but it would be dangerous to underestimate what a determined lunatic can achieve when he has easy access to a powerful handgun. Especially when scandalously bad security allows that same armed lunatic to be given a perfect opportunity to shoot someone famous.

CHANDRA LEVY

When the skeletal remains of missing former Washington intern Chandra Levy were found in a Washington, DC park in May 2002, almost 13 months after she vanished without a trace, a missing-person case became a murder investigation and a political scandal developed into a full-blown conspiracy theory.

When she came to Washington to begin an internship at the Federal Bureau of Prisons in September 2000, Levy was just 22. Within weeks, friends had introduced her to Democratic Congressman Gary Condit, who represented her home district in California. It was a fateful meeting, as the two quickly became secret lovers.

Condit, a member of the US Congress since 1989, was married and the father of two adult children. A major political player in Washington, he had founded a voting coalition of conservative and moderate congressmen. He also sat on several committees connected to espionage agencies and acted as an overseer of the CIA, through his work as a member of the House Permanent Select Committee on Intelligence. However, it was not just through her intimate relationship with Condit that Levy had access to information for which some conspiriologists would happily exchange various body parts. Her role at the Federal Bureau of Prisons involved making access arrangements for the press to view the execution of Timothy McVeigh, the man convicted of the Oklahoma Bombing. (To many conspiracy cynics, he is known as Lee Harvey McVeigh, due to their belief that he was merely a patsy.) Levy had access to sensitive Bureau and Department of Justice records relating to the condemned prisoner.

On Monday, 23 April 2001, Levy was somewhat surprisingly released from her internship. A mere week later, she was seen alive for the last time when she called in to cancel her membership of the Washington Sports Club. When her worried parents contacted the police on Saturday, 5 May 2001, they searched her apartment and found suitcases packed and ready to leave but no trace of Levy. Officially declared missing, suspicion began to build on Condit and the nature of his relationship with Levy. Questioned by both the police and her parents, at first he denied having an affair. When inconsistencies in his story surfaced, he eventually confessed to police that he was having a sexual relationship with Levy.

Over a year later, Levy was still missing and with his reputation in shreds, Condit was ousted from his seat in the Democratic primary by Dennis Cardoza, a former member of his own staff. However, the eventual discovery of Levy's body did not even begin to answer any of the questions her family, the police and conspiracy theorists had as to why she had gone missing in the first place.

THE STRANGE PART
Levy's skeleton was found by a man walking his dog in Rock Creek Park, in an area previously searched by the police and

Chandra Levy: a vegetarian with an ambition to join the FBI.

just 300 yards (274.30 metres) from a running path that she was known to have used. Police discovered Levy had looked at a website about the Klingle Mansion, a farmhouse built in 1823 and now used as park offices, on the day she disappeared, which made the park a major focus of the investigation. Given that it was not buried, how come it took almost 13 months to find her body?

THE USUAL SUSPECTS
The CIA
Given Condit's role in overseeing the CIA, many believe that it was something he discovered in this capacity that led to Levy's death. Her disappearance not only helped to remove him from any position of power over the agency, it also served as a warning of the fate that might lay in store for him, if he shared his knowledge with anyone else.

The FBI
At the time of Chandra's disappearance, questions were mounting up with regard to the FBI and their investigation of Timothy McVeigh. A court battle over evidence that the FBI had concealed led to a delay in the planned date of his execution. Did Levy's work involving that execution lead her to discover something about McVeigh that may have made the FBI take a hand in arranging her fatal vanishing act?

The Republican Party
Even the former First Lady Hillary Clinton talks about a "vast right-wing conspiracy" against successful Democrat politicians. So it is no surprise that there are those who believe that the whole Chandra Levy affair was a plot by a clique of renegade Republicans to unseat Condit and yet again drag the Democratic political establishment through the mud over sexual impropriety with young interns.

THE UNUSUAL SUSPECTS
Mossad
Ever since she had been a little girl, Levy had wanted to be a spy and she and other members of her family had strong connections with Israel. Some theorists believe that she had been recruited by Mossad – the Israeli Secret Service – to infiltrate to the highest possible levels in Washington, possibly to provide future blackmail on key politicians. If agents of the US or a country hostile to Israel had discovered this, it could certainly have been a motive for her death.

Members of Condit's Staff
Not every conspiracy needs to be about global politics.

Often they can be local and personal. If that is the case with Chandra Levy, then it is easy to understand why some have already pointed the finger at members of Condit's own staff, who may have wanted to expose the Congressman for either personal or Democratic Party benefit.

MOST CONVINCING EVIDENCE
Given Condit's sensitive position as a member of the House Permanent Select Committee on Intelligence and the access he had to highly classified intelligence, one of the most surprising and suspicious elements of the Chandra Levy case is just how little interest the US secret services took in her disappearance. In most other countries, if an intern of the Federal Bureau of Prisons who was connected to a politician with close links to foreign intelligence disappeared, it would not just be the conspiracy theorists massing to try to find out what happened to her. The absence of serious investigation by the shadowy forces responsible for security of the State convinces many that a full-blown cover-up is involved. They believe the reason they are not looking is because they already know the answers – they just do not want anyone else to know.

MOST MYSTERIOUS FACT
The lead FBI investigator in the Chandra Levy case was Special Agent Bradley J. Garrett, someone who had already come to the attention of some conspiracy researchers. Garrett had played a key role in the prosecution of Pakistan national Aimal Kasi, who was accused of murdering CIA agents in a car parked outside the Agency's HQ in Langley, Virginia. He had also investigated the suspicious death of another young female intern – Mary Caitrin Mahoney – shot in what seemed like a professional hit in a Washington, DC Starbucks. Being an FBI agent involved in two conspiracies with unresolved questions makes you either incredibly unlucky or highly suspicious in the eyes of conspiracy research, but three? Not even Fox Mulder from *The X-Files* was that unlucky.

SCEPTICALLY SPEAKING
An unknown random attacker murders a young woman; a married politician has a career-wrecking affair with an intern – sadly, these are hardly uncommon occurrences. Were it not for the coincidence that both headlines could be related to Chandra Levy, conspiracy theorists would have their work cut out finding anything to worry about. Give it up, boys! Washington, DC is convoluted and murky enough without having to invent new twists and turns through the cesspool.

DAVID KELLY

A government scientist reveals to a journalist the truth about false evidence designed to make the public accept an unpopular war and is then found dead in suspicious circumstances. It sounds like the plot of a major Hollywood thriller.

However, it happened in one of the most high-profile and intriguing conspiracies of recent times when the UK government's leading arms expert Dr David Kelly was found dead in a field near his home with his left wrist slashed.

Weeks before his death, Kelly was thrust into the media spotlight after being revealed as the man the government believed could be a source for a BBC report on Iraq. Although briefing journalists was part of his job, Kelly was shocked when he became a key public figure in the row between the government and the BBC over claims that Downing Street had "sexed up" a dossier concerning Iraq's weapons capability.

The Oxford-educated microbiologist was the scientific adviser to the government's proliferation and arms control secretariat. Kelly was also senior adviser on biological warfare for the UN in Iraq between 1994 and 1999. Nominated for a Nobel Peace Prize, he was renowned for being so bright "his brain could boil water". He had been the UN weapons inspector who had previously discovered Iraq's radioactive material and was so good at his job Saddam was reported to have said that he should be thrown out of the country.

Kelly found himself at the centre of a huge political scandal after government rules were breached and he was exposed as the source for the BBC story that questioned Prime Minister Blair's claims about weapons of mass destruction (WMDs). He was forced to give evidence in public to the Foreign Affairs Select Committee on 15 July. Two days later, Dr Kelly left his home at 3pm, telling his wife he was going for one of his regular walks. When he failed to return home by 11.45pm, his family contacted the police.

The next morning, the Thames Valley police made public his disappearance, shortly before they found a body in woodland on Harrowdown Hill, near his Oxfordshire home. As Blair struggled to answer questions about Kelly's death during a press conference in Japan, police and MI5 officers were sweeping through the germ warfare expert's house in search of "relevant documents".

Quickly reported as an apparent suicide, public speculation over the circumstances surrounding the death of Kelly and the media's focus on the case meant the government was forced to hold a judicial inquiry into the affair. Headed by Lord Hutton, the inquiry aimed to investigate the circumstances of his death and the allegation

that the government doctored intelligence reports.

One of Russia's top scientists and a former colleague of Kelly, Professor Sergei Rybakov, immediately cast doubt on the alleged suicide. Rybakov asserted: "David was optimistic and never lost his cool even under extreme pressure. He was not capable of committing suicide."

Rybakov's claims gained weight when the inquiry found that four months before his death, Kelly had predicted that if the American and British invasion of Iraq went ahead, he would "probably be found dead in the woods". His chilling and accurate prediction was made in February 2003 during a conversation with David Broucher, British Ambassador to the Disarmament Conference in Geneva.

THE STRANGE PART

Aside from prophecising his own death, not leaving a note to his beloved wife and being a member of the Ba'hai faith, which is opposed to suicide, there is the question of an email Dr Kelly sent before his death. At the Hutton Inquiry, it emerged that he had sent an email to an American journalist warning that "many dark actors are playing games" hours before he walked to the woods where he bled to death.

THE USUAL SUSPECTS
MI6

Many parapolitical researchers believe that Kelly was murdered by security services as an example to others tempted to reveal elements of their shadowy world. Whether or not an elected official sanctioned the killing, many feel that the most likely executioners would have been MI6 personnel, especially given their links to Kelly and his work for them debriefing Russian and Iraqi defectors.

DEFENCE INTELLIGENCE AGENCY

Dr Kelly's work with the Iraq Survey Group, set up by America and Britain to track down Saddam's alleged WMD arsenal, meant he came into contact with the Pentagon's Defence Intelligence Agency (DIA). Kelly had vast experience of Iraq and was one of the few people to have ever questioned Dr Rihab Taha, the head of Saddam's biological weapons programme. After the war, he could have proved that the DIA's evidence to justify the war was false. With their reputation at stake, the DIA not only had a motive, but are viewed by many conspiriologists as one US security agency competent enough to have organized the murder.

THE UNUSUAL SUSPECTS
Iraqi Secret Service
Kelly was a thorn in the side of the Iraqi military and intelligence forces. His work had enraged Saddam and had done much to create the view in America that Iraq had never fully abandoned its WMD programme. In the aftermath of the invasion, Iraqi sleeper agents may have been awakened and sent to kill Kelly in reprisal for helping bring about the invasion. If this was true, the Iraqi Secret Service not only got revenge against Kelly and embarrassed Blair's government, but created a suspicious climate in which their rivals in US and UK secret services were thought most likely to have been involved in Kelly's murder.

Unit 13
Alleged to be name of Britain's black ops death squad, formed from SAS members working for rogue elements of MI6 with strong links to the US military industrial complex, Unit 13 has been accused of politically motivated assassinations and removal of "embarrassing" individuals. Infamous for a range of "death from above wet operations" – especially in Northern Ireland – it has a notorious dislike for those it regards as traitors to its country. Some of its members may have taken it upon themselves to punish Kelly for his perceived disloyalty to Blair or to protect the interests of those involved in biological warfare research.

MOST CONVINCING EVIDENCE
Michael Page, the Assistant Chief Constable of Thames Valley Police, told the Hutton Inquiry he did not think anyone else could have been involved in Kelly's death. However, this is not the view of some of his officers as expressed in off-the-record conversations with the author David Southwell. Suspicions were first raised because, despite his position as a security threat, there were apparently no police, MI5 or security service observing Kelly's movements – a breach of standard protocol.

Some officers have doubts that Kelly could have slashed his wrist and then walked yards to conceal himself without leaving a trail of blood. They are worried about reports of three men dressed in black in the area where Kelly's body was found. Explained away as policemen, testimony by one of the officers alleged to be one of the three men to the Hutton inquiry clearly proves that whoever the three MIBs were, they were not Thames Valley's finest. Also troubling is that Mr Page had to tell the inquiry how Dr Kelly's dentist contacted the police after his death. Mysteriously, the scientist's dental records had gone missing from a locked filing cabinet on the day of his death and eventually reappeared the following Sunday.

Stop the War Coalition

♠ A

B.liar

A ♠

When asked, "Have you got blood on your hands?", Blair refused to answer.

MOST MYSTERIOUS FACT
Some conspiracy researchers feel that Kelly's death had little to do with Iraq and is actually part of a much larger conspiracy involving the deaths of at least twenty of the world's top microbiologists within a year of each other. Many of the scientists – such as Russian defector Vladimir Pasechnik, whom Kelly had debriefed for MI6 – had worked with Kelly. Among the strange deaths recorded are Benito Que (beaten in Miami); Robert M. Schwartz (stabbed in a "ritualistic slaying"); Nguyen Van Set (died in a lab freezer); and Tanya Holzmayer, killed by a microbiologist colleague, Guyang Huang, who shot her before apparently turning the gun on himself.

SCEPTICALLY SPEAKING
The Hutton Inquiry failed – some might say deliberately – to answer many outstanding questions surrounding the suspicious elements of Dr Kelly's demise. Ultimately, however, blame for the tragic death of this decent man has been laid at the door of the scientist himself. Lord Hutton found that the Ministry of Defence had not failed in its care of duty to its employee and, certainly for the foreseeable future, the case is now closed.

DOROTHY KILGALLEN

Of all the mysterious deaths that swirled around the assassination of John F. Kennedy in 1963, few are as curious as that of Dorothy Kilgallen.

She has her own star on Hollywood's Walk of Fame and Joan Crawford attended her funeral.

What separates the tragic loss of Kilgallen from the scores of officially unrelated deaths connected to that fateful day in Dallas, is that Kilgallen was a popular member of the media, very much in the public eye long before her involvement in the investigation surrounding the assassination. But as her death may prove, even celebrity may not be enough to protect you if you cross the wrong people.

Kilgallen's media career began in 1931 when she signed on to work for the Hearst newspaper syndicate as a fledgling writer. At first, she was relegated to writing about "woman

things", but her ambition and skill soon overrode the chauvinistic limits placed upon her, and she moved on to far meatier stories, including covering the legendary Sam Sheppard trial. (Sheppard's story was the basis for the popular sixties television series *The Fugitive*, and the subsequent Harrison Ford movie of the same name.) Not content with simply being a top-notch writer, Kilgallen moved into other media, working as a panellist on the popular television show *What's My Line?* as well as hosting her own radio show in New York – a programme so successful that it ran for some twenty years after first hitting the airwaves in 1945. Her popularity, buoyed by her sharp wit and intelligence, endeared her to many fans.

But it was during the trial of Jack Ruby for the murder of alleged Kennedy assassin Lee Harvey Oswald that Kilgallen may have taken the first steps that would lead to her death. After attending Ruby's murder trial in Dallas, in 1964, Kilgallen became convinced that there was more to the story than was being reported in the press. After voicing her doubts in her daily newspaper column, "The Voice of Broadway", Kilgallen returned to Dallas to interview Ruby. Excited by what she learnt, she returned to New York and wrote a column that linked Dallas police officer JD Tippet (thought to have been shot dead by Oswald shortly after the assassination as he tried to flee) to Jack Ruby and to Bernard Weissman – a man who was publicly known to dislike Kennedy. In her column, Kilgallen revealed that all three men had met in Ruby's strip club just one week before Kennedy was shot.

After she revealed more ominous material, the FBI launched an investigation into Kilgallen. But still she persevered, undeterred. She travelled to New Orleans, ostensibly to gather further proof of a cover-up, then returned home with plans to reveal all in a book. The threat that Kilgallen posed to the forces behind Kennedy's assassination may have caused her demise. Dorothy Kilgallen was found dead in her bed on 8 November 1965. The official explanation of her death was "accidental". An autopsy found an acute mix of ethanol and barbiturates in her system, so suicide could have been the cause of death. But why would Kilgallen commit suicide when the book of her career was set to be published? Was her death truly accidental? Or was she silenced, as were so many, because of her knowledge of the truth surrounding the Kennedy assassination?

THE STRANGE PART
None of the files Kilgallen had compiled, including the transcripts of her interview with Jack Ruby and the information she gleaned in New Orleans, were ever released to the media.

THE USUAL SUSPECTS
The FBI
J. Edgar Hoover himself ordered the investigation into Kilgallen, determined to discover just how she was uncovering her information, especially her publication of Ruby's testimony to the Warren Commission. Before Kilgallen broadcast that to the world, it had been classified "Top Secret". Kilgallen's refusal to be cowed by the FBI combined with her determination to reveal the truth behind Kennedy's death – including suspected FBI involvement – may have sealed her fate.

The Mob
Another suspect in the Kennedy assassination, the Mafia, may have silenced Kilgallen, trying to make her death look like a suicide. The Mob may have been acting on its own, or under orders from the FBI or the CIA.

Also suspected: agents of the military–industrial complex; pro-Castro Cubans; and anti-Castro Cubans.

THE UNUSUAL SUSPECTS
Richard Kollmar
Kollmar, Kilgallen's husband, was in the apartment at the time of her death, and reportedly didn't find her body until noon the next day. There are rumours that she was romantically involved with singer Johnny Ray. Allegedly, she called him from a public payphone to say that she had the story of the century, but that she didn't feel comfortable talking about it over the phone. Her husband's jealousy as a result of this affair may have played a role in Kilgallen's demise.

Jealous Rivals
Kilgallen made no secret of the impact she felt her investigations would have. In the cut-throat world of journalism, where a single scoop can make or break a career, someone may have decided to trim the competition.

MOST CONVINCING EVIDENCE
Kilgallen was found in bed, apparently having died while reading a book. Her glasses – which she needed in order to read – were not on her face, nor within her reach. The book was one she had told friends she had already finished reading, and she was still wearing make-up, which Kilgallen always removed before retiring.

MOST MYSTERIOUS FACT
Shortly after Kilgallen's death, Mrs Earl T. Smith, a close friend of Kilgallen, also died mysteriously.

SCEPTICALLY SPEAKING
It's OK to report the truth – just make sure it's the approved truth.

LORD LUCAN

One of the most mysterious vanishing acts ever accomplished by a fugitive was the disappearance of Richard Bingham, the Seventh Earl of Lucan. "Lucky" Lucan was a member of the aristocracy and a professional gambler, a man with a well-known taste for the easy life.

A popular socialite in well-to-do London circles, Lucan's expensive hobbies had left him heavily in debt. He had become estranged from his wife, and the couple were in the process of fighting a bitter custody struggle over their three children.

On the night of 7 November 1974, the 29-year-old nanny who looked after Lucan's children, Sandra Rivett, was brutally murdered in the family's home with a length of lead piping. When Lady Veronica Lucan went to investigate, she too was attacked and badly injured. The alarm was raised when she staggered into a pub close to the house, covered in blood, declaring that her husband had murdered the nanny.

Penniless and without his passport, that same night Lord Lucan left a letter saying that he was innocent. He borrowed a friend's car (the bloodstained vehicle was later retrieved at Newhaven Docks) and then vanished. The last sighting in the UK of the man himself had him some 18 miles away, in the town of Uckfield. Many find it significant that although his children eventually had Lucan declared financially dead, his eldest son was not allowed to have him declared legally dead until the day after the hereditary peerage was abolished in 1999. If this had happened before, his son could have inherited his father's seat in the House of Lords.

THE STRANGE PART

Much like Elvis, Lucan is regularly sighted around the world. Reports have placed him walking on mountain slopes in Sicily and in permanent residence in Southern Africa. Scotland Yard still investigate supposed sightings of the Earl, and has had as many as 70 different sighting reports under investigation at once. If he is still alive and in hiding, Lucan would be in his seventies, having been penniless and on the run for a quarter of a century.

THE USUAL SUSPECTS
Lord Lucan – Dead

The most common theory is that the Earl is dead, having committed suicide in despair and remorse after bungling his attempt to kill his wife. He drove to the English coast, and then swam out into the English Channel to drown.

Lord Lucan – Alive

In this version, Lucan was helped out of the county by a rich friend – possibly the now-deceased Sir James Goldsmith – who flew him from the South of England to France in a private plane. The benefactor also provided money and clothing. Once within Europe, it would have been relatively simple to move around without a passport – border controls are often lax – and slowly make his way down to Botswana, where he now lives. Funded by people who would rather not see the peerage dragged into disrepute by a trial, he lives in modest comfort.

THE UNUSUAL SUSPECTS
Freemasons

While it is uncertain whether or not Lucan was a Freemason, many members of the nobility are part of the ancient fraternity. Uncertain of Lucan's guilt but desperate to prevent a hugely embarrassing trial, the Masons helped "Lucky" out of the country, and set him up with a peaceful life somewhere out of the way.

Meonia

Lucan may have been a member of the mysterious organization dedicated to preserving the bloodline of certain aristocratic British families and ensuring the continuation of Britain through mystic means. If one of their own was in trouble, the secret order would have seen it as their sacred duty to protect him from the threat of prison.

MOST CONVINCING EVIDENCE

Even though his children eventually managed to have Lucan declared legally dead, the English police were far from convinced. In interviews conducted by author David Southwell, in 1999, some detectives at Scotland Yard announced a suspicion that Lucan is living in Botswana in Southern Africa and that frequent trips made by his children to the area have been observed. Lack of funds made an investigation difficult to carry out. Lucan's children, however, dismissed the suggestion as absurd.

MOST MYSTERIOUS FACT

In 2003, a furore was caused when a photograph of an elderly man, claimed to be Lord Lucan, was published as part of the publicity for a book claiming that the missing Earl had died in Goa, India, in 1996. However, it later turned out that the photograph of a dishevelled man with a long beard bearing a resemblance to the 7th Earl of Lucan – taken in 1991 – was actually that of ancient hippie and one-time folk singer Barry Halpin. Also known as "Mountain" or "Jungle Barry", Halpin was a heavy-drinking, banjo-playing ardent socialist, who went to live in India because it was cheap, sunny and more spiritual than St Helens.

SCEPTICALLY SPEAKING

As the publicity around the mistaken Halpin photo showed, Lucan has become something of a popular tragic-heroic figure. He has even adorned the album cover of England pop band Black Box Recorder and been the subject of one of their songs. Given that his theoretical backers are now dead, if Lucan revealed himself today he could make a fortune and the publicity surrounding his case would make a trial almost impossible. If he returned and was exonerated of charges, there's little doubt he would become a genuine English folk hero. There's simply not enough scandal left to make hiding worthwhile any more.

LEE HARVEY OSWALD

The history books tell us that on 22 November 1963, in Dallas, Texas, Lee Harvey Oswald shot and killed John F. Kennedy from a window in the Texas School Book Depository.

His last words to his protection squad were, "Nobody's going to shoot at me!"

The history books go on to recount that roughly 45 minutes later, Oswald then shot and killed Officer J. D. Tippit of the Dallas Police Force, and was later apprehended in a movie theatre. Two days later, Oswald was himself shot by Jack Ruby, apparently outraged at the murder of the President. According to the Warren Commission, which investigated the assassination, there the story ends – the late Oswald was the lone gunman, there was no conspiracy, case closed.

However, conspiracy theories continue to swirl around the incidents of that fateful day in Dallas, suggesting that the least probable theory is that Oswald acted alone. There also remains the mystery of Oswald himself. Even the most cursory of glances at him and his alleged activities around Dallas in the days preceding the assassination, is rife with inconsistencies and bizarre elements worthy of a conspiracy all on their own.

On 26 October 1957, Oswald joined the Marines in San Diego, California. While he was in the Marines he became enamoured of Russia and its politics. After a dishonourable discharge on 13 September 1960, he announced he was going to renounce his American citizenship and move to the USSR. He arrived in Moscow a little more than a month later. Travelling to Minsk, he married Marina, the daughter of a KGB colonel. The glorious life in Russia apparently soured and Oswald returned to the US with his wife in 1962. Back in the US, Oswald drifted from one job to another and was suspected of an assassination attempt on Major General Edwin Walker on 10 April 1963, in Dallas.

His political views got him arrested in New Orleans on 9 August that same year when he was involved in a fight with angry Cubans while passing out "Fair Play for Cubans" pamphlets. A friend of his wife – a Russian exile with CIA connections – arranged for him to get an interview back in Dallas at the Texas School Book Depository. Lying about his past, Oswald was hired on 15 October 1963. The rest, as the books tell us, is history. Or is it?

THE STRANGE PART

There are conflicting reports, of Oswald's activities before the Kennedy assassination. A Texas car salesman, Albert Guy Bogard, reported that Oswald took a car for a test-drive before the shooting, remarking about a large amount of money he would be getting soon – yet, Oswald never had a driver's licence. Another sighting has Oswald showing off at a Dallas area rifle range, expertly shooting the bull's-eyes in other patrons' targets – this, despite Oswald's inferior record as a marksman while in the Marines. Maybe these "Oswalds" were actors hired by the true parties behind the assassination to ensure the real Oswald would pay for the crime.

THE USUAL SUSPECTS
The Mafia

Jack Ruby originally claimed he shot Oswald to spare Jackie Kennedy the pain of a public trial. However, plenty of evidence abounds that Ruby was a member of the Mob. With several of the most believable conspiracy theories surrounding the assassination of JFK involving the Mafia, it probably is not coincidence that Ruby took out Oswald. Ruby killed Oswald to prevent the Mafia's role in the President's death being exposed.

The FBI and the CIA

Even before Oswald left for the USSR, he was under FBI scrutiny. The reason for his dishonourable discharge from the Marines – for wanting to be a Russian – was public knowledge, so the CIA would have the perfect fall guy: a lone assassin working for the dreaded Russians, which would play extremely well with the media.

THE UNUSUAL SUSPECTS
KGB

The KGB knew that if Oswald was ever brought before a court, his communist background and links to the KGB would emerge. If this happened, the Soviets would be suspected of organizing the Kennedy shooting, so they employed Ruby to ensure Oswald never went on trial.

MOST CONVINCING EVIDENCE

If Oswald had killed Kennedy for political reasons, then why did he never proudly take credit? Instead, he insisted until his death that he had been set up – hardly the actions of a fanatic. His murder by Jack Ruby – preventing the truth from ever coming to light – was far too convenient.

MOST MYSTERIOUS FACT

The CIA reportedly experimented with LSD on troops in Atsugi, Japan, as part of their mind-control tests in 1957. Oswald was serving with the Marines there at the time.

SCEPTICALLY SPEAKING

Of course Oswald shot Kennedy and therefore it is not impossible that an outraged American might want to take revenge. If you listen to some of the conspiracy theories about him you might also believe Oswald sank the Titanic and stole your newspaper this morning.

HIT-MAN MISSING

Glenn Miller and his band were one of the most successful American recording acts of all time, with a track record to dwarf that of the later Elvis Presley. Between 1938 and 1942, when he volunteered for the US Army, Miller had 70 Top Ten hits, as many as 23 of them becoming Number 1s.

This compared with Presley's record of 38 songs in the Top Ten, with 18 of those making the Number 1 position. Once he had joined the army, Miller organized concerts and radio shows to help boost morale. Having recorded what would turn out to be his swan-song at London's Abbey Road Studios – later made so famous by The Beatles – Miller set out to find a flight to France, where he was due to organize a string of concerts entitled I Sustain the Wings. However, the way things turned out for Miller, this proved to be a highly inappropriate title…

Miller drove from London to the Milton East airbase outside Northampton, thinking he would be able to hitch a flight to Paris. However, having no luck there, he drove on to the Twinwood Farm airfield, just outside Bedford, where USAF Lt Col. Norman Baessell offered him a seat on his pre-arranged flight for the next day – 15 December 1944. Baessell's pilot, Flight Officer John Morgan, arrived the next day at 1:30pm. All three men then took off in thick fog at 1:55pm in Morgan's single-engined Norseman, never to be seen again.

THE STRANGE PART

Given that Glenn Miller was such a highly valued PR asset and morale builder for the American forces, it is odd that he was wandering the UK alone, trying to secure a seat on an aeroplane bound for Paris. Surely, what with the concerts being a military enterprise, his transfer would have been arranged as part of the basic logistical planning? Unless, of course, Miller's brother Herb was right about Glenn being at death's door at the time. This might explain why, as has been suggested, he wanted an insignificant flight in a small plane from which he could jump to his death. It is a matter of record that Miller seemed strangely pleased by the absence of parachutes on the Norseman that day.

THE USUAL SUSPECTS
Assorted

There is a popular theory about Glenn Miller's death which claims that mechanical failure was to blame for the aeroplane crash. It has been alleged that cold weather iced up the Norseman's wings or possibly its carburettor. However, this

theory can be quickly dismissed for, although the day in question was undoubtedly foggy, the temperature was a steady 41°F – which was far too warm for any such icing to occur.

Some have maintained that the Germans, furious at Miller making anti-Nazi broadcasts in their language, dispatched a hit squadron to bring down his plane. However, with his travel arrangements being both so haphazard and last-minute, how could they possibly know his intentions? Others have suggested that, reluctant to fly in a single-engined plane in the fog, Miller backed out of the flight at the last minute to make alternative arrangements. Notionally, he then made it to Paris by other means, where he was either shot in the dark by a trigger-happy American military policeman or overcome by a heart-attack in a brothel, while engaged in some rather frantic 'horizontal jogging'. Either way, the American authorities felt obliged to brush Miller's death under the carpet and maintain that he had stuck to his original plans to fly with Baessell in the ill-fated Norseman.

Miller's own younger brother, Herb, waded into the debate with his assertion that Miller had in fact died of lung cancer in a military hospital. This matter-of-fact death was then covered up, as a mysterious disappearance made for better PR than a national icon suffering a lingering and unpleasant demise. To be fair, Miller was not a well man at the time of his death or disappearance; a heavy smoker, he was losing so much weight that his uniform simply hung on him. In the summer of 1944, Miller had written to Herb to say that he was emaciated and having trouble breathing. At the same time, he was telling friends, "I think you guys will be going home without me."

THE UNUSUAL SUSPECTS
The RAF

The smart money suggests that Glenn Miller's plane was knocked out of the air by a returning flight of 138 Lancaster bombers heading for their base at Methwold in Norfolk, after they had been recalled from their raid on Siegen in Germany due to lack of fighter cover. In accordance with normal practice in such circumstances – it was far too dangerous to land with a full load of primed bombs – the flight was directed to Jettison Area South, a 10-mile square patch of the English Channel to the south of Beachy Head, where they could dump their ordnance. Three members of the crew of Lancaster NF937 – the bomb-aimer, the tail gunner and the navigator – would later confirm that, as they shed their load at 4,000ft, they saw a Norseman directly below at about 2,500ft. Caught in the lethal shower of bombs, they saw the small plane flip over and go down.

Instructed to follow the SHAFE shuttle-route to Paris, Miller's plane headed south from the airfield to skirt the London no-fly zone before heading for Beachy Head. There it would have had to turn southeast for Dieppe to take the plane within five miles of the bomb-dump zone. Therefore, if Flight Officer John Morgan allowed the Norseman to veer even a shade off-course in the fog at this point, then he, Baessell and Miller would have been left flying straight through the middle of the Jettison Area at the right time. The Lancasters from 149 Squadron had taken off at 11:30am for Seigen, about 40 miles to the northeast of Bonn, but 90 minutes into their flight they were recalled and ordered to dump their bombs in Jettison Area South. According to the flight logs of 149 Squadron, this dumping commenced at 1:43pm.

MOST CONVINCING EVIDENCE

Miller's disappearance was hushed up at the time and, as nobody from Lancaster NF937 was running around boasting of having 'bombed' a light aircraft, no one made the connection. It was only after the war that the NF937 navigator, Fred Shaw, saw the film *The Glenn Miller Story* (1954) and started to get a very uneasy feeling. He dug out all his old flight logs and went public with his theory, only to be met with a hail of derision from both the RAF and the Glenn Miller Appreciation Society. As there were only five Norsemen in the UK at the time, how would he, Shaw, know one from a hole in the ground? Apart from that, the timings were all wrong by at least an hour for the Norseman and Squadron 149 to have met so calamitously in Jettison Area South.

Nevertheless, Shaw was openly supported by the well-known RAF historian Roy Conyers Nesbit, who pointed out that during World War II the Americans in the UK logged their flight times in accordance with Local Time, which always put them one hour ahead of the RAF, which instead flew on Greenwich Mean Time (GMT). Take that one-hour difference into account and the Norseman was spot on track to have been in the wrong place at the right time. As for Shaw's recognition of the Norseman, he had grown up and completed his flight training in Canada, starting out on a Norseman, which was pretty ubiquitous in such climes. Besides, the locations of the other four Norsemen in the UK at the time were all documented.

The row also brought Captain Vincent Gregory of NF937 to the fore to back up Shaw's account. He said, "Please don't think me callous but, at the time, I simply told everyone to forget about it; he shouldn't have been there. It was a war; people were dying all about us and my job was to get my plane and my crew home safe."

MOST MYSTERIOUS FACT

In 1985, a British diver named Clive Ward found the wreckage of a Norseman aircraft under the English Channel and, with the other Norsemen in the UK all accounted for, this can only have been the one in which Miller and his two companions disappeared. Nevertheless, for all Ward's diligent searching, there were no skeletal remains to be found within the flight or passenger compartment nor on the seabed anywhere near the plane.

SCEPTICALLY SPEAKING

It is highly likely that the RAF, albeit inadvertently, knocked the most famous American of the time out of the air by showering his plane with their unwanted bombs. However, it must also be said that, had they not done so, Miller himself might have had some "terminal" plans of his own for jumping "sans-'chute" from the plane to avoid the horrors of a lingering death from cancer. Perhaps all three men managed to get out of the plane after it hit the water only to drown, which would explain why Clive Ward found no human remains in that sunken Norseman.

"I think you guys will be going home without me?"

INDEX

(Page numbers in italics refer to photographs and captions)

A

Adanson, James 167
Ahnenerbe 126, 142
AIDS 63, 90–1, 102
Al Fayed, Dodi 166, *167*
al Qaeda 56–7, 95, 105
Albert Victor, Prince ("Eddy") 86–7, *86*
aliens, *see* extra-terrestrial life (ET)
All-Fathers 113
Anglo-American cabal 17, 45, 95, 166–7
Antarctica 126–7, *127*
Anunnaki 175
Arlington Farms 139
Armunier, Leon 146
Arthurian Magus 144
Assassins 70
Atlantis 76, 127, 129, 144

B

Bacon, Francis 135
Baker, Gladys 161
barcodes 116
BATF 100
Bavarian Illuminati 43, 60–1, *60*, *61*, 63, 76–7 (*see also* Illuminati)
Beakers 144
Beatles 157, 158–9, 204
Bermuda Triangle 128–9, *128*
Bernard, Dr Raymond 131
Bilderberg Group 10, 40–1, *41*, 95
bin Laden, Osama 56–7, *57*, 106
Bingham, Richard 200–1, *201*
Bioethics Advisory Commission 113
black helicopters *18*, 63, 118–19, *119*, 172
black ops 6, 63, 65, 105, 197
Blair, Tony *41*, 196, *197*
Bletchley Park 148–9
Bogard, Albert Guy 203
Boisselier, Dr Brigitte 113
Branch Davidians 100, *101*
Brazel, W. W. "Mac" 182
Briand, Roche 146
British Shadow Government 50
Brotherhood of Death 76, 77
Bruni, Georgina 181
Bryan, William 193
Brzezinski, Zbigniew 10
burger chain companies 165
Burgess, Michael 167

Burrell, Paul 166, *167*
Burroughs, William S. 153
Bush, George H. W. 25–6, *25*, 175
Bush, George W. ("Dubya") 27–8, 102, 175

C

Camp Hero 132, *133*
Campbell, William 158, *159*
Casico, Carolyn 129
Catesby, Robert 74–5, *74*
Catholic Church 26, 46, 51, 52–3, *53*, 58, 64, 65, 74–5, 79, 80, 81, 161
cattle mutilations 172–3, *173*
Cecil, Robert, Earl of Salisbury 74, 75
Cesaro, Richard 121
Challenger, SS 92–3, *92*, 184
Chapman, Mark David 156, 157
Chelsea Hotel 169
Childs, Stephen 103
China 55, 94–5, 107, 122, 123, 143
Chow, Raymond 155
Christian Identity 37, 99
Chrononauts 129
Churchill, Winston 148, *148*, 149
CIA 14, 25–6, *25*, 36–7, *36*, 45–9 *passim*, 97, 166
 and AIDS 91
 and al Qaeda 56
 and Beatles 157, 158
 and JFK, RFK 30–1, 193, 203
 and Ku Klux Klan 62
 and MH370 108–9
 and mind control 120–3
 and Monroe 160–1
 and 9/11 106–7
 and oil companies 28
 and Oklahoma Bombing 99
 and OSS 68–9
 and Pont-Saint-Esprit 146–7
Clinton, Bill 99, 101, 112
Clinton, Hillary 23–4, *23*, 33, *182*, 195
cloning 112–13
Cobain, Kurt 152–3, *152*
Columbus, Christopher 128
Condit, Gary 195
Conway, Kellyanne 121
Coolidge, Calvin 62
Coronation Street 51
Courson, Pamela 162
Coventry 148–9, *148*
Crowley, Aleister 20, 87, 132, *133*, 139, 143
Cuba 6, 14, 25, 28, 30, 91, 107,

120, 121, 199, 203
cyber-jacking 108, 109

D

Dalai Lama 143
Dance Mania 146
Dee, Dr John 81
Dennis, Glenn 182, 183
Denver International Airport 136–7, *137*
Deros 131
Devil, *see* Satan
Devil's Triangle 128–9, *128*
DIA 196
Diana, Princess of Wales 6, 46, 50–1, *51*, 166–7
Dick, Phillip K. 114, 115
DiSalvo, Albert 193
Disney, Walt 38, *38*
Dolly the Sheep 112–13, *112*
D'onston Stephenson, Dr Roslyn 87
Draconians 175
Dream Machine 153
drug barons 107
Druids 144
Dugas, Gaetan 91
Dulles Commission 31

E

earthquake in Antarctica, unexplained 127
Eckhardt, Dietrich 77
Egypt 140–1, 144
Einhorn, Ira 114
Einstein, Albert 132
El Chupracabra 172
El Faro, SS 129
Elder Race 67, 126, 140, 143
Elders of Zion 77
Elizabeth II 50–1, 137, 166
Enigma code 148–9
Enter The Dragon 154
Equagesics 155
ergot 146
European Union (EU) 57
Eve (clone) 113
extra-terrestrial life (ET) 10–11, 39, 41, 49, 53, 67, 87, 93, 105, 113, 114–15, 116, 126, 129, 130–1, *130*, *131*, 137, 143, 144, 172–3, 175, 179, 180–1, 182–3, *182*, 184–5, 193

F

"false flag" operations 6, 107
FBI 13, *98*
FEMA 119

Filatov, Nikolai 94
Flight 77 (American Airlines) 138
Flight 800 (TWA) 104–5, *104*, *105*
Flight MH370 (Malaysia Airlines) 108–9, *109*
Founding Fathers 139
Fouquet, Nicholas 79
Fourth Reich 113
Frankos, Donald ("Tony the Greek") 189
free energy 117, 179
Freedom of Information 36, 157, 180
Freemasons 10, 28, 37, 39, 43, 45, 49, 58–9, *58*, 61, *61*, 64, 70, 81, 83, 87, 126, 136, 139, 140, 166, 200
fundamentalism 93, 99, 116, 139, 157, 166

G

Gardner, Marshall B. 131
Geller, Uri 114, 115, *115*
Generation X 152
Glastonbury 145
Global Strategy Council (GSC) 120
God 91, 115, 157
Goldsmith, Sir James 200
Grant, Tom 153
Great Galactic Ghoul 93, 184, 185
Greys, *see* extra-terrestrial life (ET)
GRID 90
Grose, Dr Vernon 105
Guantanamo Bay 108
Gulf War Syndrome (GWS) 102–3, *103*
gun control (US) 101, 157
Gunpowder Plot 74–5, *74*
Gurdjieff, George I. 143

H

Halpin, Barry 201
Halt, Lt Col. Charles 180, 181
Hawass, Zahi 141
Hess, Rudolf 18–20, *19*
Hicks, Bill 101
Hilton, J, 142
Hitler, Adolf 76–7, *77*, 149, 179
Hoffa, Jimmy 188–9, *188*, *192*
Hofmann, Dr Albert 146
Hollow Earth 130–1, *130*, *131*, 143, 183
homosexuality 87, 90–1, *90*
Hong Kong 71, 94, 155

Hoover, J. Edgar ("Mary") 13, 157, 161, 162, 190, 199
Hussein, Saddam 21–2, *21*, 28, 43, 46, 102, 166, 174, 196
Hutton, Lord 196, 197

I

Illuminati 10, 39, 41, 43, 59, 60–1, *60*, *61*, 63, 76–7, 119 (*see also* Bavarian Illuminati)
impostors 50, 51, 78–9, 158, 159
Inca 135
IRA 166
Ismaeli Sect of Islam 70

J

Jack the Ripper 86–7, *87*
James I (VI) 74, 75, 81
Jason Society 126
Jesus Christ 53, 67, 96, 100, 158
Jianlin, Lia 94
Jones, Jim 96–7
Jonestown Massacre 96–7, *96*
Judas Priest 124

K

Kelly, David 196–7
Kennedy, John F. ("JFK") 6, 12, 14, 25, 29–31, *29*, *30*, 45, 156, 160, 161, 192, 193, 198, 198–9, 199, 202–3
Kennedy, Robert F. ("Bobby") ("RFK") 160, 161, 188–9, 191, 192–3, *192*
Key, Wilson Bryan 124
KGB 22, 31, 32, 42–3, *42*, *44*, 47, 50, 120, 121, 203
Kidd, Capt. William *134*, 135
Kilgallen, Dorothy 198–9, *198*
King, Dr Martin Luther 190–1, *191*
Knights of Malta 26, 37, 45
Knights Templar 11, 43, 45, 59, 70, 76, 126, 135
Kollmar, Richard 199
Koresh, David 100, *101*
KORN 149
Kremlin 91
Ku Klux Klan (KKK) 62–3, *63*, 99, 190

L

LaBour, Fred 159
LAPD 193
Lateran Treaty 52
Lauzun, Jean-Michel 167
Lawford, Peter 161
Lawson, Revd James 191
Lee, Brandon 155
Lee, Bruce 154–5, *154*
Lennon, John 156–7, *156*, 159, 169
Levy, Chandra 194–5, *195*
ley lines 144, 145

lizard people, *see* extra-terrestrial life 175
Louis XIV 78, 79
Love, Courtney 152, 153
LSD 124, 146, 147, 203
Lucan, Lord 200–1, *201*

M

McAuliffe, Christa 92
McCartney, Paul 157, 158–9, *159*
McGinnis, Daniel 134–5
McLaren, Malcolm 168, 169
McNulty, Mike 101
McVeigh, Timothy 98–9, *99*, 195
Mafia 13, 31, 64–5, *65*, 161, 188, 189, 193, 199, 203
Mahoney, Mary Caitrin 195
Majestic 12, *see* MJ-12
MAJI (MAJESTY) 67
Man in the Iron Mask 78–9, *79*
Marcel, Maj. Jesse 182
Marlowe, Christopher 80–1
Martians 185
Mary Celeste 129
Maya 135
Meacher, Michael 106–7
Memphis Police 190
Men in Black (MIBs) 161, 176–7, *177*
Meonia 200
Merlin 144
Microsoft 121
military–industrial complex (MIC) 22, 153, 157, 166, 193, 197, 199
Miller, Glenn 204–5, *205*
mind-control 97, 115, 120–1, 122, 132, 203
MI6 19, 20, 44–5, 47, 147, 149, 166, 167, 196, 197
MJ-12 26, 37, 48, 66–7, *66*, 93, 126, 129, 136, 139, 165, 175, 184, 193
MK-Ultra 115, 124, 146, 147
Mob, *see* Mafia; Russian Mob
Mole Men 183
Molière 79
Monroe, Marilyn 160–1, *160*
Montauk Point 132–3
Moon:
    landings 7
    secret bases 178–9, *178*
Moon, Peter 132
Moonlight Sonata 149
Mootoo, C. Leslie 97
Morrison, Jim 162–3, *163*
Mossad 46–7, 49, 107, 166, 195
Mozart, Wolfgang Amadeus 82–3
MW audiogram induction 120, 121

N

NASA *7*, 38–9, 68, 69, 92–3, 117, *130*, 132, 136–7, *137*,

140–1, *178*, 179, 184–5
Nation of Islam 13
National Association of Food Chains (US) 116
National Security Council (NSC) 126, 132
Nazis 16, 17, 20, 27, 28, 38–9, 43, 46, 52, 62, 68–9, *69*, 76–7, *77*, 101, 113, 126, 130, 131, 133, 136, 139, 143, 178–9, 183, 193, 204
Neuschwabenland 126
New World Airport Commission 136
New World Order 11, 21, 22, 23, 27–8, 40, 50, 59, 63, 69, 101, 113, 119, 136, *137*, 165, 172
9/11 6, 27–8, 56–7, 57, 106–7, 138, *138*, 156
Nirvana 152, *152*
NORAD 106, 129
NSA 48–9, *48*, 106, 115, 116, 120, 137, 140, 181

O

O-rings 93
Oak Island 134–5
O'Brien, Chuckie 189
Odessa 68–9, *68–9*
Ogle, Tom 117
oil interests 22, 25, 27, 28, 56, 57, 107, 175
Oklahoma Bombing 98–9, *99*
Oldendorff, Louis 78
Order of the Green Dragon 63, 143
Organization of Former SS Members 69
Orpheus 38, 137
OSS 68
Oswald, Lee Harvey 15, 25–6, 29, 30–1, 84, 193, 199, 202–3, *202*

P

Page, Michael 197
Pasechnik, Vladimir 197
Patient O (Patient 0) 91
Paul, Henri 166, 167
Pearl Harbor 16–17, *16*
Pentagon 56, 99, 105, 106, 107, 121, 138–9, *138*, 196
People's Temple 96–7, *96*
Phobos 184
Phoenicians 144
Piri Reis Map 127
Plan Red 6
Polanski, Roman 157
Pont-Saint-Esprit 146–7, *147*
Porton Down 147
Preseli Mountains 144
Presley, Elvis Aron 155, 158, 164–5, *164*, 169, 200, 204
Process Church 97
Proctor and Gamble (P&G) 124

Profanes 59
Project Pandora 121
Project Phoenix 105, 126, 181
Provenzano, Tony ("Tony Pro") 189
P2 45, 53, 58, 64
Putin, Vladimir 32–3, *42*, 43
Pythagoreans 139

Q

Queen Maud Land 127

R

Raelians 113
RAF 204–5
Rasputin 84–5
Ray, James Earl 190, 191
Ray, Johnny 199
Red Eyebrows 71
Rendlesham 180–1, *181*
Reno, Janet 99, 100
Reza, Zahid 109
Rockefeller Family 10, 15, 28, 40, 45
Roddenberry, Gene 115
Roosevelt, Franklin D. 139
Rosemary's Baby 157
Rosicrucians 45
Roslin Institute 112
Roswell 179, 180, 182–3, *183*
Rotten, Johnny 168, 169
Royal Family (UK) 19, 20, 28, 45, 50–1, *51*, 59, 166
Ruby, Jack 31, 199, 203
Russian Mob 32, 33
Ryan, Leo 96–7
Rybakov, Prof. Sergei 196

S

Saint Mars 78
Salieri, Antonio 82, *82*, 83
Sandoz Pharmaceuticals 146
Sarfatti, Dr Jack 114
SARS 94–5, *95*
Satan 59, 70, 76, 85, 116, 123, 128, 139, 156, 157, 158, 172
Saudi Arabia 55, 57
Scientology 97
Secret Earth 126
Shah, Zaharie Ahmad 108–9
Shakespeare, William 81, 135
Shambhala (Shangri-La) 142, 143
Shaver, Richard 131
Shaw, Fred 205
Shea, Robert 61
Single Bullet theory 31
Sirhan, Bashira Sirhan 192–3
Sirius 176
Sitchin, Zecharia 175
Skull and Bones 25, 26, 28, 77
Smith, Earl T. 199
Southwell, David 200
Space Command (US Air Force) 136–7

Space Race 7, 92–3
space sabotage 184–5, *185*
Space Shuttle 92–3, *92*, 184
SPECTRA 114, 115
Sphinx 140–1, *141*
Spring-Heeled Jack 87
Spungen, Nancy 169
Stanford Research Institute (SRI) 140
Star Trek 115
Stephens, Charles 191
Stephenson, Sir William 149
Stonehenge 144–5, *145*
Stride, Elizabeth 86, *87*
subliminal messages 123–4

T
Taha, Dr Rihab 196
Taliban 57, 107
Taranto, Italy 146
Tate, Sharon 157
Taylor, Lt Charles Carroll 128
Teamsters 188, 189
Teutonic Knights 43
Texas School Book Depository 31, 202, 203
Thatcher, Margaret 181
Third Reich 68, 101, 178, 179
Thule Gesellschaft 76, 126, 130
Tibet 142–3, *142*

time travel 114–15, 133, 181
Tingpei, Betty 155
Tippit, J. D. 203
tobacco lobby 75
Too Bizarre To Believe factor 131, 132
transvestism 13, 84
Triads 64, 71, 155
Trilateral Commission 10–11, *11*, 15, 45, 173
Triton Alliance 135
Truman, Harry S. 67, 182
Trump, Donald 32–3, 121
Tumblety, Dr Francis 87
Turing, Alan 148
28 IF 159
Twin Towers 56, 106–7

U
UFOs 26, 37, 39, 66–7, *66*, 93, 105, 113, 114, 119, 129, 131, 136, 138, 140, 161, 165, 172, 174–5, *174*, 176, 178–9, *180*–1, *181*, 182–3, *183*, 193
Unit 13 197
United Nations (UN) 12, 13, 101, 113, 126, 129, 137, 175, 196
UPC 116

V
VALIS 114–15
Vatican 52–3
Vicious, Sid 168–9, *168*
Virginia Company 50
Von Braun, Werner 139
Von Neumann, Janus Eric 132, 133
Vril Society 20, 179

W
W-105 105
Waco 100–1, *101*
Walker, Edwin 203
Walsegg zu Stuppach, Count von 83
Walsingham, Sir Thomas 80, 81
Ward, Clive 205
Warren Commission 31, 193, 199, 203
WASPs 37
Watergate 14–15, 25, 26, 27, 30
Weishaupt, Adam 60, *60*
White Aryan Resistance 99
WHO 95
Wickramasinghe, Prof. Chandra 95
Wiesenthal, Simon 69
Wilcox, George 182
Wilson, Harold 44–5, *44*

Wilson, Robert Anton 61
Wilson, Woodrow 63
Winterbotham, Grp Capt. F. W. 149
witchcraft 139, 163
WMDs 28, 102, 175, 196, 197
World Trade Center 56, 98, 106–7
Worldvision 97
WRAIR 120

X
X, Malcolm 12–13, 62
The X-Files 138, 166, 195

Y
Yakuza 64
Yellow Hats 143
Yusupov, Prince Felix 85

Z
Zeta Reticula 181
Zhironovsky, Vladimir 43
ZOG (Zionist Occupation Government) 63
ZPE (zero-point energy) 117
Zwack, Xavier 60

CREDITS

The publishers would like to thank the following sources for their kind permission to reproduce the pictures in this book.

4-5. Aero Icarus/Wikimedia Commons, 7. NASA, 8-9. Library of Congress, 11. Public Domain, 12. Al BurleighAP/REX/Shutterstock, 15. Granger/REX/Shutterstock, 16. Library of Congress, 19. Sipa Press/REX/Shutterstock, 21-25. REX/Shutterstock, 29. Penn Jones Photograph, Baylor University Collection, 30. Bettmann/Getty Images, 32. ITAR-TASS News Agency/Alamy Stock Photo, 34-35. Shutterstock. com, 36. Public Domain, 38. NASA, 41-42. Shutterstock.com, 44. Michael Stroud/Daily Express/Hulton Archive/Getty Images, 47. Times Newspapers/REX/Shutterstock, 48. Linda R. Chen/Touchstone/Kobal/REX/Shutterstock, 51. Jack Guez/AFP/Getty Images, 53. Keystone Pictures USA/Keystone/REX/Shutterstock, 54-55. Keystone Pictures USA/Keystone/REX/Shutterstock, 57. Sipa Press/REX/Shutterstock, 58. Shutterstock.com, 60-61. Public Domain, 63. Shutterstock.com, 65. Keystone/Getty Images, 66. Shell R. Alpert/Library of Congress, 68-69. NASA, 72-77. Public Domain, 79. Library of Congress, 82-86. Public Domain, 87. REX/Shutterstock, 88-89. Bruce Weaver/AP/REX/Shutterstock, 90. Barbara Alper/Getty Images, 92. Bruce Weaver/AP/REX/Shutterstock, 95. Christian Keenan/Getty Images, 96. David Hume Kennerly/Getty Images, 98. Bob Daemmerich/AFP/Getty Images, 101. Greg Smith/Corbis via Getty Images, 103. Corbis via Getty Images, 104-105. Jon Levy/AFP/Getty Images, 108. Aero Icarus/Wikimedia Commons, 110-111. NASA, 112. Jeremy Sutton Hibbert/REX/Shutterstock, 115. Hulton-Deutsch Collection/CORBIS/

Corbis via Getty Images, 118. RichardBaker/Alamy Stock Photo, 119. Shutterstock.com, 120. Adalberto Roque/AFP/Getty Images, 124-128. Shutterstock.com, 130. Chronicle/Alamy Stock Photo, 132. Shutterstock.com, 133. Public Domain, 134. Library of Congress, 137. Shutterstock.com, 138. U.S. Navy, 141-145. Shutterstock.com 147. REX/Shutterstock, 148. Galerie Bilderwelt/Getty Images, 150-151. AP/REX/Shutterstock, 152. Robert Sorbo/AP/REX/Shutterstock, 154. Kobal/REX/Shutterstock, 156. George Konig/REX/Shutterstock, 159. Shutterstock.com, 160. SNAP/REX/Shutterstock, 163. CBS Photo Archive/Getty Images 164. AP/REX/Shutterstock, 167. Scott Barbour/Getty Images, 168. Richard E. Aaron/Redferns/Getty Images, 170-173. Shutterstock.com, 174. U.S. Air Force, 177. Melinda Sue Gordon/Columbia/Kobal/REX/Shutterstock, 178. NASA, 181. General Images/UIG/REX/Shutterstock, 182. Steve Back / Daily Mail /REX/Shutterstock, 183. Sipa Press/REX/Shutterstock, 185. NASA, 186-187. David F. Smith/AP/REX/Shutterstock, 188. Robert W. Kelley/The LIFE Picture Collection/Getty Images, 191. AP/REX/Shutterstock, 192. Dick Strobel/AP/REX/Shutterstock, 194. REX/Shutterstock, 197. Helen Atkinson/REX/Shutterstock, 198. Associated Newspapers/REX/Shutterstock, 202. Topfoto.co.uk, 202. David F. Smith/AP/REX/Shutterstock, 205. Michael Ochs Archives/Getty Images.

Every effort has been made to acknowledge correctly and contact the source and/or copyright holder of each picture and Carlton Books Limited apologises for any unintentional errors or omissions, which will be corrected in future editions of this book.